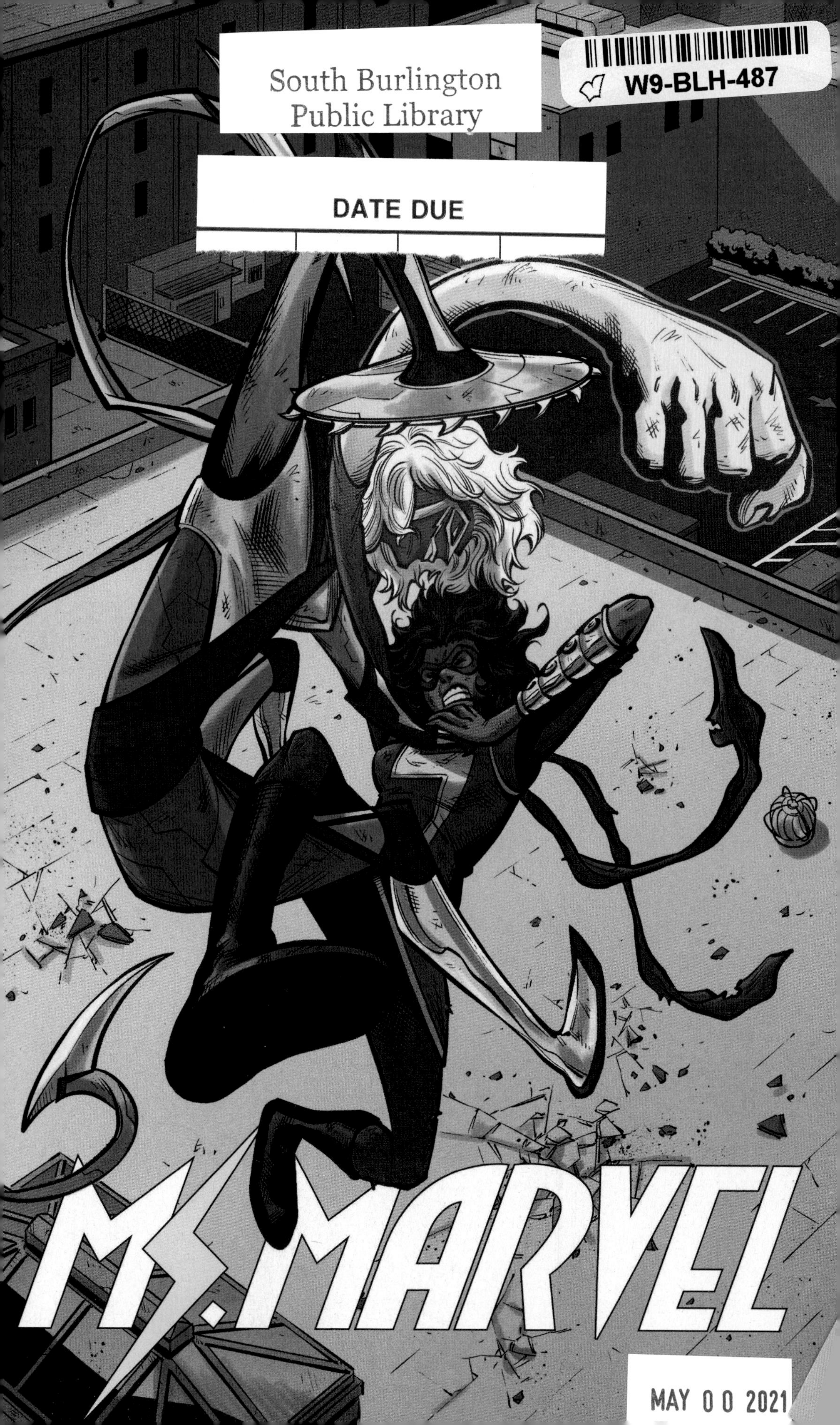
MS. MARVEL

RECENTLY, KAMALA'S FATHER FELL ILL WITH A SEEMINGLY INCURABLE DISEASE, BUT NOT ALL HOPE WAS LOST: DOCTOR STRANGE AGREED TO OPERATE AFTER THEORIZING THAT MR. KHAN'S ILLNESS STEMMED FROM LATENT INHUMAN DNA.

DOCTOR STRANGE DETERMINED THAT ABU COULD RECOVER WITH THE AID OF A BLOOD TRANSFUSION FROM KAMALA, BUT KAMALA TOOK TOO LONG TRYING TO STOP HER NANOTECH COSTUME FROM KILLING HER CLASSMATE TURNED NEMESIS, DISCORD, AND DIDN'T RETURN TO THE HOSPITAL IN TIME FOR THE TRANSFUSION TO HAVE ITS FULL IMPACT.

FOR NOW, ABU CAN COME HOME. BUT HAVE KAMALA'S ACTIONS CAUSED PERMANENT HARM?

COLLECTION EDITOR JENNIFER GRÜNWALD
ASSISTANT MANAGING EDITOR MAIA LOY
VP PRODUCTION & SPECIAL PROJECTS JEFF YOUNGQUIST
SVP PRINT, SALES & MARKETING DAVID GABRIEL

DANIEL KIRCHHOFFER ASSISTANT EDITOR
LISA MONTALBANO ASSISTANT MANAGING EDITOR
STACIE ZUCKER & JAY BOWEN BOOK DESIGNERS
C.B. CEBULSKI EDITOR IN CHIEF

MS. MARVEL BY SALADIN AHMED VOL. 3: OUTLAWED. Contains material originally published in magazine form as MAGNIFICENT MS. MARVEL (2019) #13-18. First printing 2021. ISBN 978-1-302-92500-0. Published by MARVEL WORLDWIDE, INC., a subsidiary of MARVEL ENTERTAINMENT, LLC. OFFICE OF PUBLICATION: 1290 Avenue of the Americas, New York, NY 10104. © 2021 MARVEL No similarity between any of the names, characters, persons, and/or institutions in this magazine with those of any living or dead person or institution is intended, and any such similarity which may exist is purely coincidental. Printed in the U.S.A. KEVIN FEIGE, Chief Creative Officer; DAN BUCKLEY, President, Marvel Entertainment; JOE QUESADA, EVP & Creative Director; DAVID BOGART, Associate Publisher & SVP of Talent Affairs; TOM BREVOORT, VP, Executive Editor; NICK LOWE, Executive Editor, VP of Content, Digital Publishing; DAVID GABRIEL, VP of Print & Digital Publishing; JEFF YOUNGQUIST, VP of Production & Special Projects; ALEX MORALES, Director of Publishing Operations; DAN EDINGTON, Managing Editor; RICKEY PURDIN, Director of Talent Relations; JENNIFER GRÜNWALD, Senior Editor, Special Projects; SUSAN CRESPI, Production Manager; STAN LEE, Chairman Emeritus. For information regarding advertising in Marvel Comics or on Marvel.com, please contact Vit DeBellis, Custom Solutions & Integrated Advertising Manager, at vdebellis@marvel.com. For Marvel subscription inquiries, please call 888-511-5480. Manufactured between 3/12/2021 and 4/13/2021 by FRY COMMUNICATIONS, MECHANICSBURG, PA, USA.

10 9 8 7 6 5 4 3 2 1

WHEN A STRANGE TERRIGEN MIST DESCENDED UPON JERSEY CITY,
KAMALA KHAN WAS IMBUED WITH POLYMORPH POWERS. USING HER NEW
ABILITIES TO FIGHT EVIL AND PROTECT JERSEY CITY, SHE BECAME…

MS.MARVEL
Outlawed

WRITER	**SALADIN AHMED**
PENCILERS	**JOEY VAZQUEZ** (#13) & **MINKYU JUNG** (#14-18)
INKERS	**JUAN VLASCO** (#13-15) & **MINKYU JUNG** (#16-18)
COLORIST	**IAN HERRING**
LETTERER	**VC's JOE CARAMAGNA**
COVER ART	**EDUARD PETROVICH** (#13-16) & **MIRKA ANDOLFO** (#17-18)
ASSISTANT EDITORS	**SHANNON ANDREWS BALLESTEROS** & **MARTIN BIRO**
EDITOR	**ALANNA SMITH**
CONSULTING EDITOR	**SANA AMANAT**

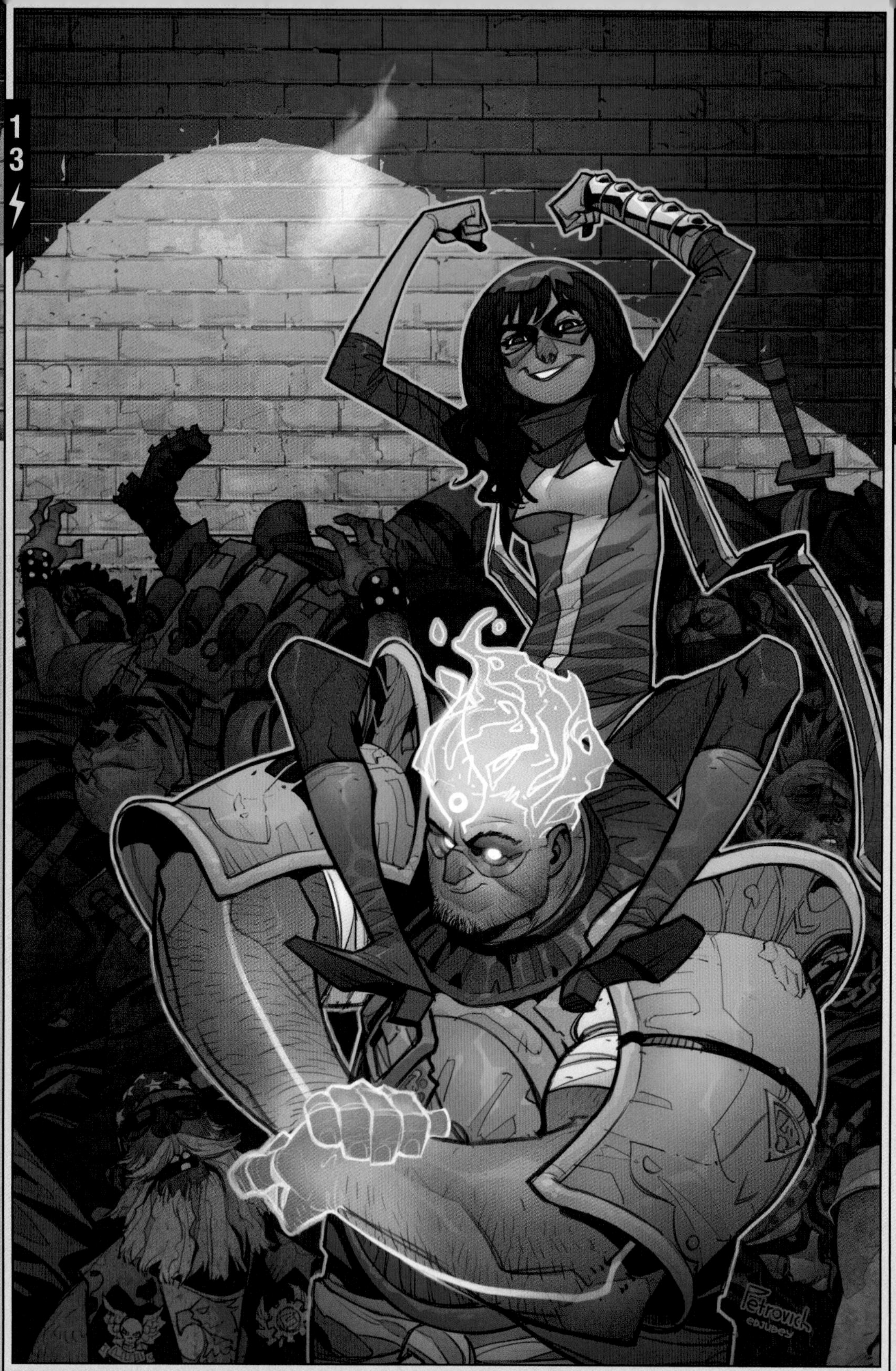
13
Petrovich

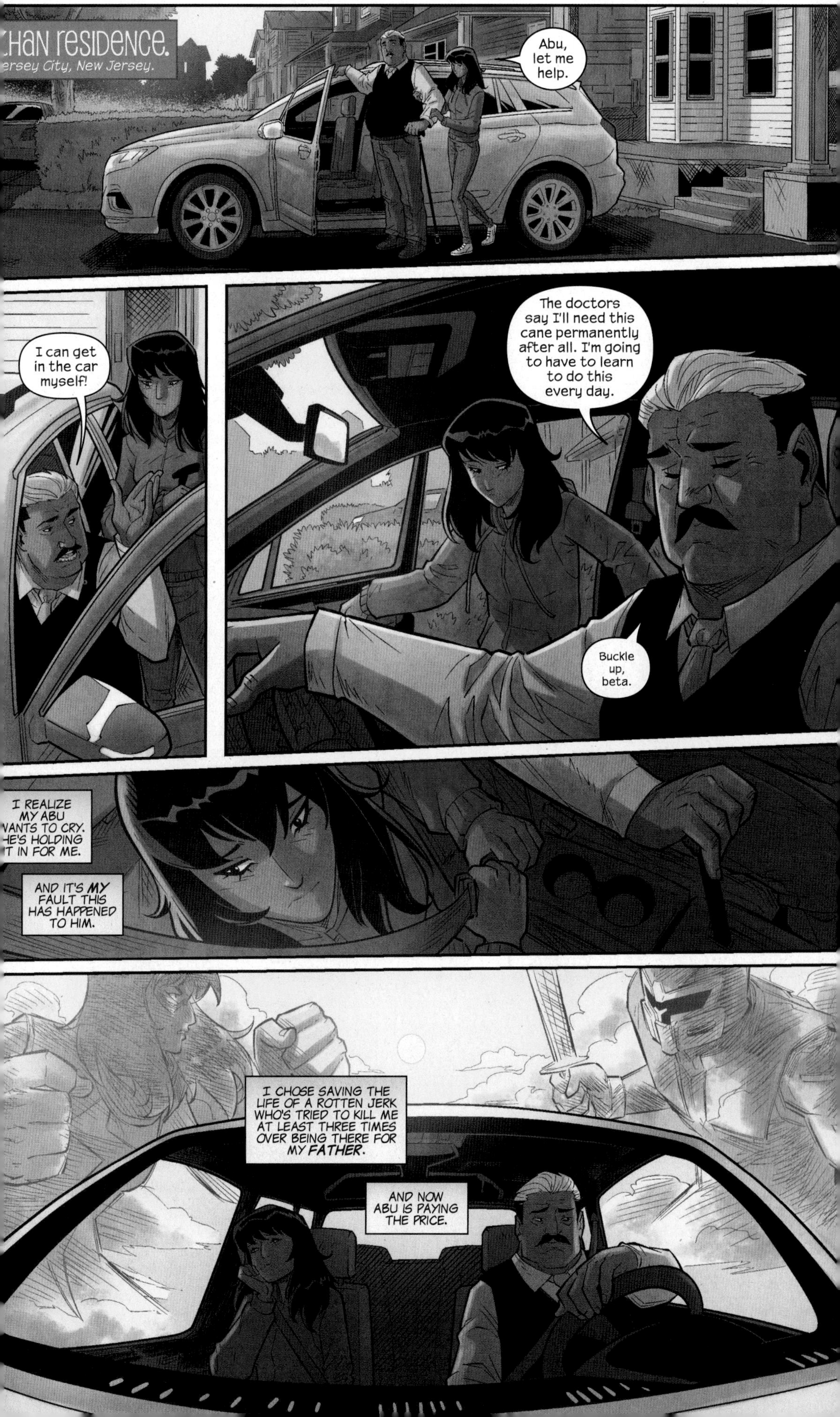

KHAN RESIDENCE.
Jersey City, New Jersey.
Abu, let me help.
I can get in the car myself!
The doctors say I'll need this cane permanently after all. I'm going to have to learn to do this every day.
Buckle up, beta.
I REALIZE MY ABU WANTS TO CRY. HE'S HOLDING IT IN FOR ME.
AND IT'S MY FAULT THIS HAS HAPPENED TO HIM.
I CHOSE SAVING THE LIFE OF A ROTTEN JERK WHO'S TRIED TO KILL ME AT LEAST THREE TIMES OVER BEING THERE FOR MY FATHER.
AND NOW ABU IS PAYING THE PRICE.

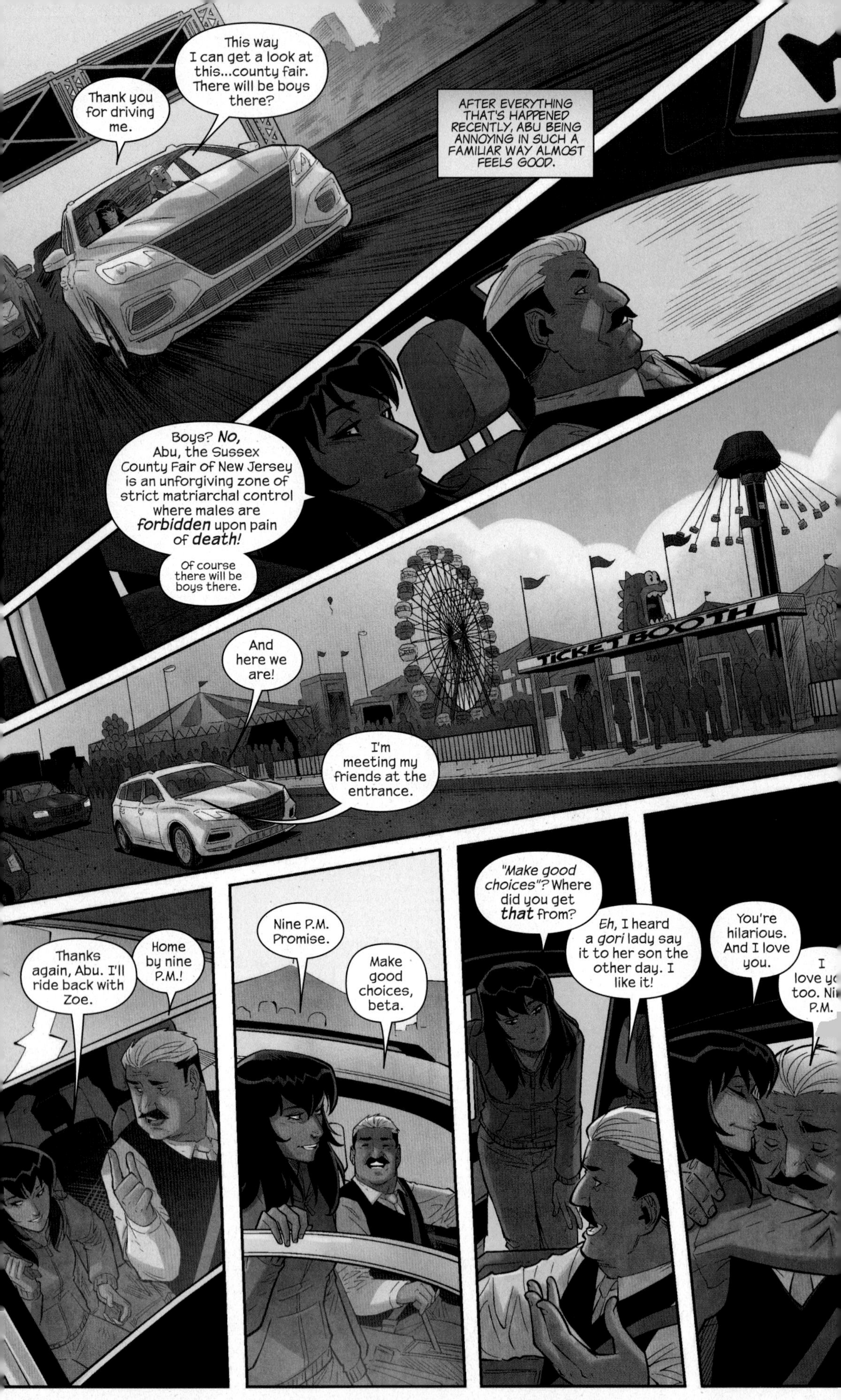
Thank you for driving me.
This way I can get a look at this...county fair. There will be boys there?
AFTER EVERYTHING THAT'S HAPPENED RECENTLY, ABU BEING ANNOYING IN SUCH A FAMILIAR WAY ALMOST FEELS GOOD.
Boys? **No,** Abu, the Sussex County Fair of New Jersey is an unforgiving zone of strict matriarchal control where males are ***forbidden*** upon pain of ***death!***
Of course there will be boys there.
And here we are!
TICKET BOOTH
I'm meeting my friends at the entrance.
Thanks again, Abu. I'll ride back with Zoe.
Home by nine P.M.!
Nine P.M. Promise.
Make good choices, beta.
"Make good choices"? Where did you get ***that*** from?
Eh, I heard a *gori* lady say it to her son the other day. I like it!
You're hilarious. And I love you.
I love yo too. Ni P.M.

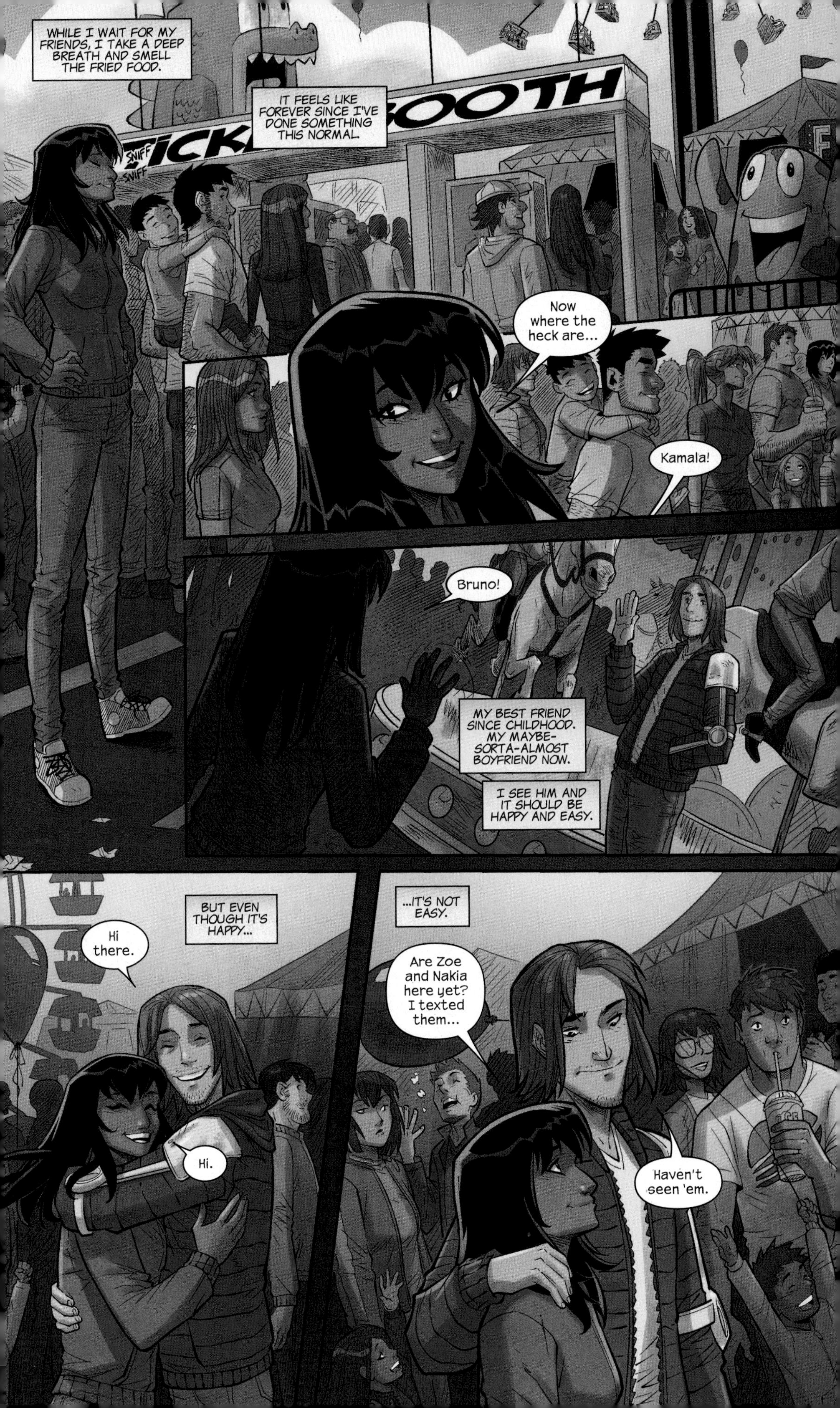
WHILE I WAIT FOR MY FRIENDS, I TAKE A DEEP BREATH AND SMELL THE FRIED FOOD.
IT FEELS LIKE FOREVER SINCE I'VE DONE SOMETHING THIS NORMAL.
SNIFF SNIFF
Now where the heck are...
Kamala!
Bruno!
MY BEST FRIEND SINCE CHILDHOOD. MY MAYBE-SORTA-ALMOST BOYFRIEND NOW.
I SEE HIM AND IT SHOULD BE HAPPY AND EASY.
BUT EVEN THOUGH IT'S HAPPY...
Hi there.
Hi.
...IT'S NOT EASY.
Are Zoe and Nakia here yet? I texted them...
Haven't seen 'em.

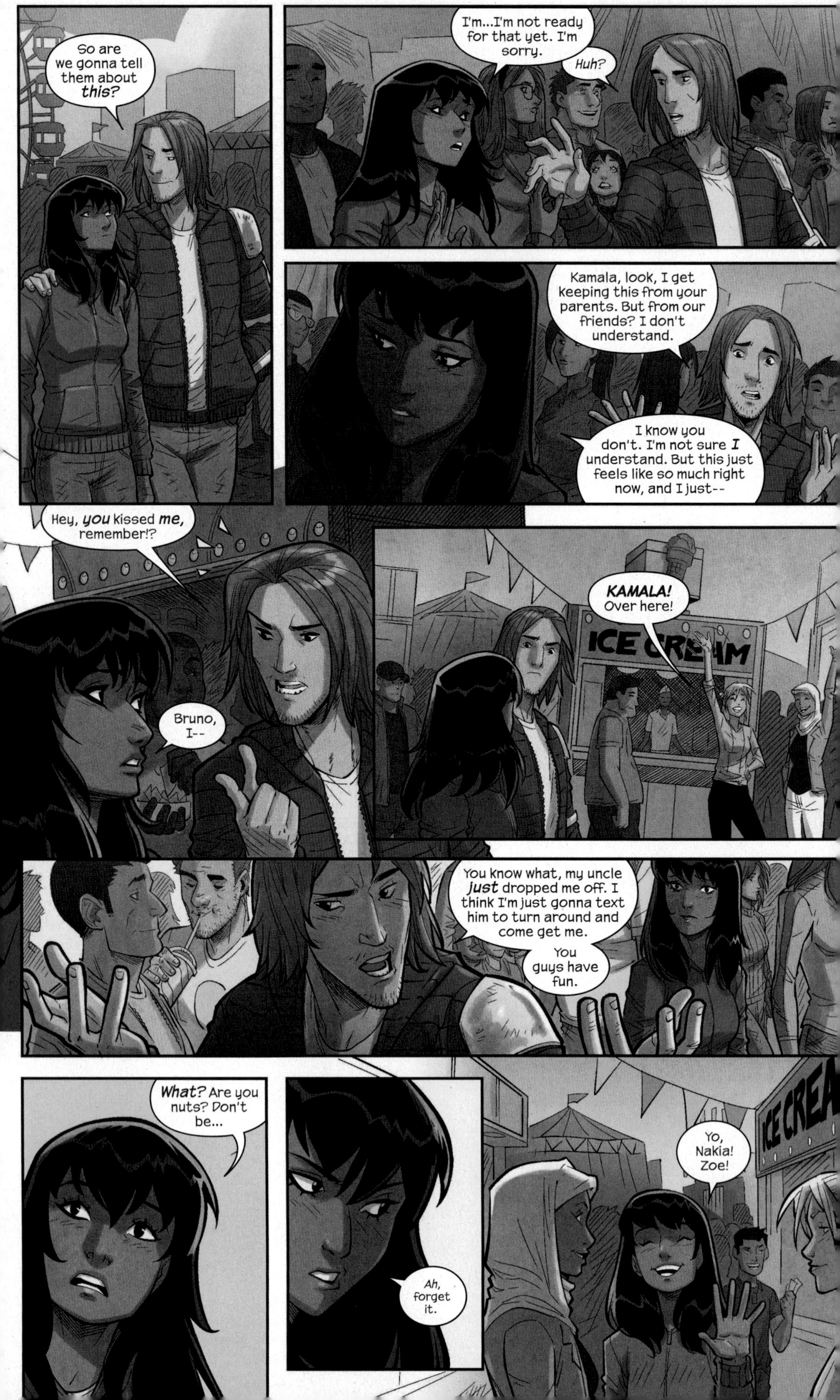
So are we gonna tell them about *this?*
I'm...I'm not ready for that yet. I'm sorry.
Huh?
Kamala, look, I get keeping this from your parents. But from our friends? I don't understand.
I know you don't. I'm not sure *I* understand. But this just feels like so much right now, and I just--
Hey, *you* kissed *me*, remember!?
Bruno, I--
KAMALA! Over here!
ICE CREAM
You know what, my uncle *just* dropped me off. I think I'm just gonna text him to turn around and come get me.
You guys have fun.
What? Are you nuts? Don't be...
Ah, forget it.
Yo, Nakia! Zoe!

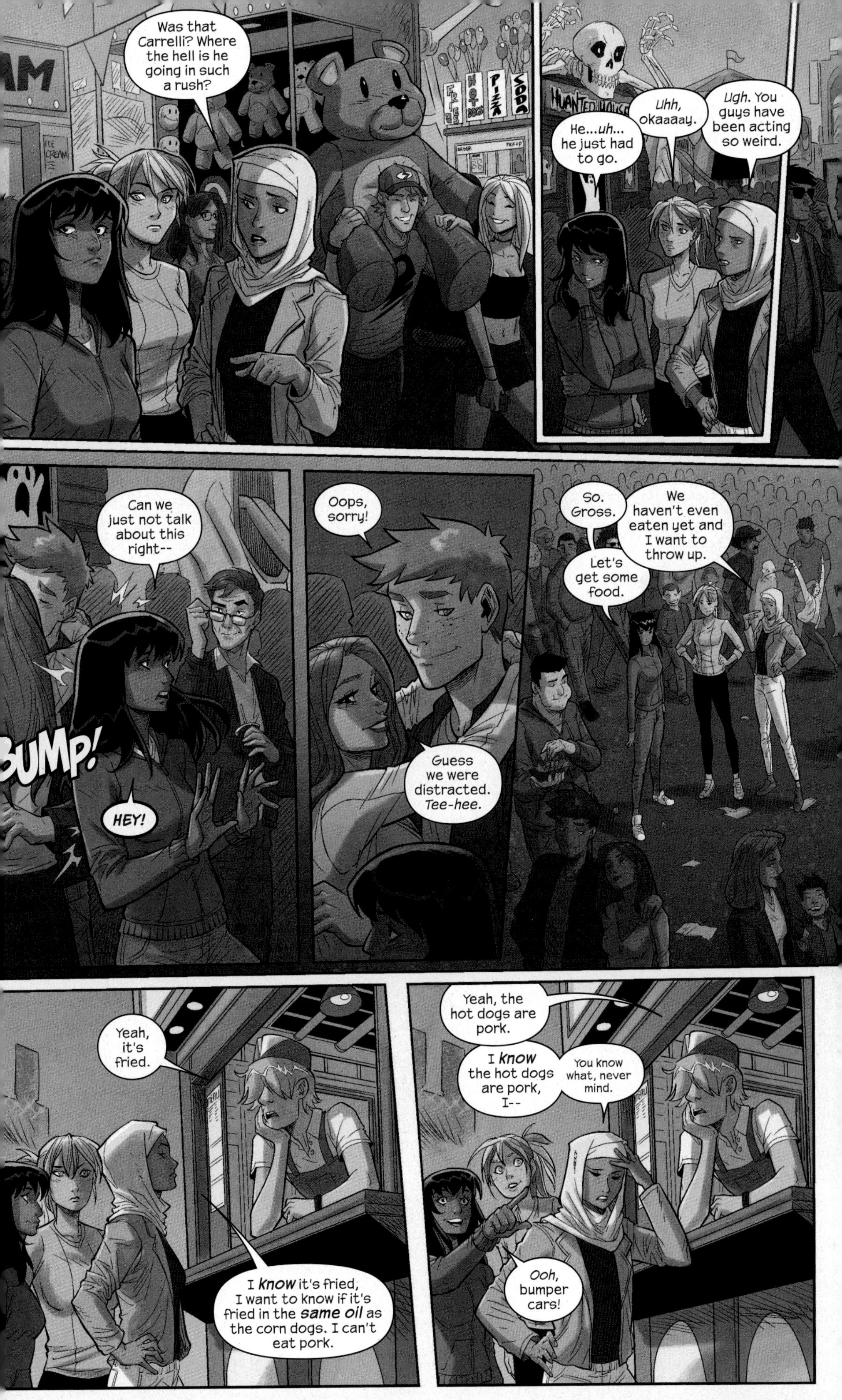
Was that Carrelli? Where the hell is he going in such a rush?
AM
ICE CREAM
FRIES
HOT DOGS
PIZZA
SODA
HUANTED HOUSE
He...*uh*... he just had to go.
Uhh, Okaaaay.
Ugh. You guys have been acting so weird.
Can we just not talk about this right--
BUMP!
HEY!
Oops, sorry!
Guess we were distracted. *Tee-hee.*
So. Gross.
Let's get some food.
We haven't even eaten yet and I want to throw up.
Yeah, it's fried.
I ***know*** it's fried, I want to know if it's fried in the ***same oil*** as the corn dogs. I can't eat pork.
Yeah, the hot dogs are pork.
I ***know*** the hot dogs are pork, I--
You know what, never mind.
Ooh, bumper cars!

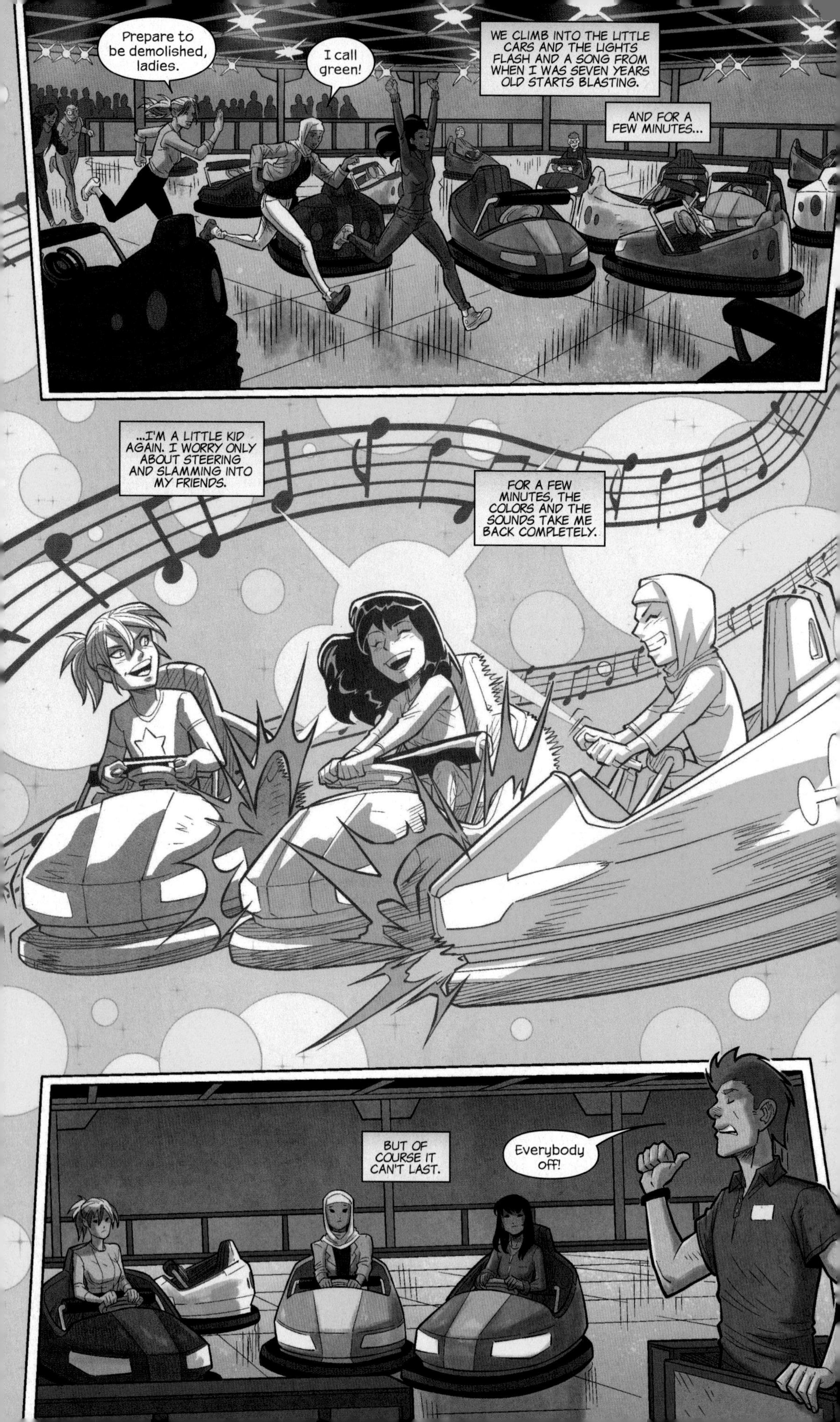
Prepare to be demolished, ladies.
I call green!
WE CLIMB INTO THE LITTLE CARS AND THE LIGHTS FLASH AND A SONG FROM WHEN I WAS SEVEN YEARS OLD STARTS BLASTING.
AND FOR A FEW MINUTES...
...I'M A LITTLE KID AGAIN. I WORRY ONLY ABOUT STEERING AND SLAMMING INTO MY FRIENDS.
FOR A FEW MINUTES, THE COLORS AND THE SOUNDS TAKE ME BACK COMPLETELY.
BUT OF COURSE IT CAN'T LAST.
Everybody off!

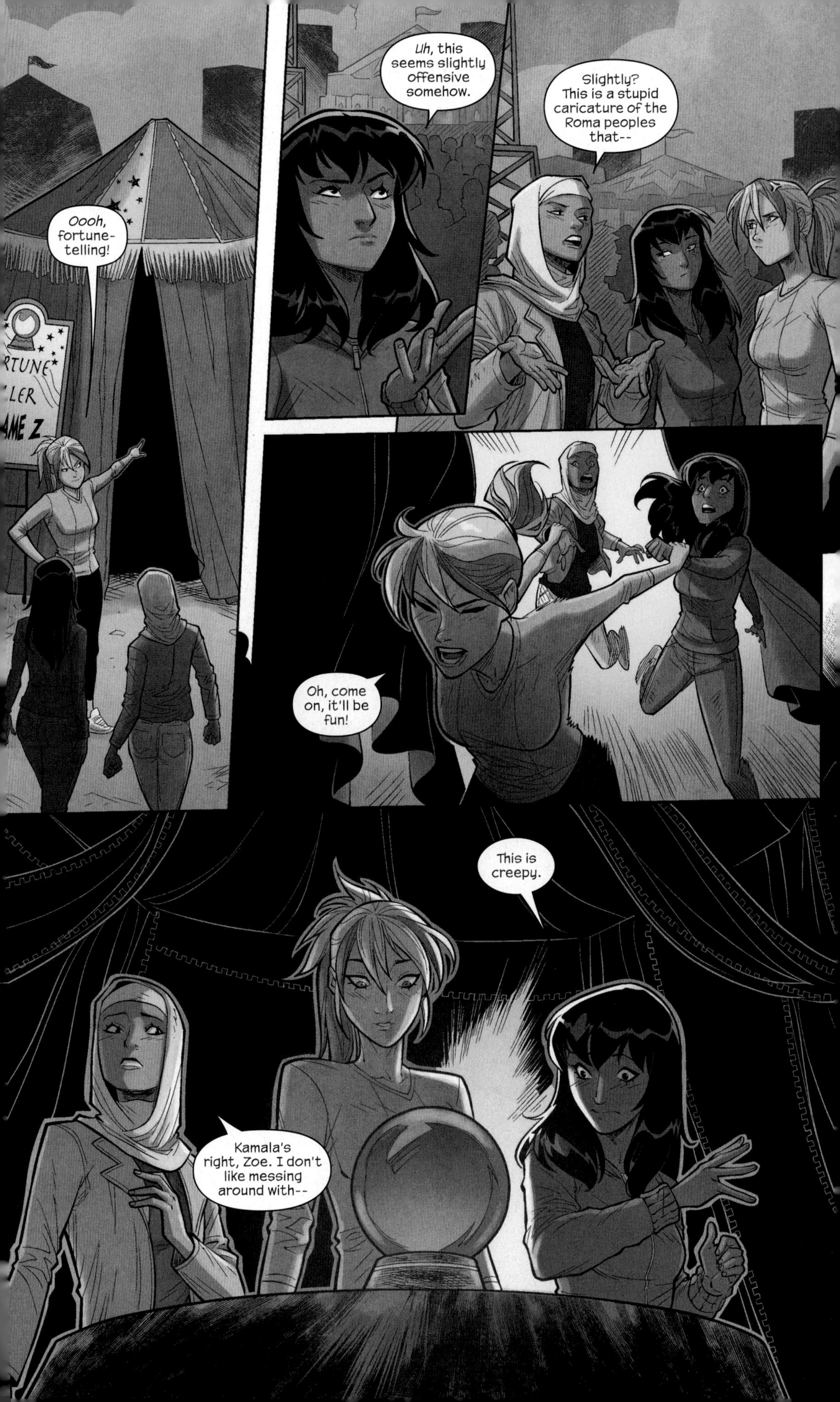

Oooh, fortune-telling!
RTUNE
LER
AME Z.
Uh, this seems slightly offensive somehow.
Slightly? This is a stupid caricature of the Roma peoples that--
Oh, come on, it'll be fun!
This is creepy.
Kamala's right, Zoe. I don't like messing around with--

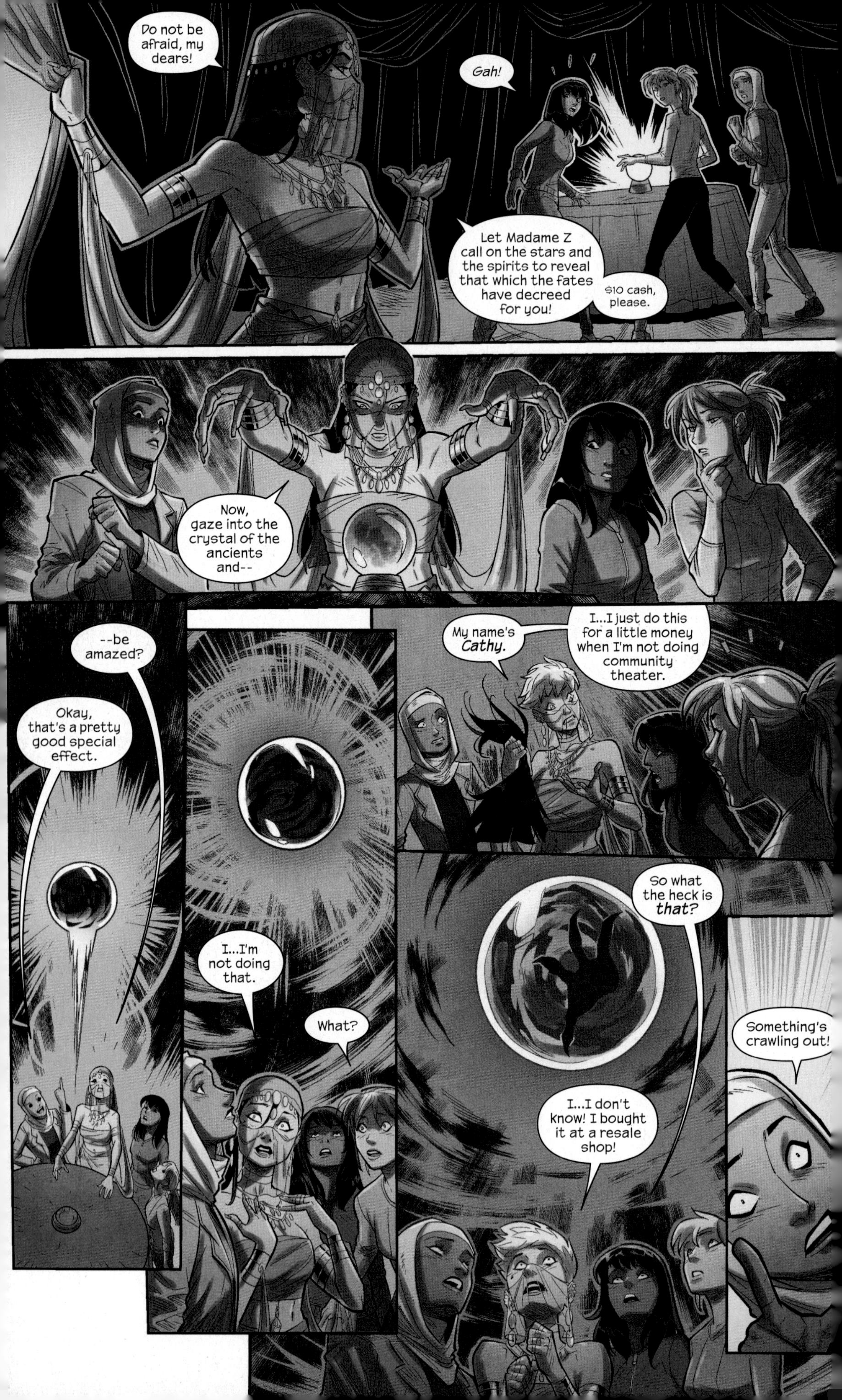

Do not be afraid, my dears!
Gah!
Let Madame Z call on the stars and the spirits to reveal that which the fates have decreed for you!
$10 cash, please.
Now, gaze into the crystal of the ancients and--
--be amazed?
Okay, that's a pretty good special effect.
I...I'm not doing that.
What?
My name's *Cathy.*
I...I just do this for a little money when I'm not doing community theater.
So what the heck is *that?*
I...I don't know! I bought it at a resale shop!
Something's crawling out!

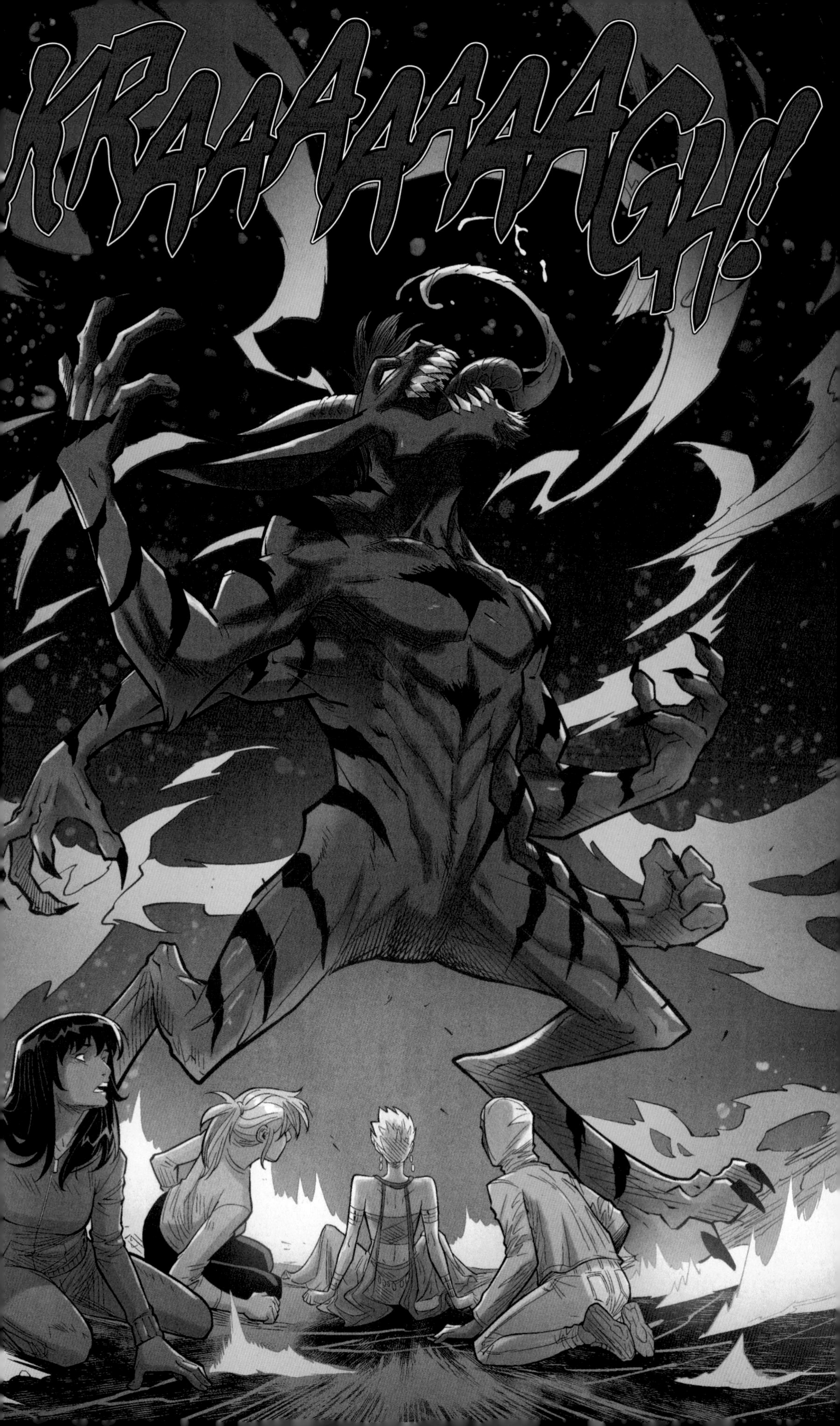
KRAAAAAAAGH!

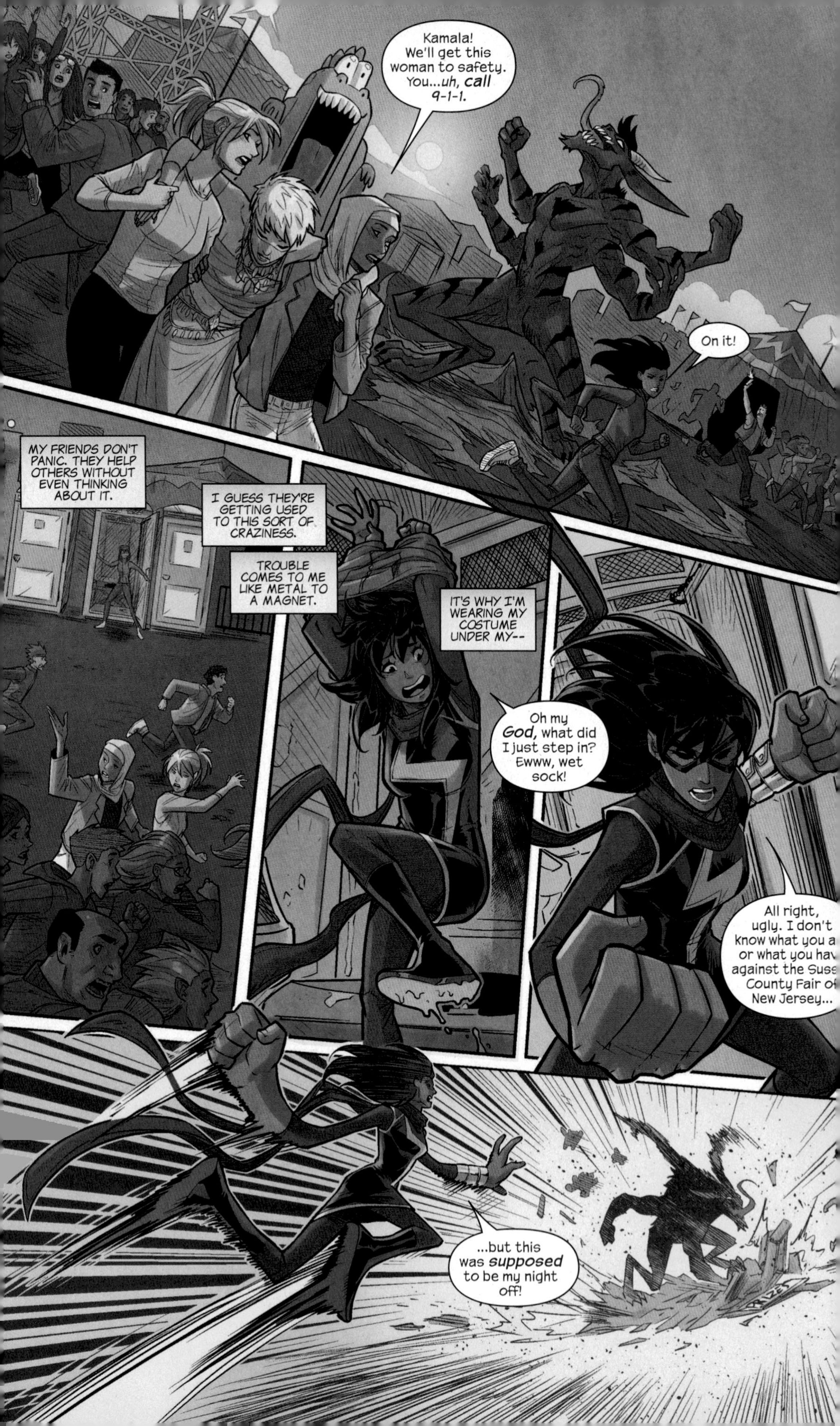
Kamala! We'll get this woman to safety. You...uh, call 9-1-1.
On it!
MY FRIENDS DON'T PANIC. THEY HELP OTHERS WITHOUT EVEN THINKING ABOUT IT.
I GUESS THEY'RE GETTING USED TO THIS SORT OF CRAZINESS.
TROUBLE COMES TO ME LIKE METAL TO A MAGNET.
IT'S WHY I'M WEARING MY COSTUME UNDER MY--
Oh my God, what did I just step in? Ewww, wet sock!
All right, ugly. I don't know what you a or what you hav against the Suss County Fair of New Jersey...
...but this was supposed to be my night off!

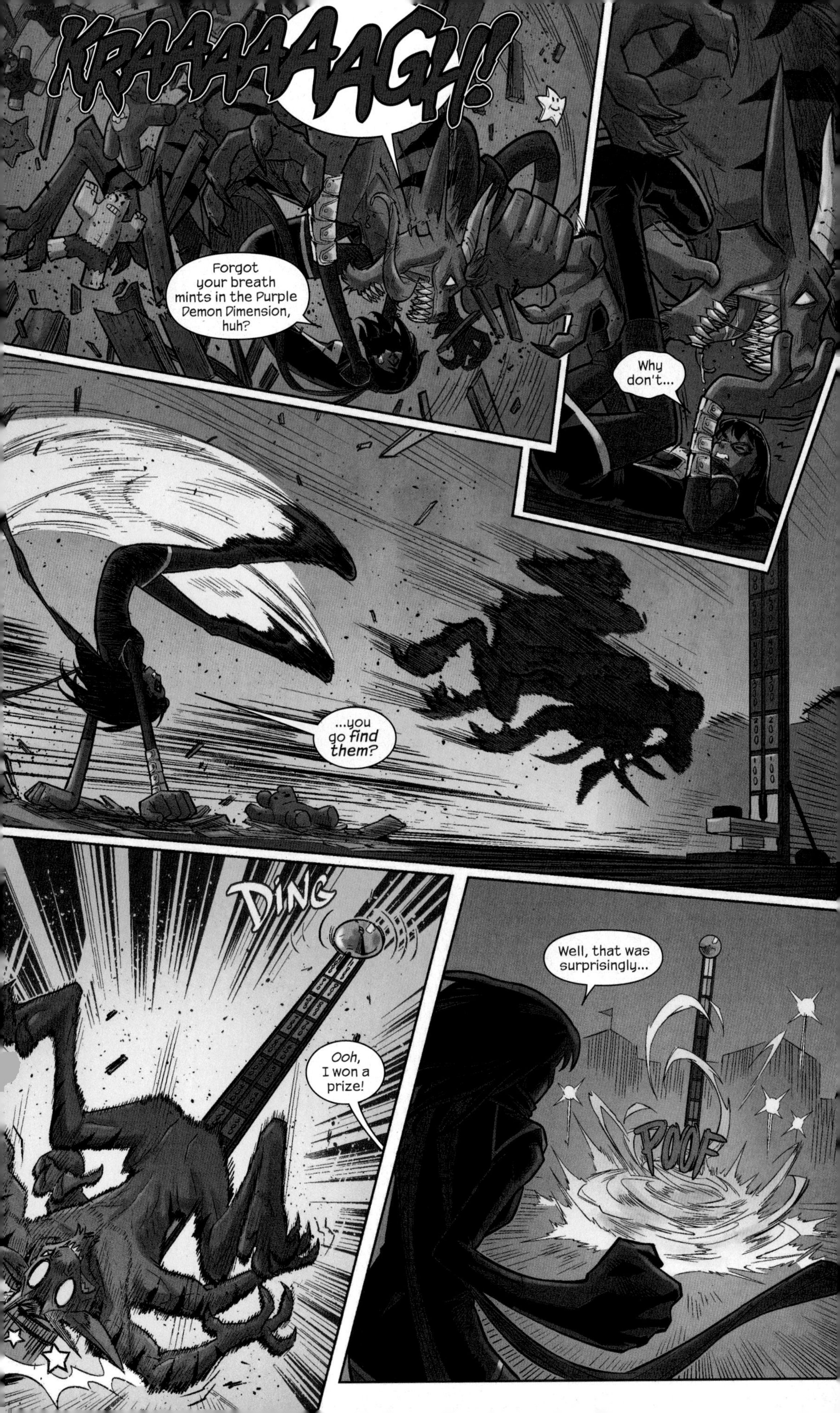
KRAAAAAAAGH!
Forgot your breath mints in the Purple Demon Dimension, huh?
Why don't...
...you go *find them?*
DING
Ooh, I won a prize!
Well, that was surprisingly...
POOF

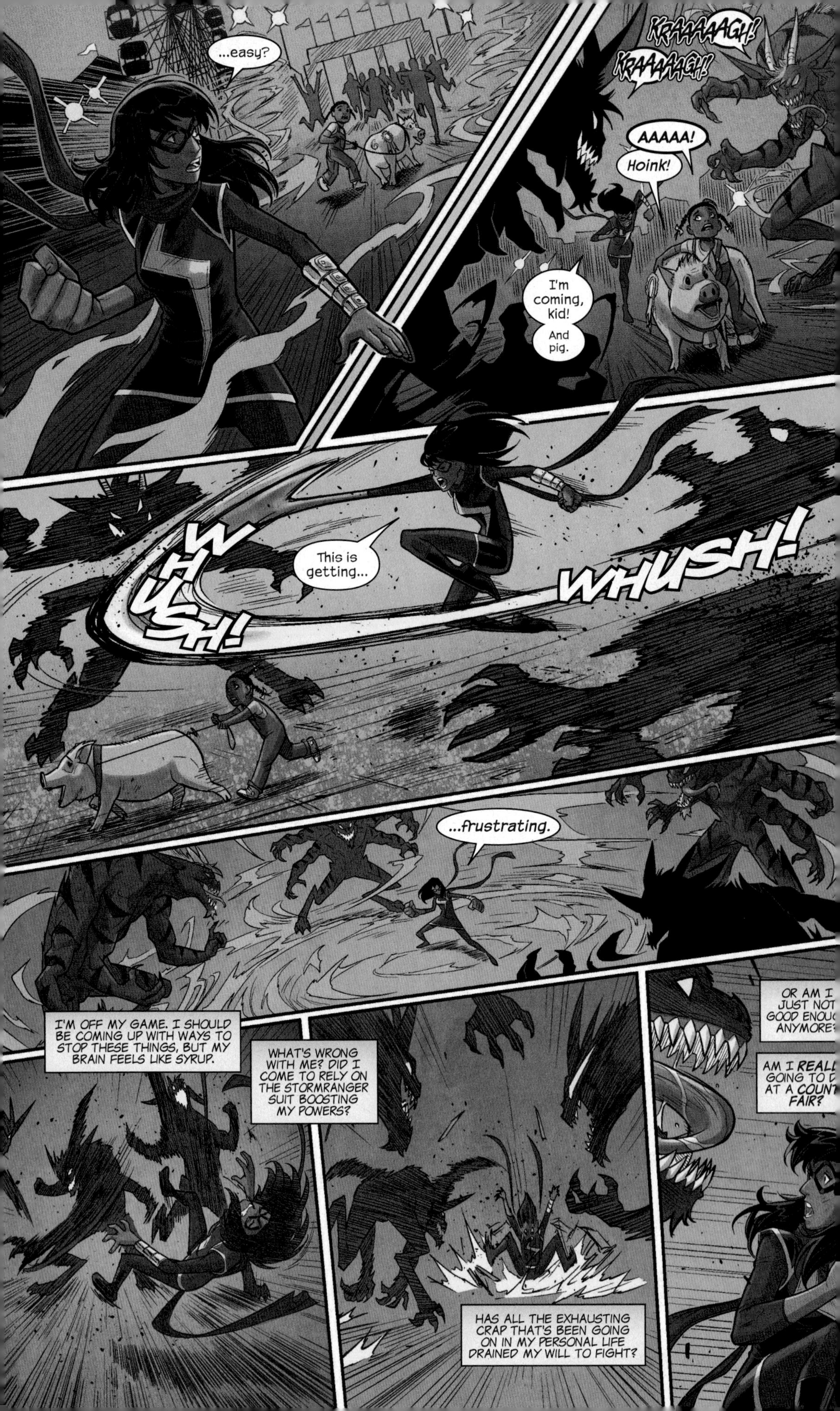

...easy?
KRAAAAAGH!
KRAAAAAGH!
AAAAA!
Hoink!
I'm coming, kid!
And pig.
WHUSH!
This is getting...
WHUSH!
...frustrating.
I'M OFF MY GAME. I SHOULD BE COMING UP WITH WAYS TO STOP THESE THINGS, BUT MY BRAIN FEELS LIKE SYRUP.
WHAT'S WRONG WITH ME? DID I COME TO RELY ON THE STORMRANGER SUIT BOOSTING MY POWERS?
HAS ALL THE EXHAUSTING CRAP THAT'S BEEN GOING ON IN MY PERSONAL LIFE DRAINED MY WILL TO FIGHT?
OR AM I JUST NOT GOOD ENOU ANYMORE
AM I REALL GOING TO D AT A COUNT FAIR?

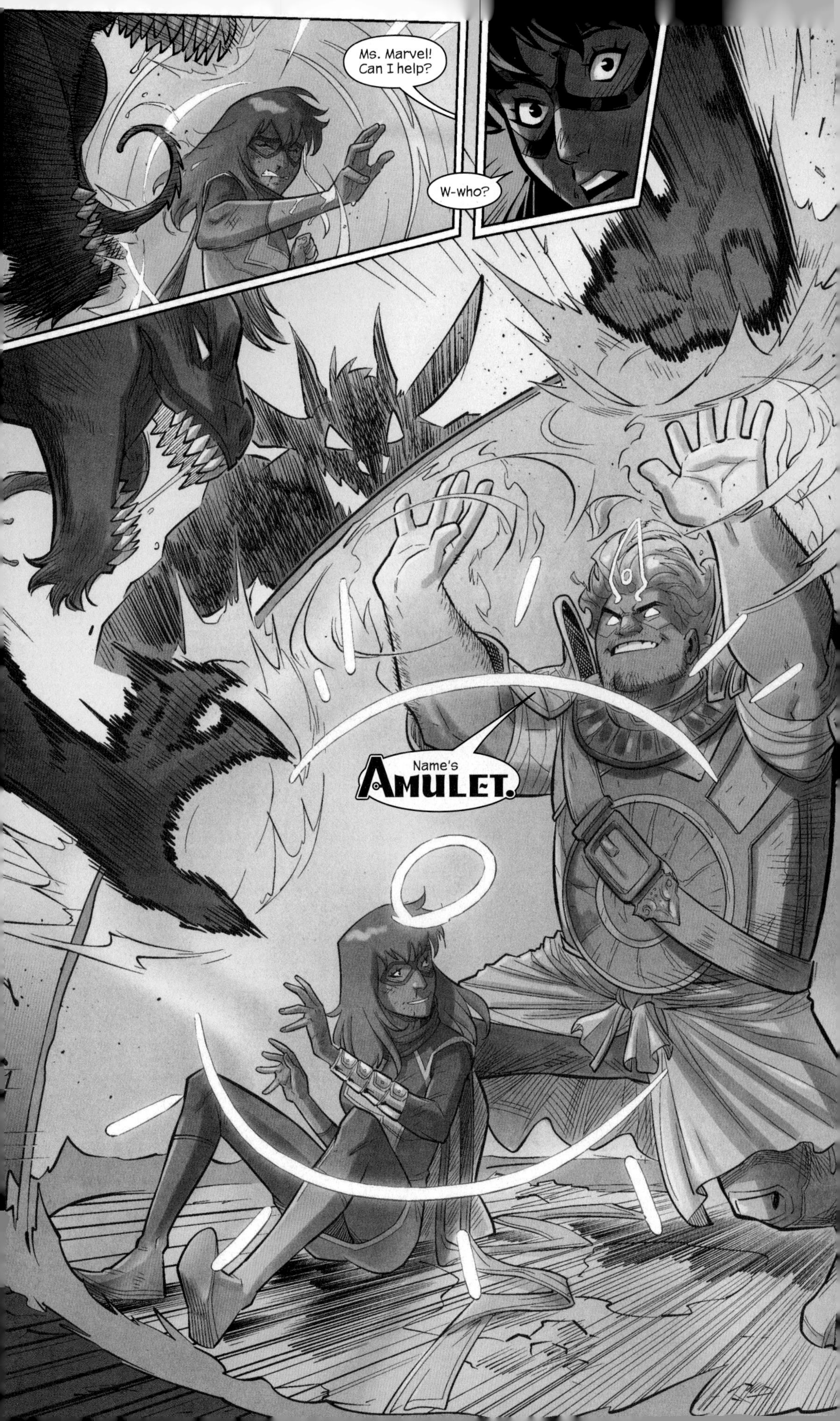
Ms. Marvel! Can I help?
W-who?
Name's AMULET.

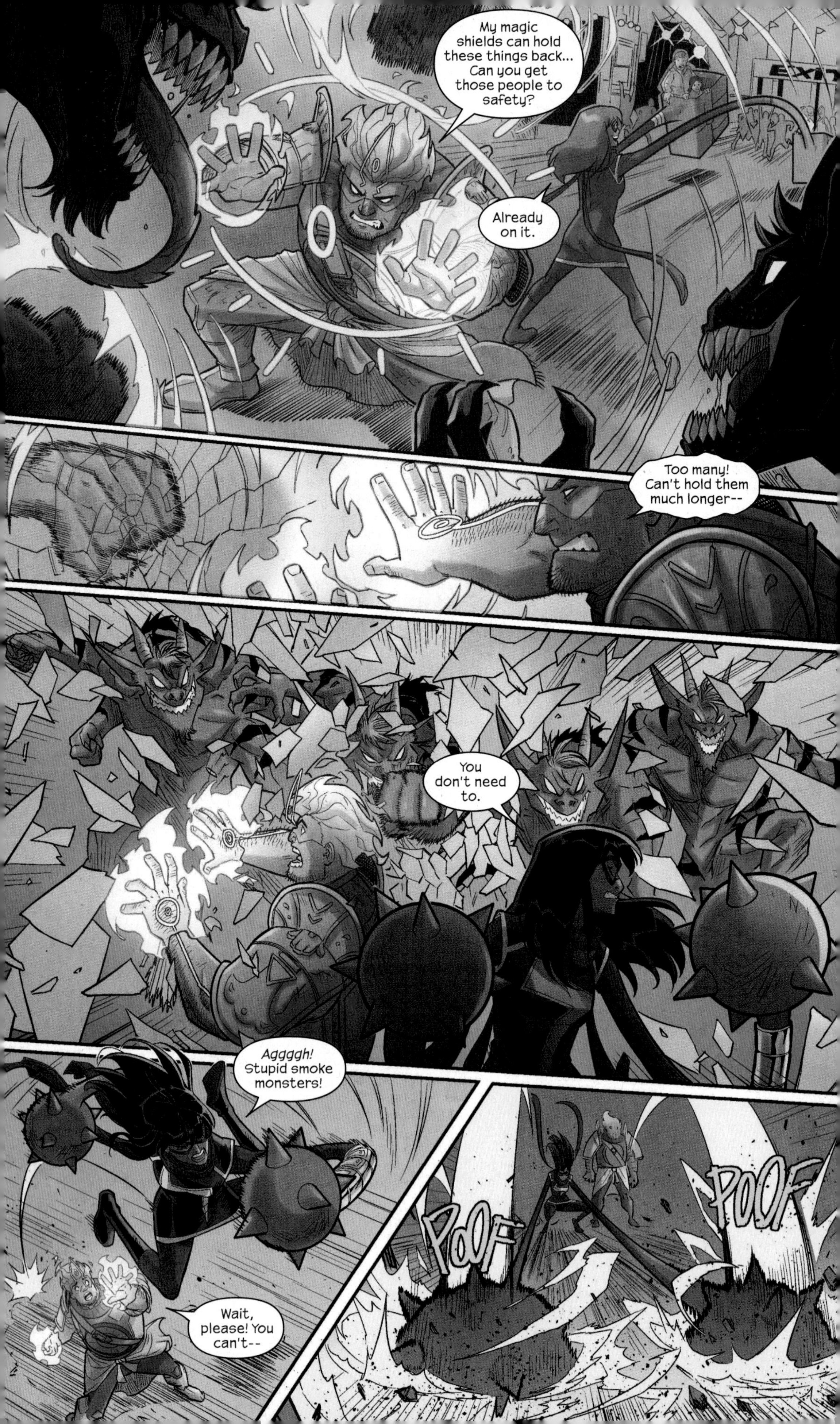
My magic shields can hold these things back... Can you get those people to safety?
EXIT
Already on it.
Too many! Can't hold them much longer--
You don't need to.
Aggggh! Stupid smoke monsters!
Wait, please! You can't--
POOF
POOF

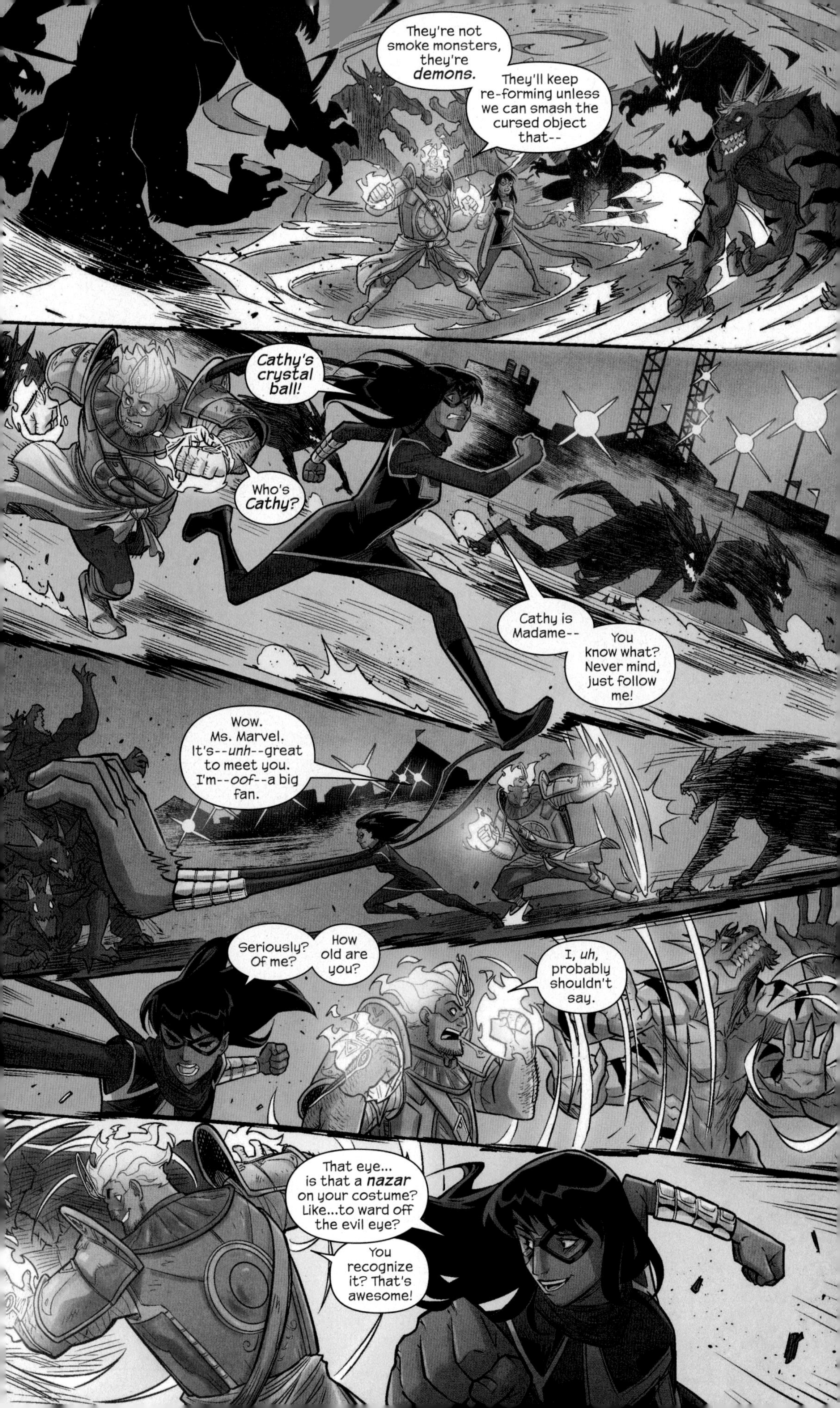
They're not smoke monsters, they're *demons.*
They'll keep re-forming unless we can smash the cursed object that--
Cathy's crystal ball!
Who's *Cathy?*
Cathy is Madame--
You know what? Never mind, just follow me!
Wow. Ms. Marvel. It's--*unh*--great to meet you. I'm--*oof*--a big fan.
Seriously? Of me?
How old are you?
I, *uh*, probably shouldn't say.
That eye... is that a ***nazar*** on your costume? Like...to ward off the evil eye?
You recognize it? That's awesome!

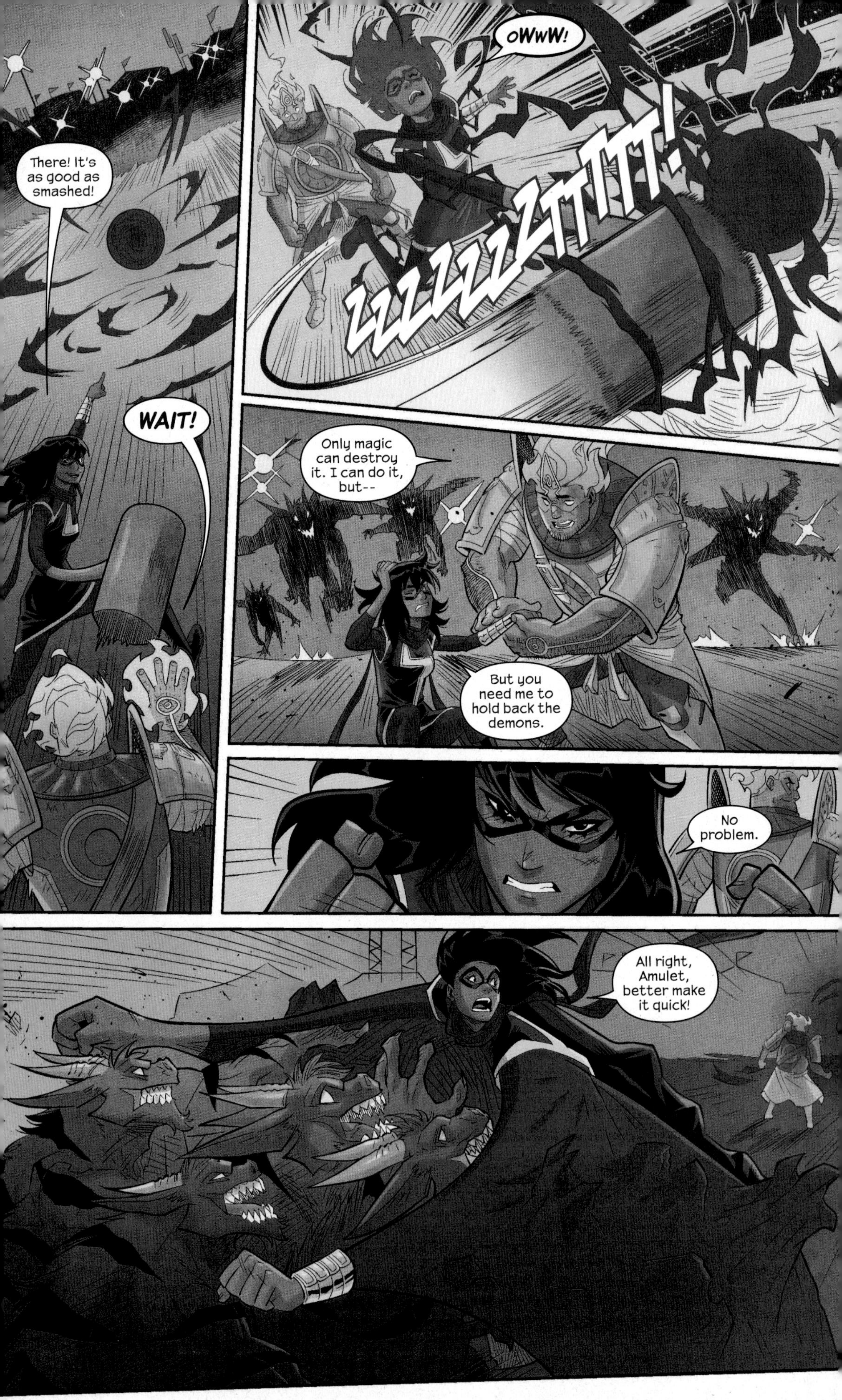
There! It's as good as smashed!
WAIT!
OWWW!
ZZZZZZZTTTTT!
Only magic can destroy it. I can do it, but--
But you need me to hold back the demons.
No problem.
All right, Amulet, better make it quick!

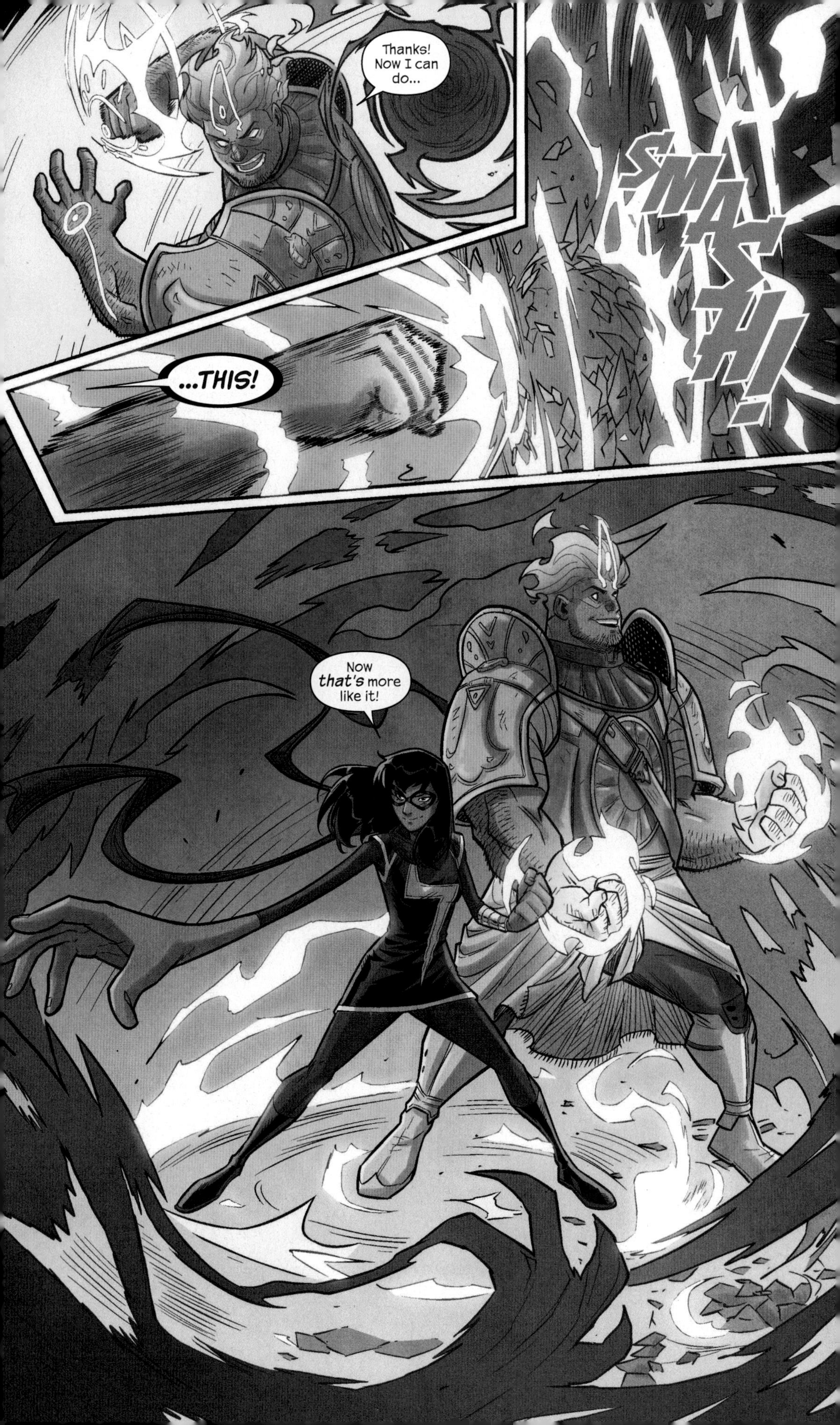
Thanks! Now I can do...
...THIS!
SMASH!
Now that's more like it!

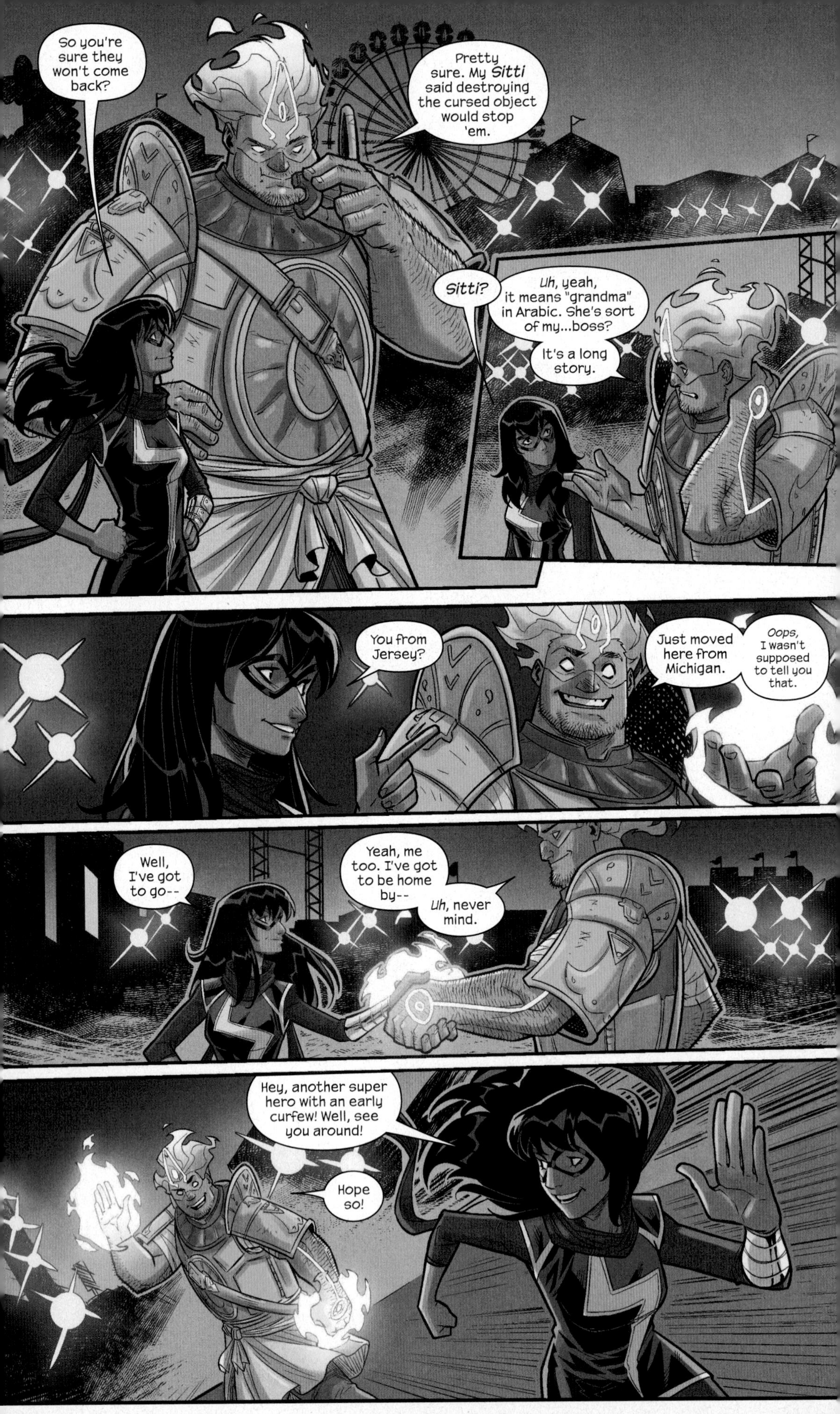

So you're sure they won't come back?
Pretty sure. My *Sitti* said destroying the cursed object would stop 'em.
Sitti?
Uh, yeah, it means "grandma" in Arabic. She's sort of my...boss?
It's a long story.
You from Jersey?
Just moved here from Michigan.
Oops, I wasn't supposed to tell you that.
Well, I've got to go--
Yeah, me too. I've got to be home by--
Uh, never mind.
Hey, another super hero with an early curfew! Well, see you around!
Hope so!

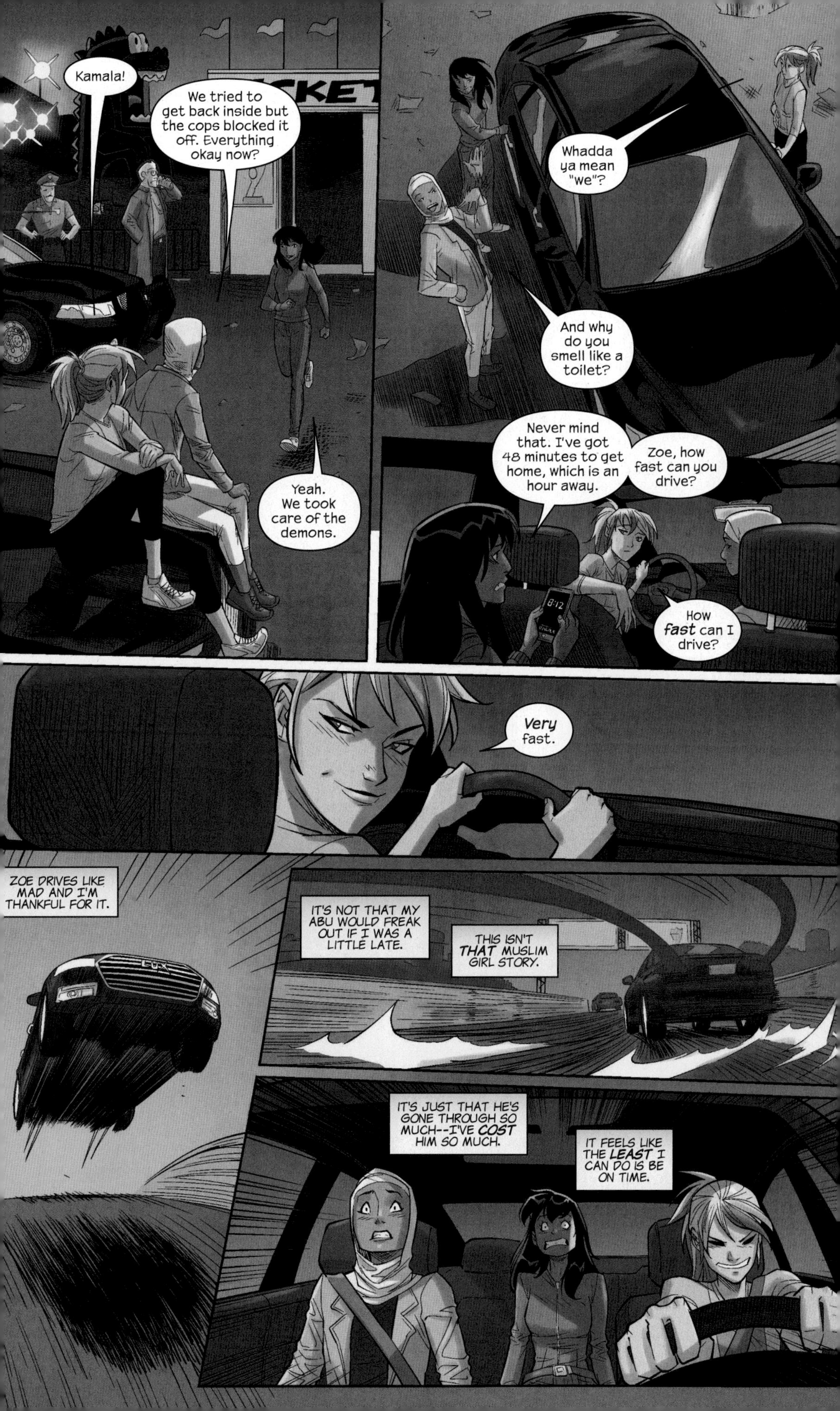
Kamala!
We tried to get back inside but the cops blocked it off. Everything okay now?
Yeah. We took care of the demons.
Whadda ya mean "we"?
And why do you smell like a toilet?
Never mind that. I've got 48 minutes to get home, which is an hour away.
Zoe, how fast can you drive?
How fast can I drive?
Very fast.
ZOE DRIVES LIKE MAD AND I'M THANKFUL FOR IT.
IT'S NOT THAT MY ABU WOULD FREAK OUT IF I WAS A LITTLE LATE.
THIS ISN'T THAT MUSLIM GIRL STORY.
IT'S JUST THAT HE'S GONE THROUGH SO MUCH--I'VE COST HIM SO MUCH.
IT FEELS LIKE THE LEAST I CAN DO IS BE ON TIME.

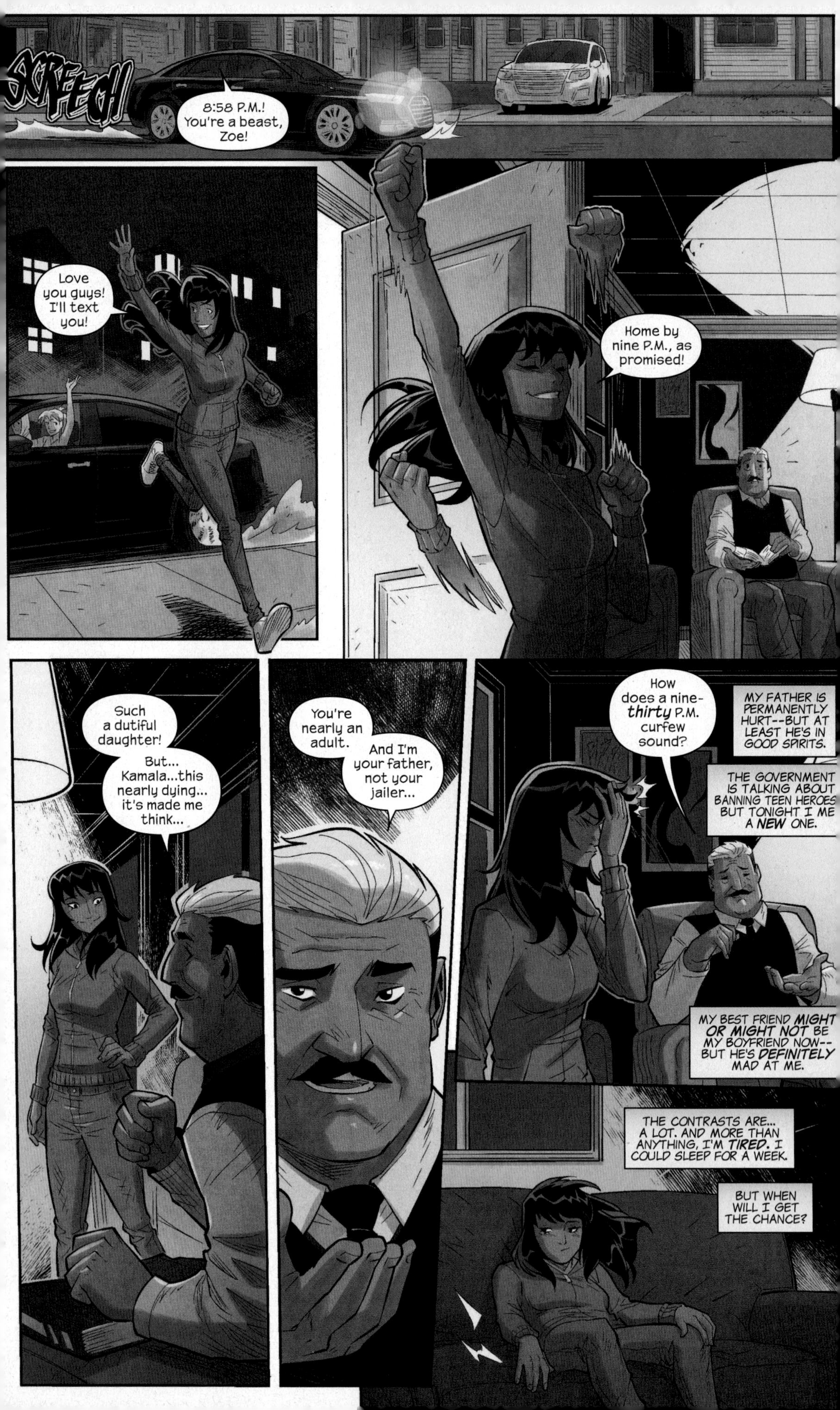
SCREECH
8:58 P.M.! You're a beast, Zoe!
Love you guys! I'll text you!
Home by nine P.M., as promised!
Such a dutiful daughter!
But... Kamala...this nearly dying... it's made me think...
You're nearly an adult.
And I'm your father, not your jailer...
How does a nine-thirty P.M. curfew sound?
MY FATHER IS PERMANENTLY HURT--BUT AT LEAST HE'S IN GOOD SPIRITS.
THE GOVERNMENT IS TALKING ABOUT BANNING TEEN HEROES BUT TONIGHT I ME A NEW ONE.
MY BEST FRIEND MIGHT OR MIGHT NOT BE MY BOYFRIEND NOW--BUT HE'S DEFINITELY MAD AT ME.
THE CONTRASTS ARE... A LOT. AND MORE THAN ANYTHING, I'M TIRED. I COULD SLEEP FOR A WEEK.
BUT WHEN WILL I GET THE CHANCE?

PROTECT OUR CHILDREN
PROTECT OUR FUTURE
Math
DOES YOUR SENATOR SUPPORT
KAMALA'S LAW?
Contact C.R.A.D.L.E. to find out more.

This issue takes place after *Outlawed #1*.

Kamala's life was finally getting back to normal — her father is recovering from his illness, and she even took the first steps toward a romantic relationship with her longtime friend Bruno. But it couldn't last...

Kamala and the Champions were serving as protection for a young environmental activist during a scientific summit at Coles Academic when the school was attacked by both a dragon and a group of armed mercenaries. The team managed to defeat the dragon, but a series of strategic miscalculations led to a disaster that destroyed half the school with Kamala inside.

Kamala was mistaken for an innocent victim of teen vigilantism and rushed to the hospital, and the senate passed a law in her honor that banned underage super heroes. Through it all, Kamala remained in a coma, unaware of just how quickly and drastically her world had changed...

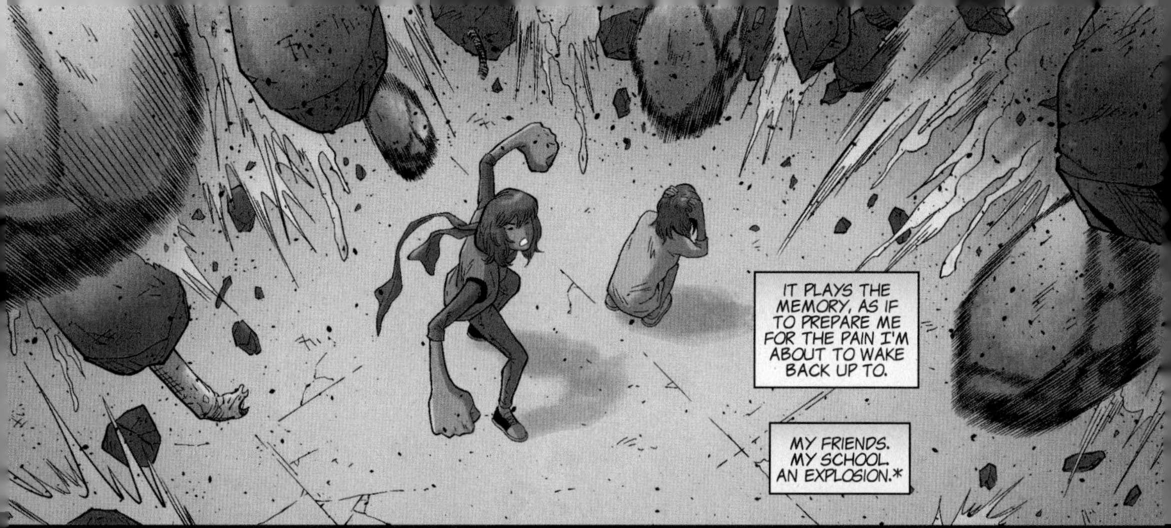
IT PLAYS THE MEMORY, AS IF TO PREPARE ME FOR THE PAIN I'M ABOUT TO WAKE BACK UP TO.
MY FRIENDS. MY SCHOOL. AN EXPLOSION.*

*Seen in **Outlawed #1**. -Alanna

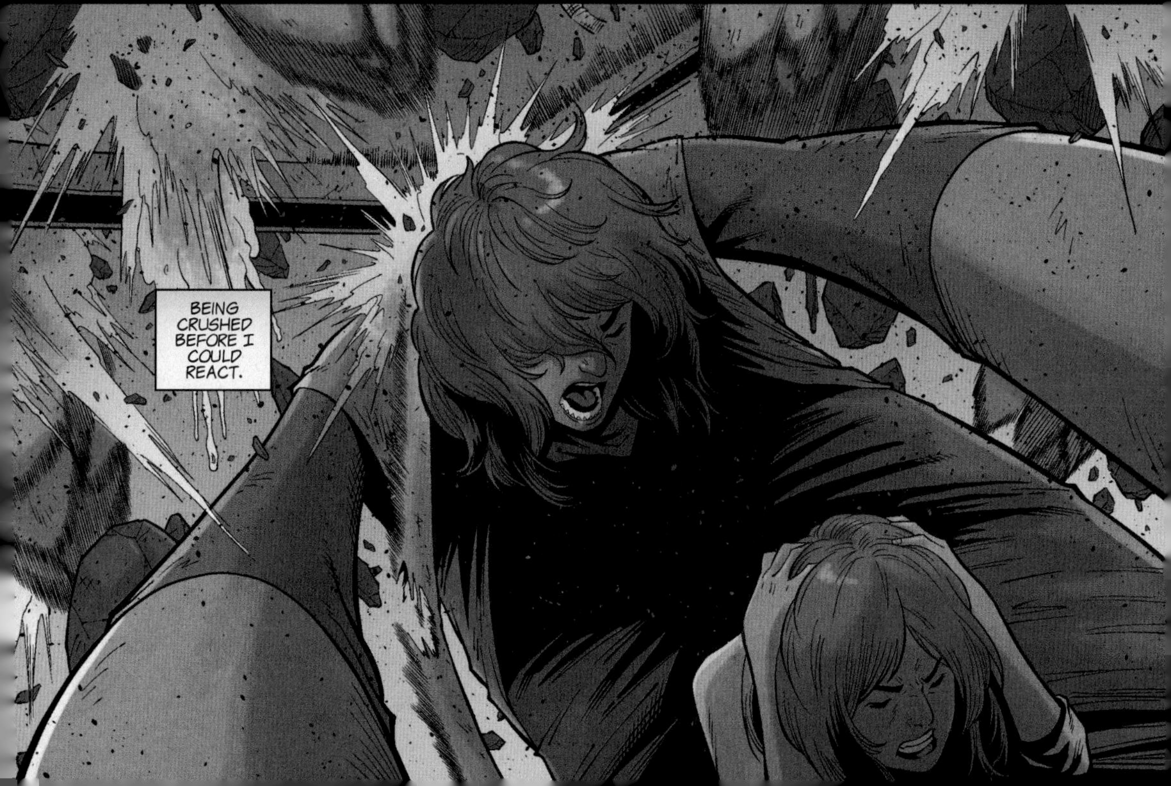
BEING CRUSHED BEFORE I COULD REACT.

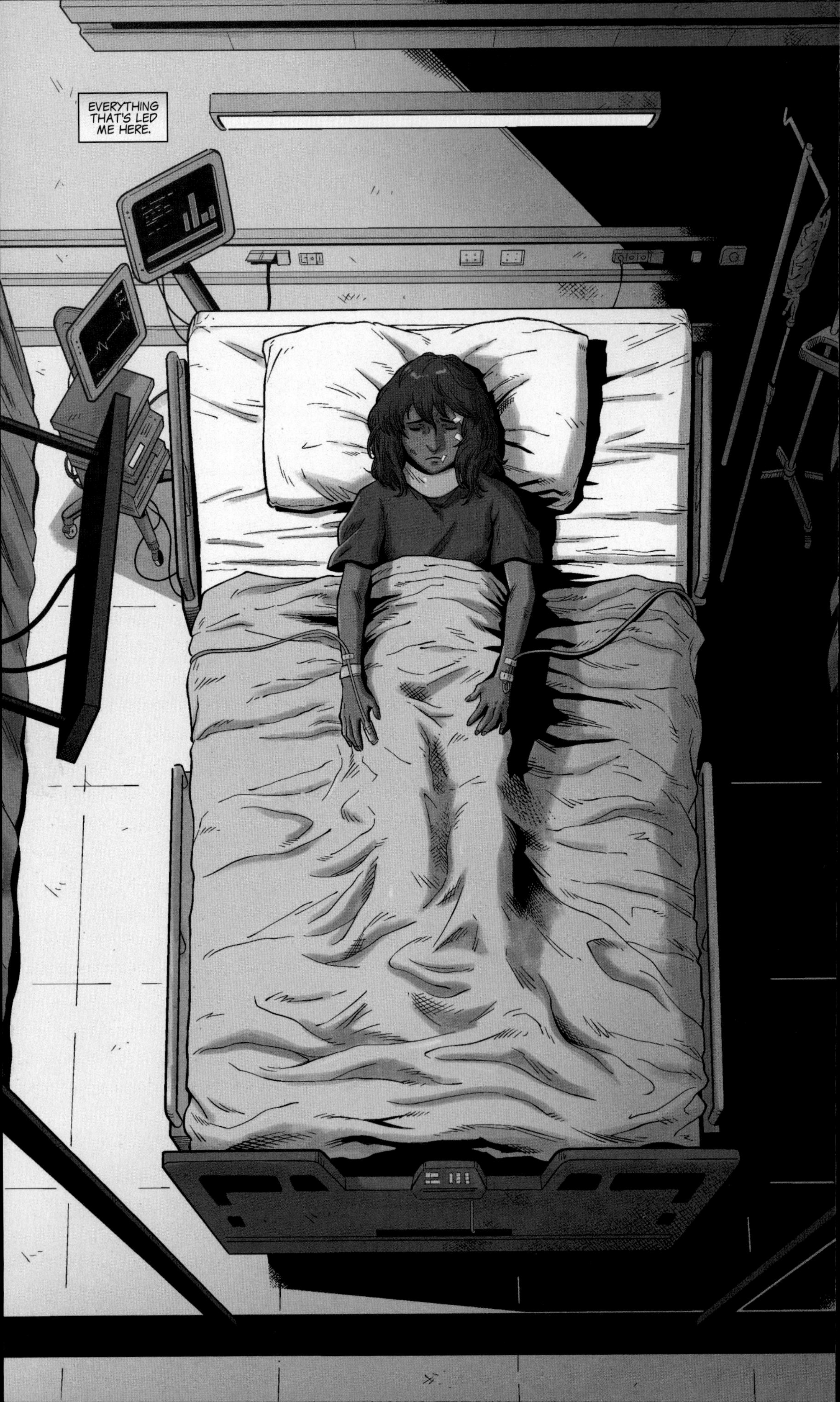
EVERYTHING THAT'S LED ME HERE.

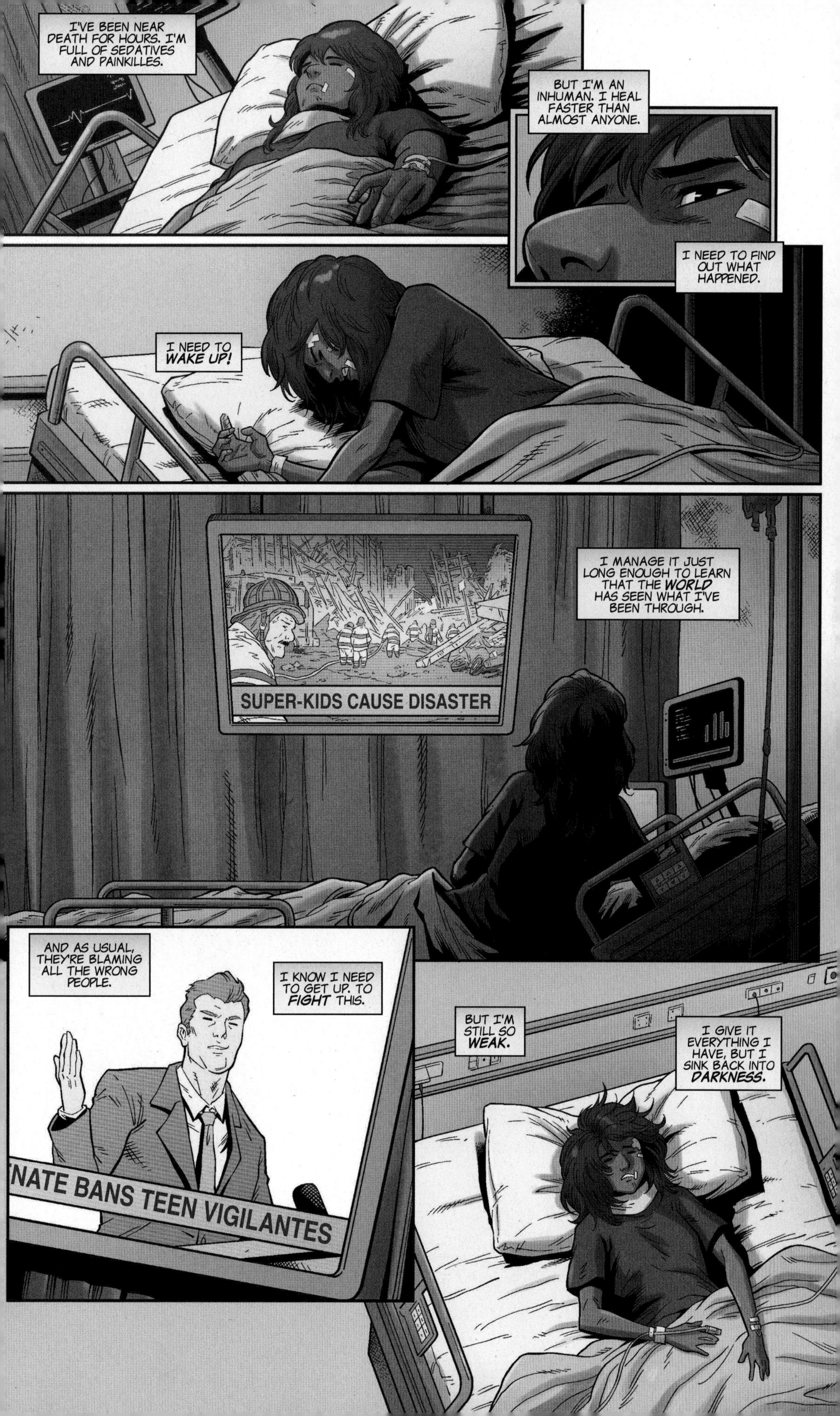
I'VE BEEN NEAR DEATH FOR HOURS. I'M FULL OF SEDATIVES AND PAINKILLES.
BUT I'M AN INHUMAN. I HEAL FASTER THAN ALMOST ANYONE.
I NEED TO FIND OUT WHAT HAPPENED.
I NEED TO *WAKE UP!*
I MANAGE IT JUST LONG ENOUGH TO LEARN THAT THE *WORLD* HAS SEEN WHAT I'VE BEEN THROUGH.
SUPER-KIDS CAUSE DISASTER
AND AS USUAL, THEY'RE BLAMING ALL THE WRONG PEOPLE.
I KNOW I NEED TO GET UP. TO *FIGHT* THIS.
NATE BANS TEEN VIGILANTES
BUT I'M STILL SO *WEAK.*
I GIVE IT EVERYTHING I HAVE, BUT I SINK BACK INTO *DARKNESS.*

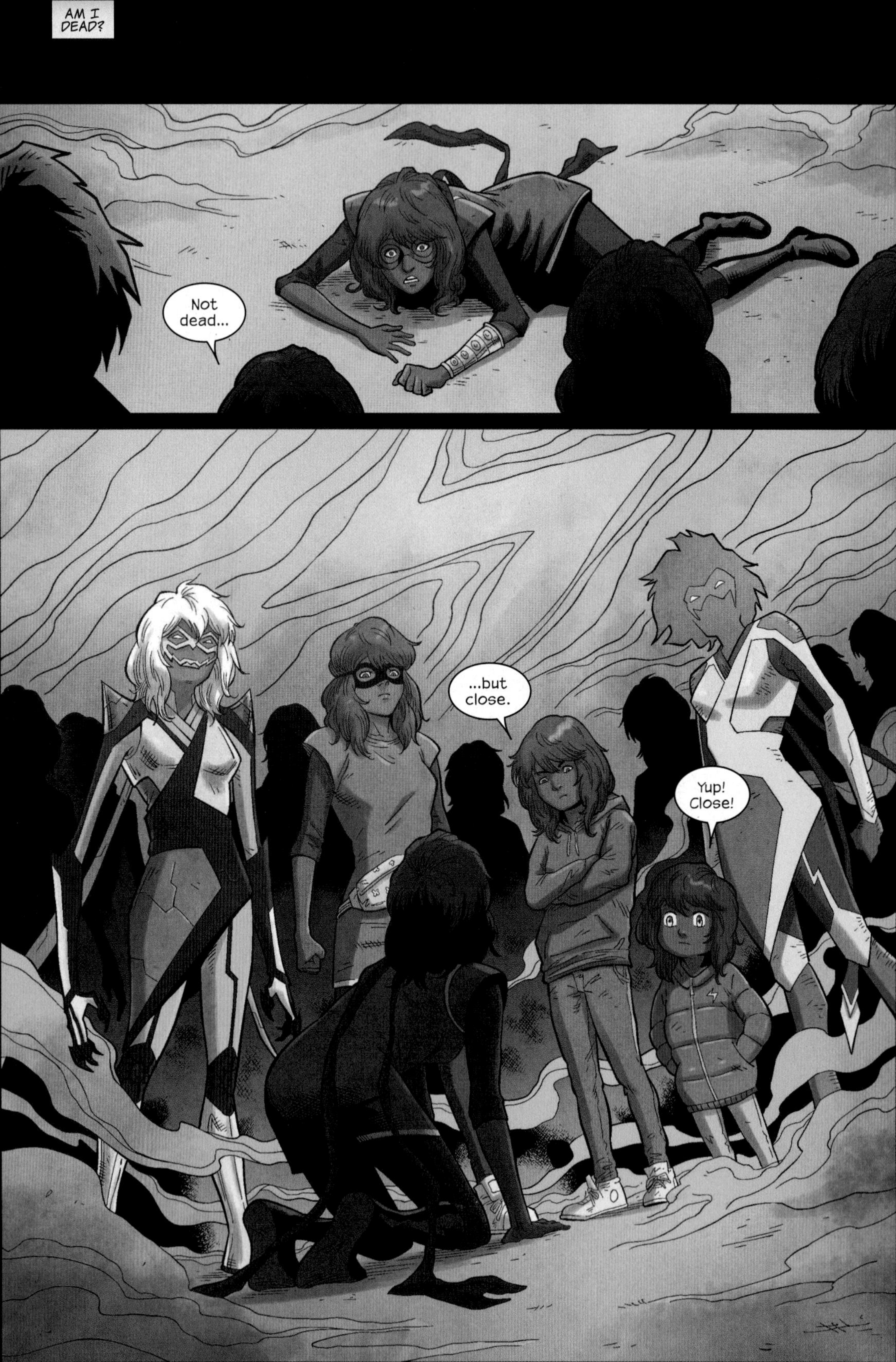
AM I DEAD?
Not dead...
...but close.
Yup! Close!

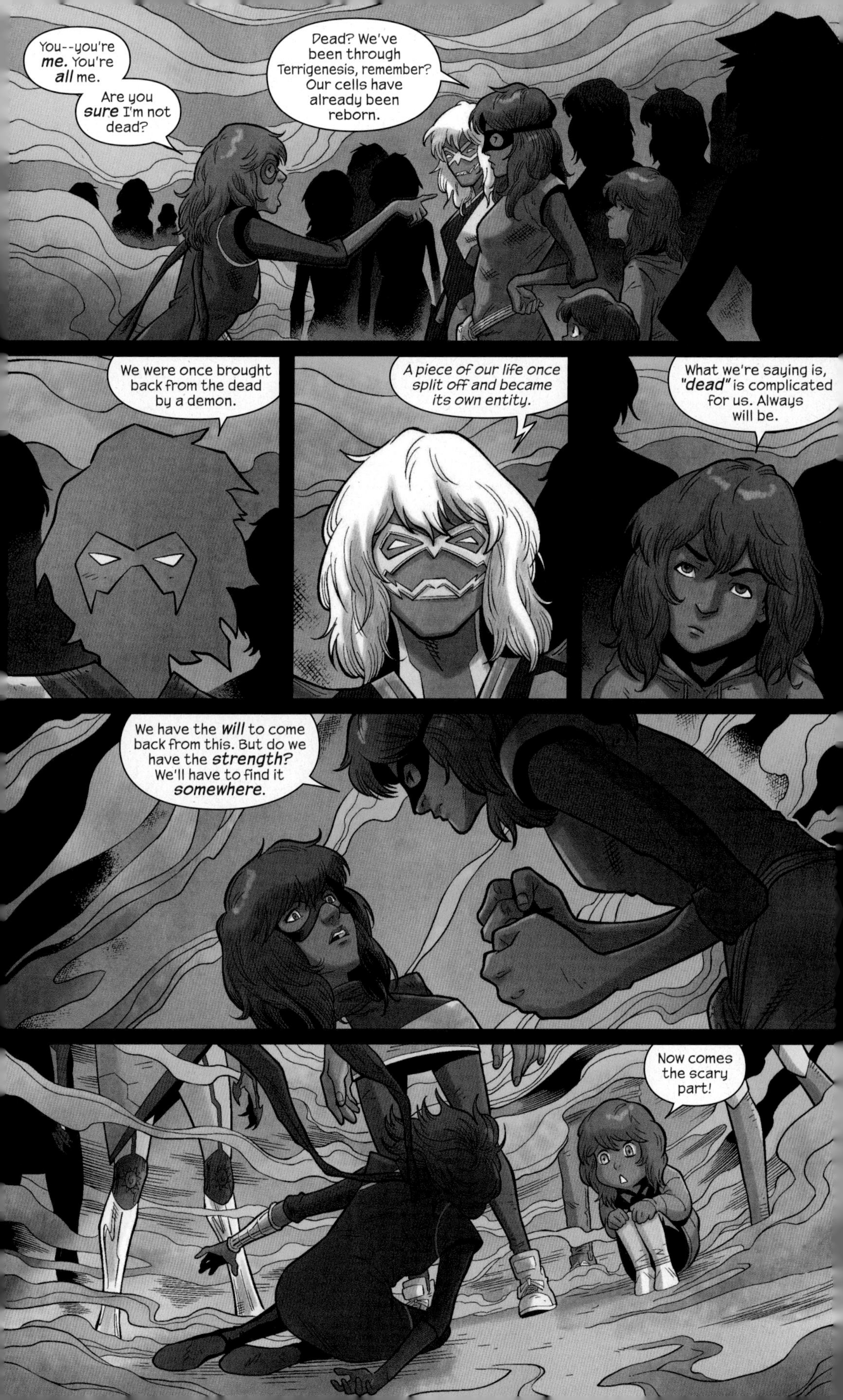
You--you're *me.* You're *all* me.
Are you *sure* I'm not dead?
Dead? We've been through Terrigenesis, remember? Our cells have already been reborn.
We were once brought back from the dead by a demon.
A piece of our life once split off and became its own entity.
What we're saying is, ***"dead"*** is complicated for us. Always will be.
We have the *will* to come back from this. But do we have the *strength?* We'll have to find it *somewhere*.
Now comes the scary part!

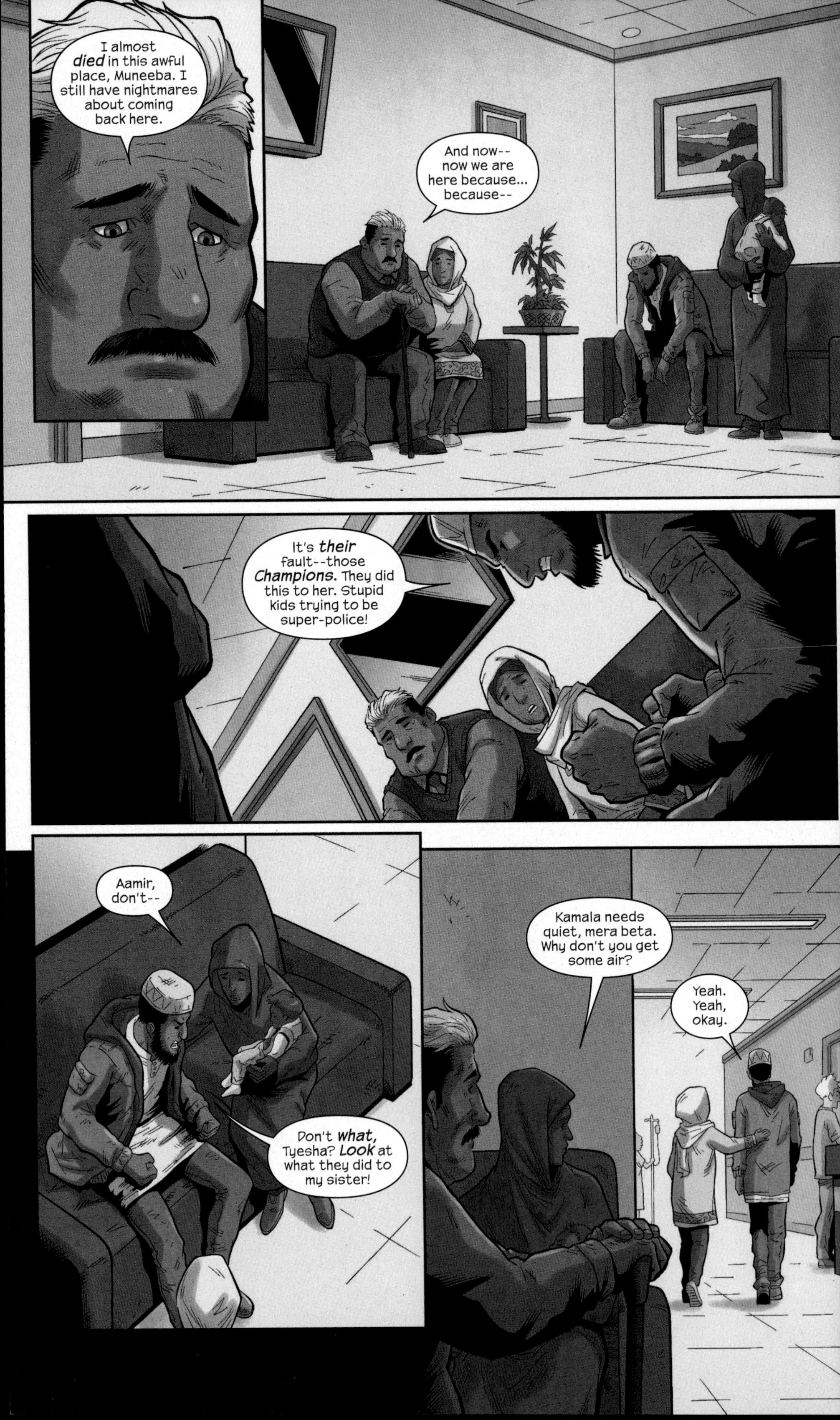
I almost *died* in this awful place, Muneeba. I still have nightmares about coming back here.
And now-- now we are here because... because--
It's *their* fault--those *Champions.* They did this to her. Stupid kids trying to be super-police!
Aamir, don't--
Don't *what,* Tyesha? *Look* at what they did to my sister!
Kamala needs quiet, mera beta. Why don't you get some air?
Yeah. Yeah, okay.

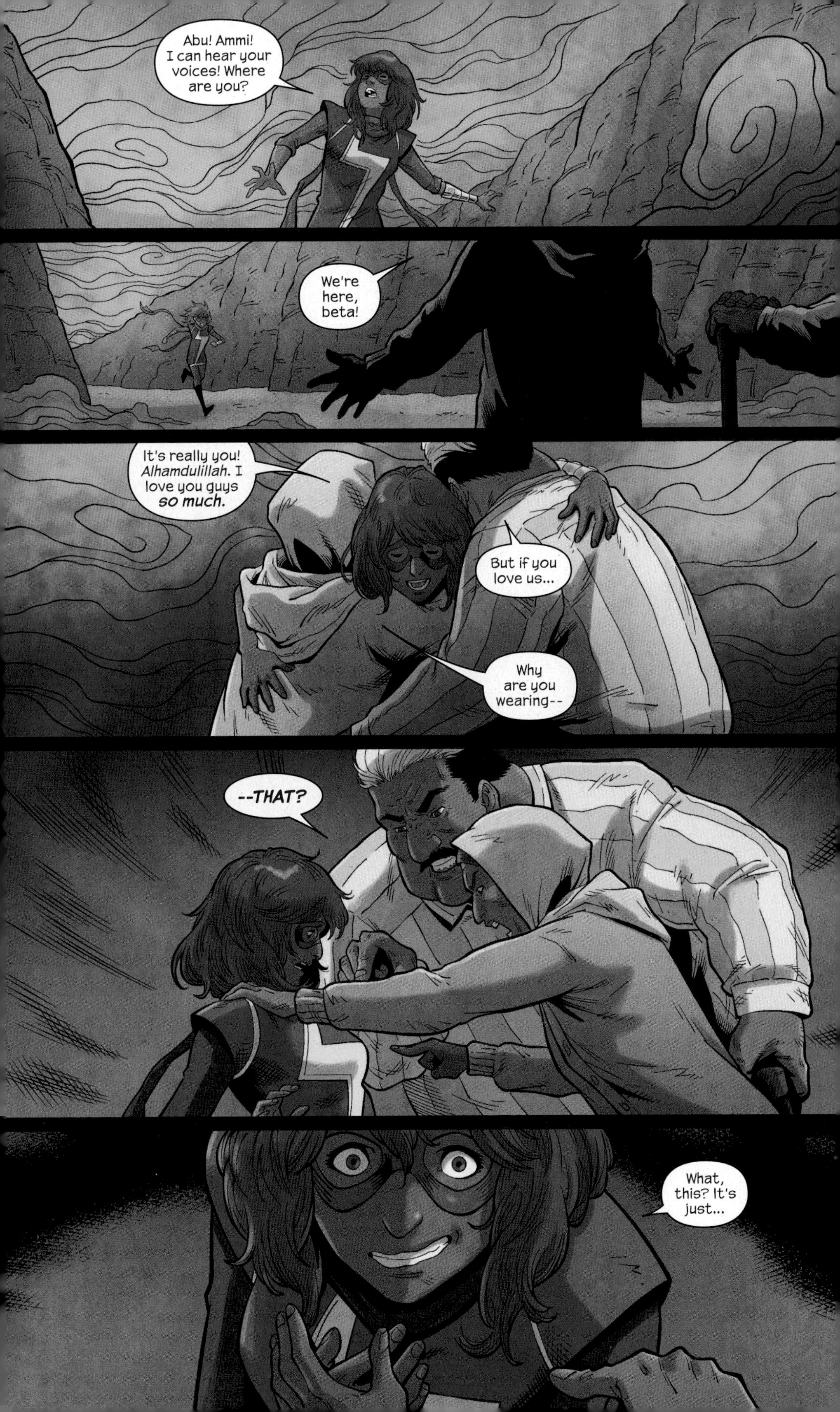

Abu! Ammi! I can hear your voices! Where are you?
We're here, beta!
It's really you! *Alhamdulillah.* I love you guys **so much.**
But if you love us...
Why are you wearing--
--THAT?
What, this? It's just...

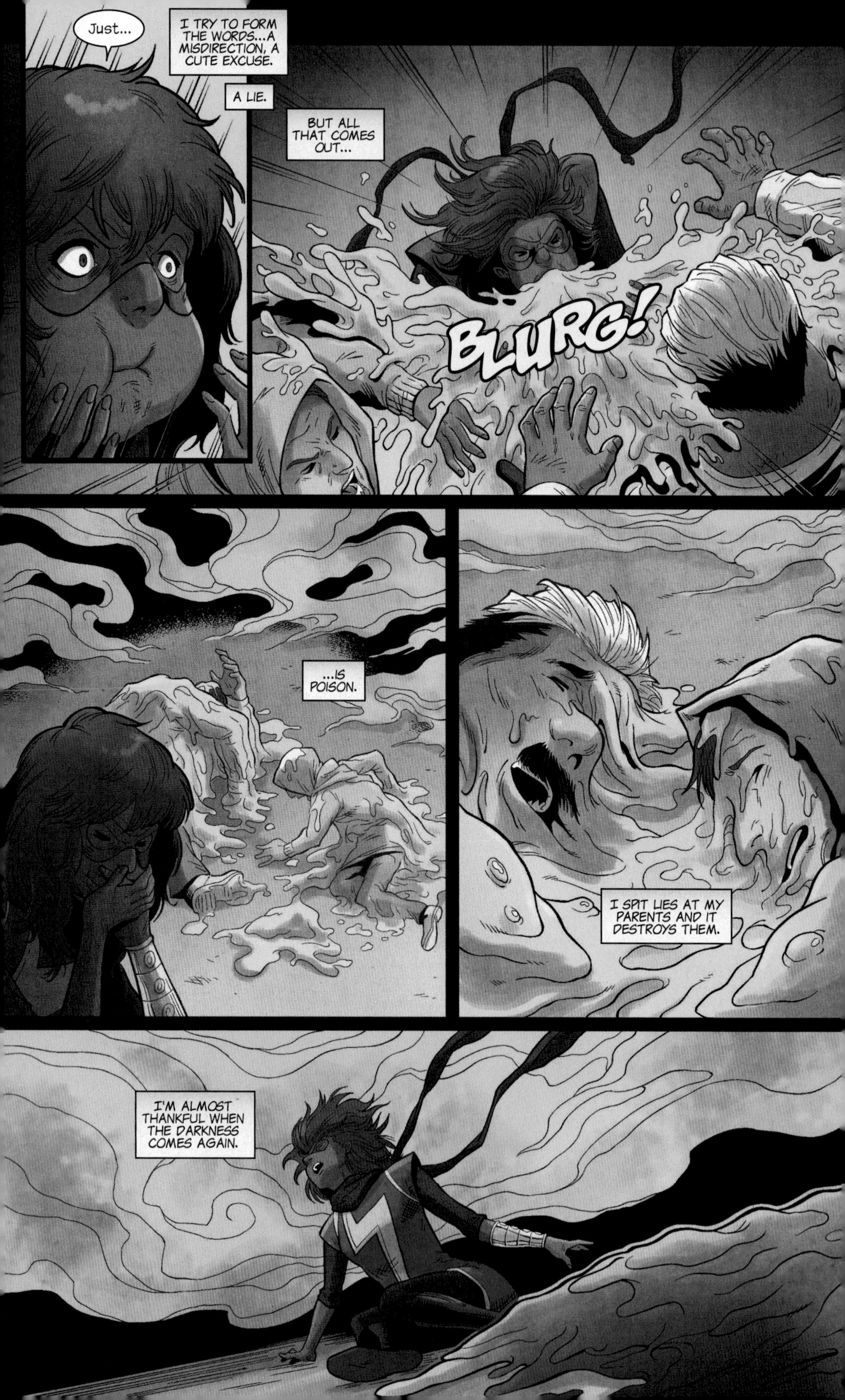
Just...
I TRY TO FORM THE WORDS...A MISDIRECTION, A CUTE EXCUSE.
A LIE.
BUT ALL THAT COMES OUT...
BLURG!
...IS POISON.
I SPIT LIES AT MY PARENTS AND IT DESTROYS THEM.
I'M ALMOST THANKFUL WHEN THE DARKNESS COMES AGAIN.

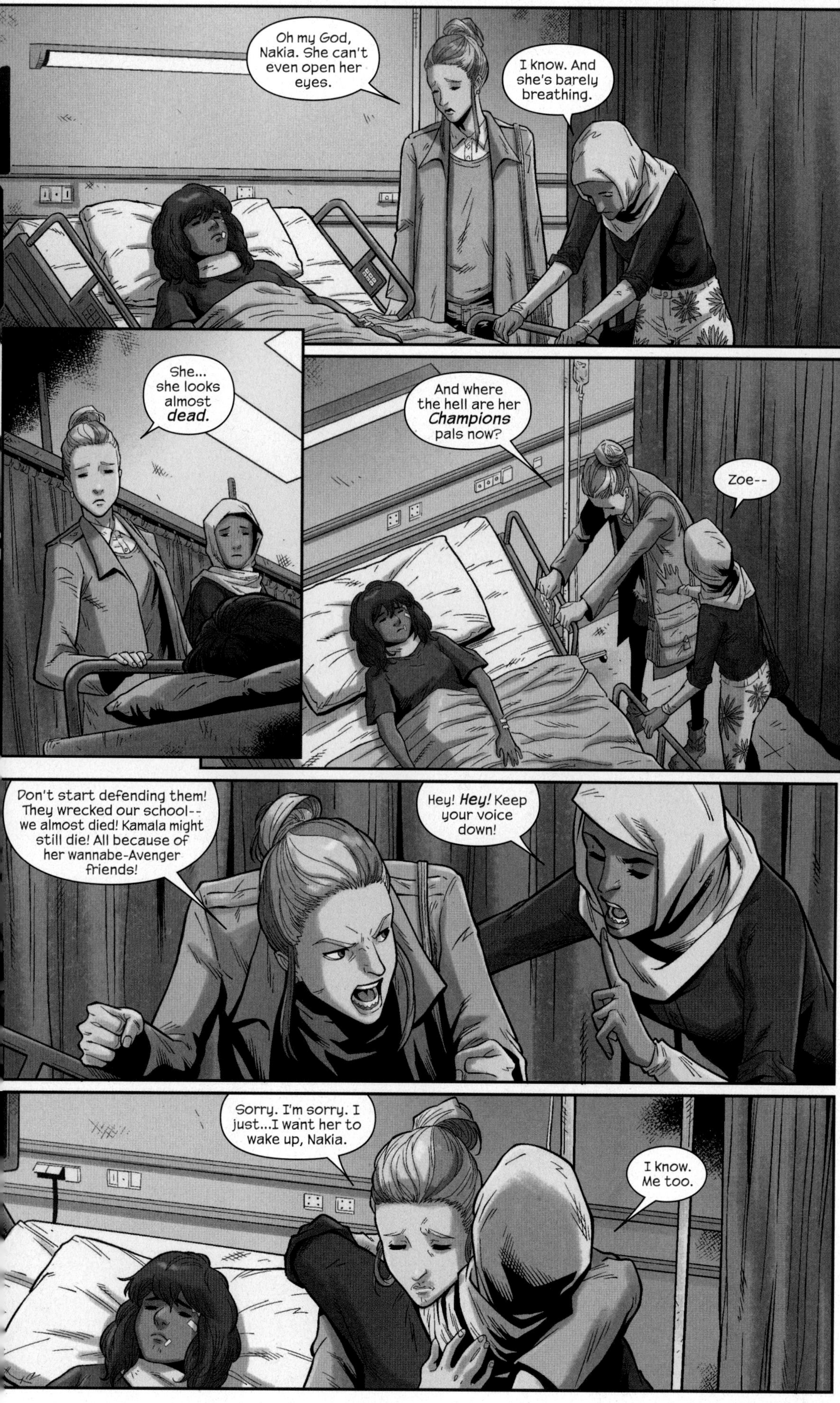

Oh my God, Nakia. She can't even open her eyes.
I know. And she's barely breathing.
She... she looks almost *dead.*
And where the hell are her *Champions* pals now?
Zoe--
Don't start defending them! They wrecked our school-- we almost died! Kamala might still die! All because of her wannabe-Avenger friends!
Hey! *Hey!* Keep your voice down!
Sorry. I'm sorry. I just...I want her to wake up, Nakia.
I know. Me too.

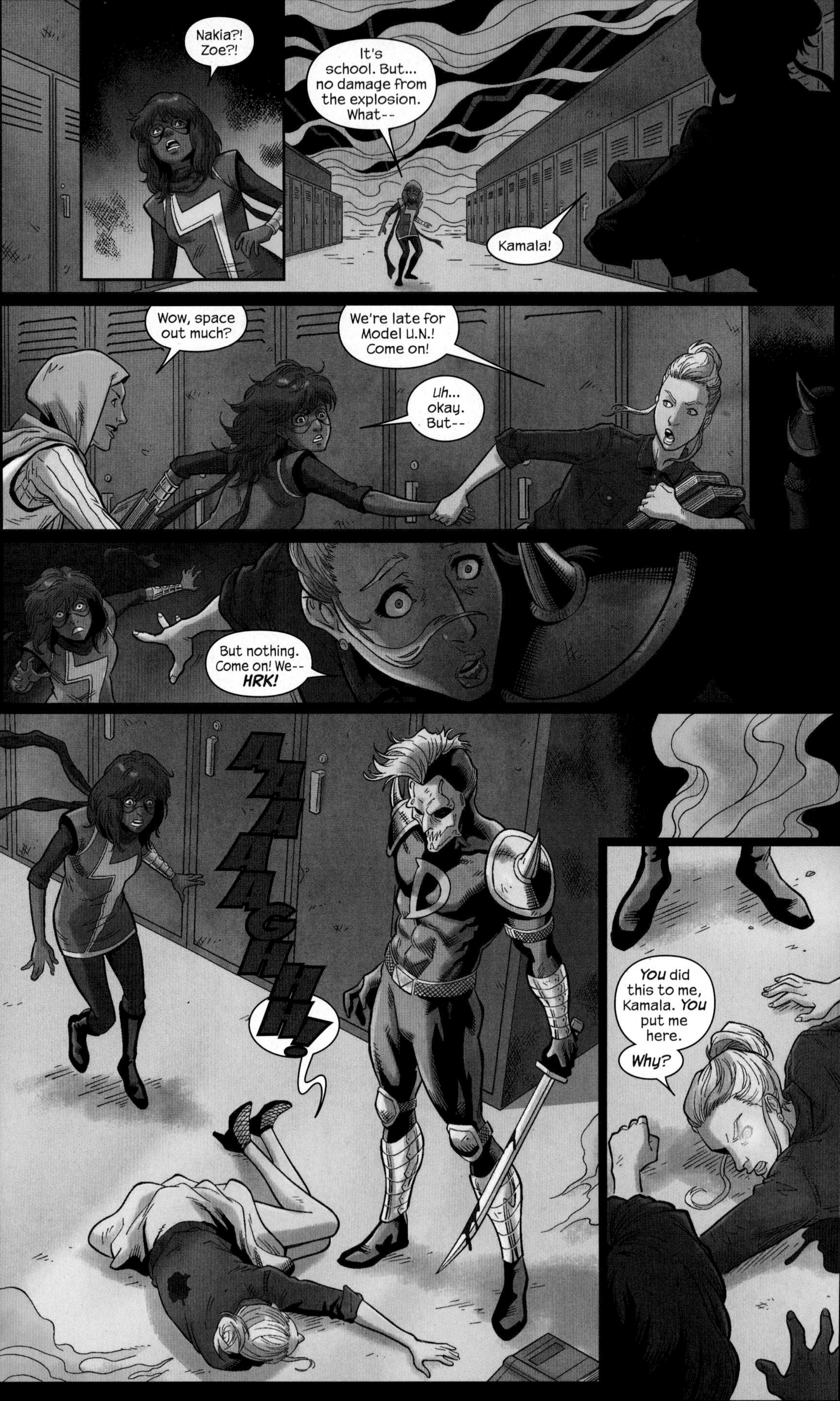

Nakia?! Zoe?!
It's school. But... no damage from the explosion. What--
Kamala!
Wow, space out much?
We're late for Model U.N.! Come on!
Uh... okay. But--
But nothing. Come on! We-- **HRK!**
AAAAAAGHHH!
You did this to me, Kamala. *You* put me here. *Why?*

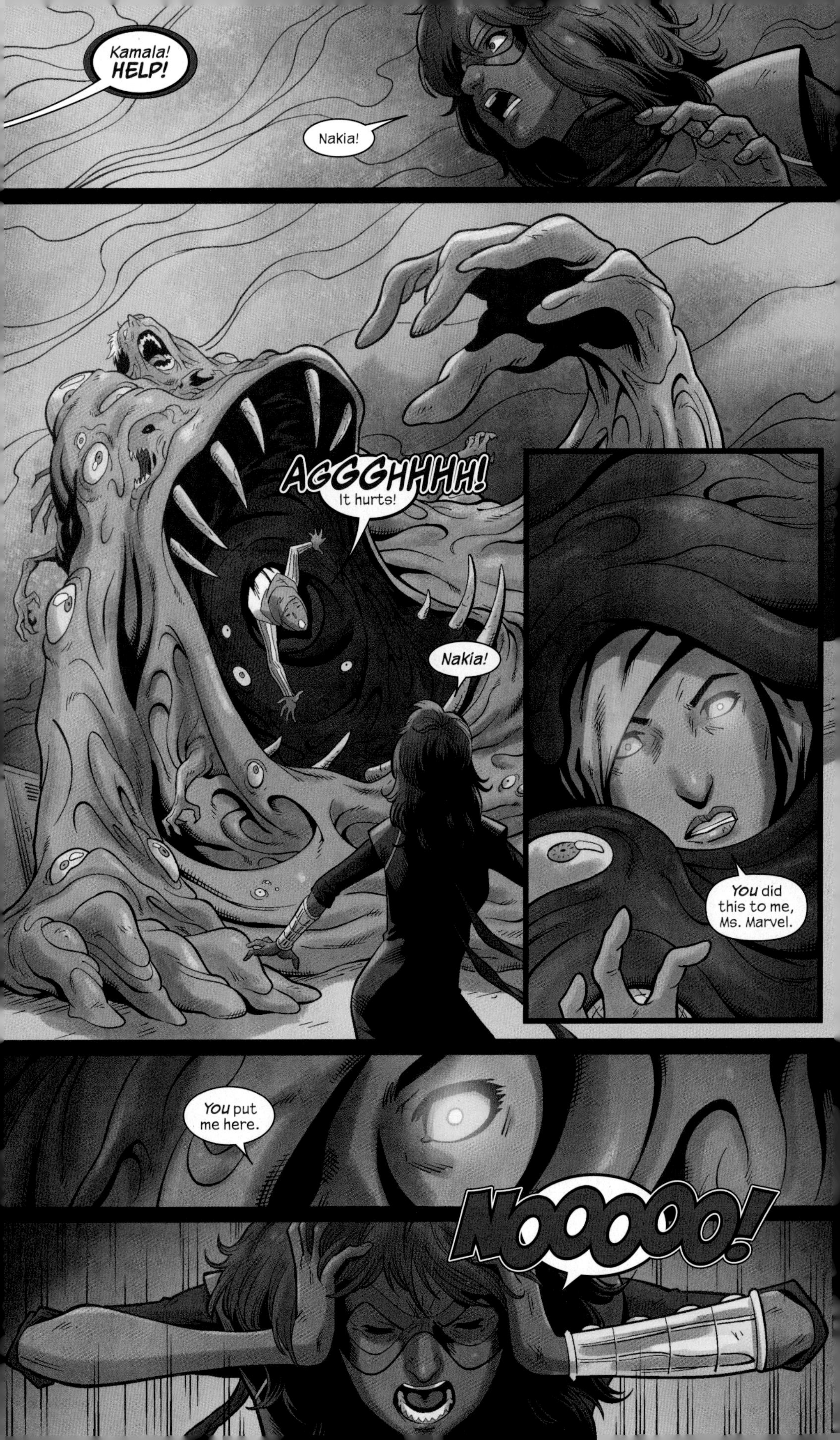
Kamala! HELP!
Nakia!
AGGGHHHH! It hurts!
Nakia!
YOU did this to me, Ms. Marvel.
YOU put me here.
NOOOOO!

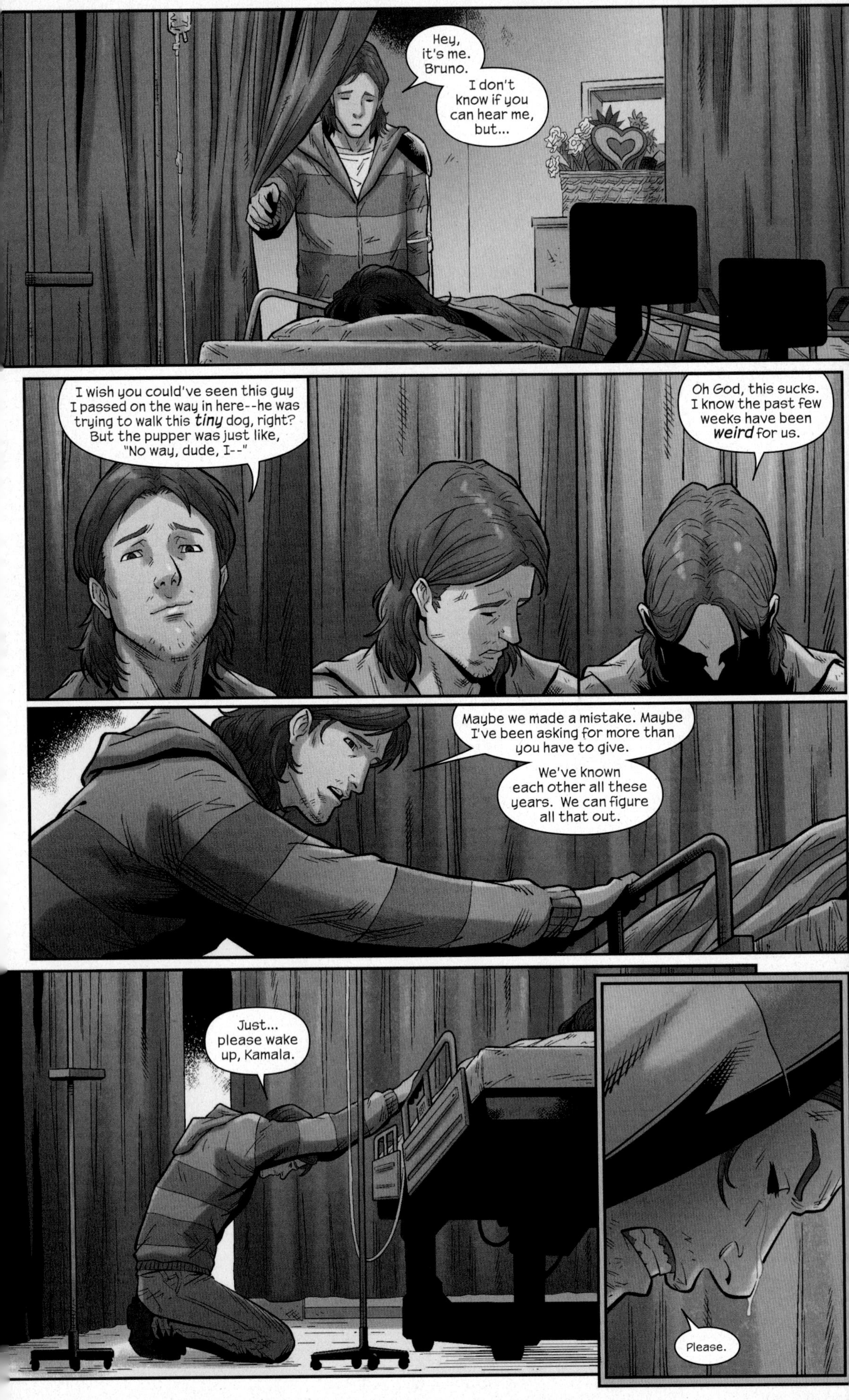
Hey, it's me. Bruno.
I don't know if you can hear me, but...
I wish you could've seen this guy I passed on the way in here--he was trying to walk this *tiny* dog, right? But the pupper was just like, "No way, dude, I--"
Oh God, this sucks. I know the past few weeks have been *weird* for us.
Maybe we made a mistake. Maybe I've been asking for more than you have to give.
We've known each other all these years. We can figure all that out.
Just... please wake up, Kamala.
Please.

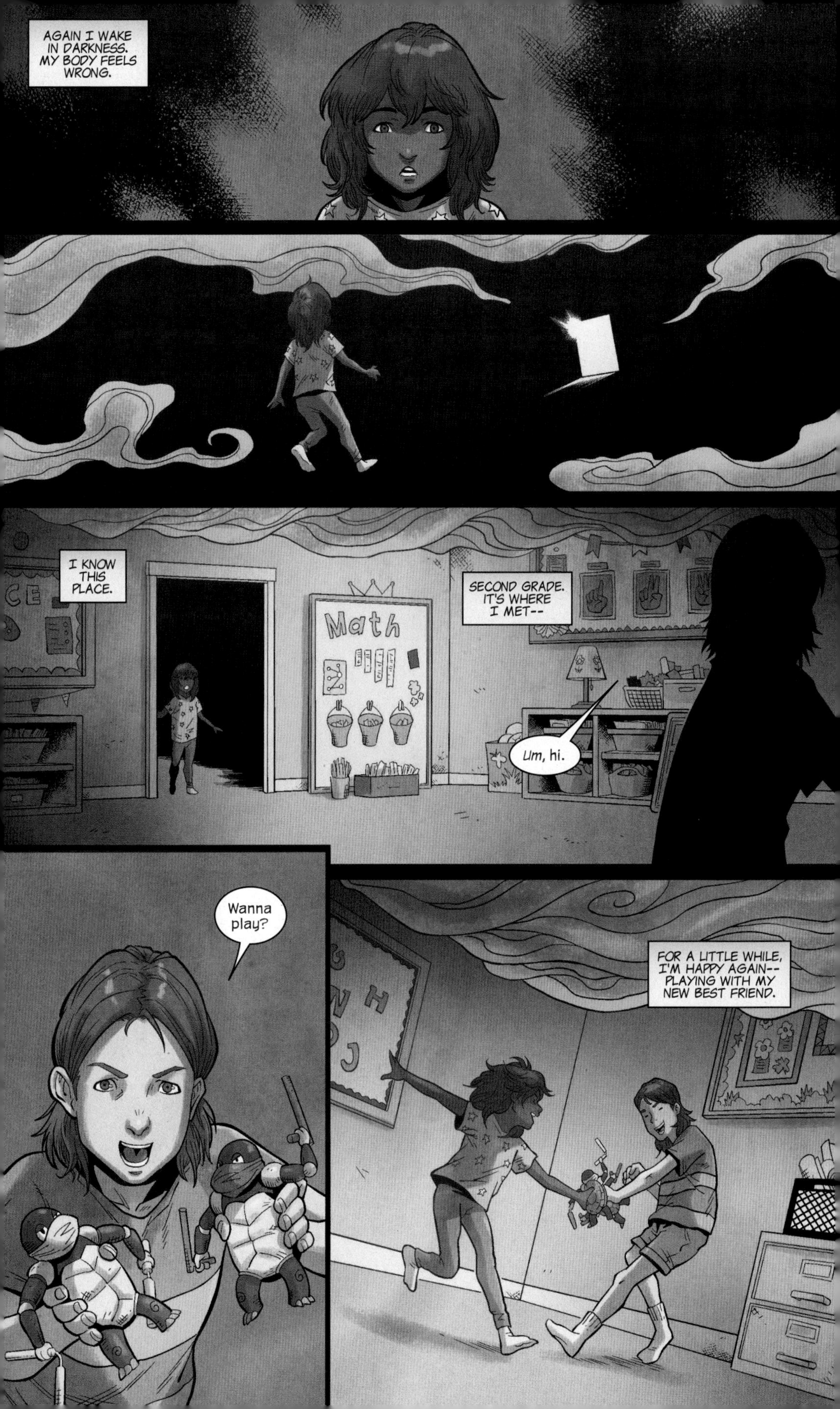
AGAIN I WAKE IN DARKNESS. MY BODY FEELS WRONG.
I KNOW THIS PLACE.
Math
SECOND GRADE. IT'S WHERE I MET--
Um, hi.
Wanna play?
FOR A LITTLE WHILE, I'M HAPPY AGAIN-- PLAYING WITH MY NEW BEST FRIEND.

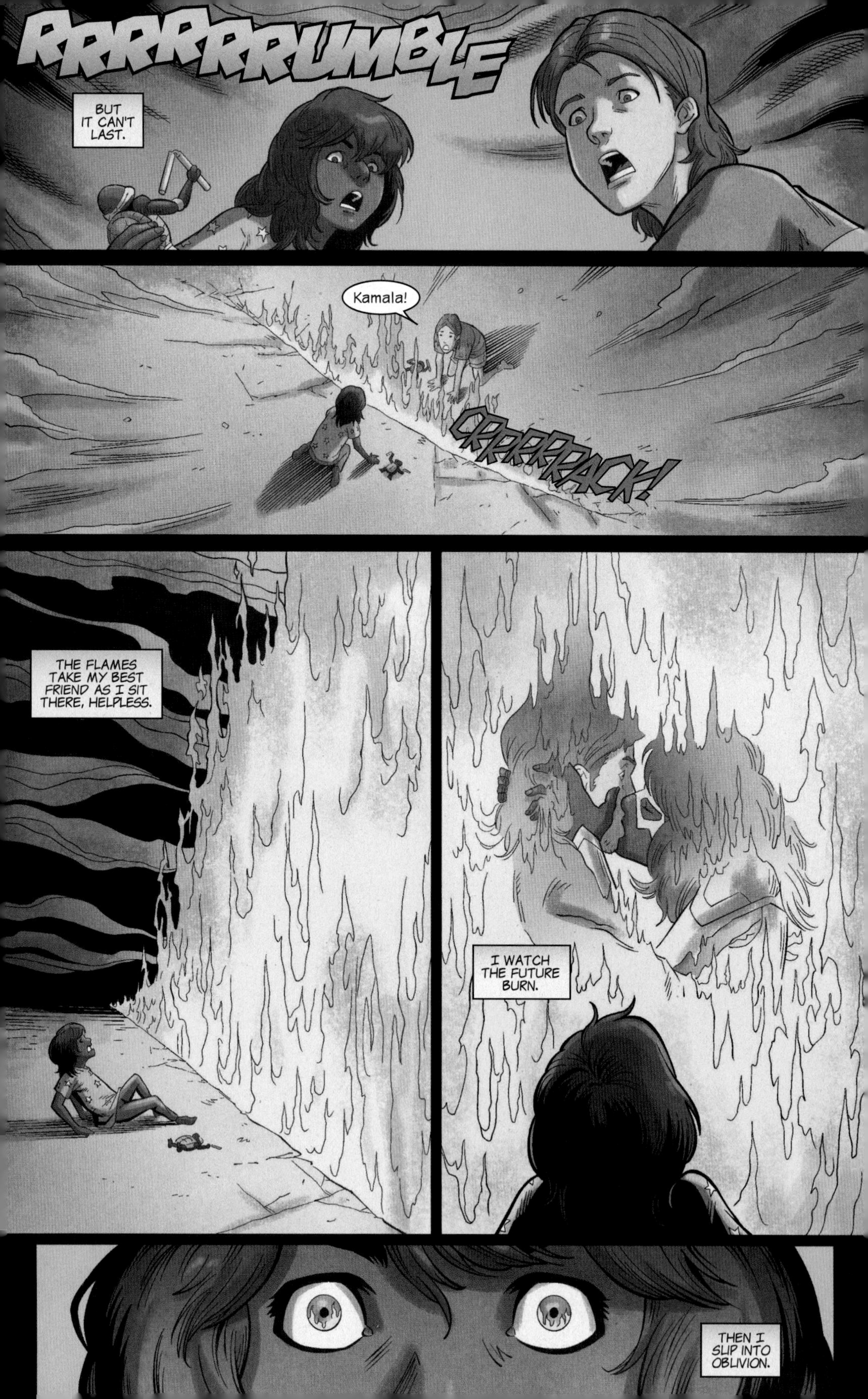
RRRRRRRUMBLE
BUT IT CAN'T LAST.
Kamala!
CRRRRRACK!
THE FLAMES TAKE MY BEST FRIEND AS I SIT THERE, HELPLESS.
I WATCH THE FUTURE BURN.
THEN I SLIP INTO OBLIVION.

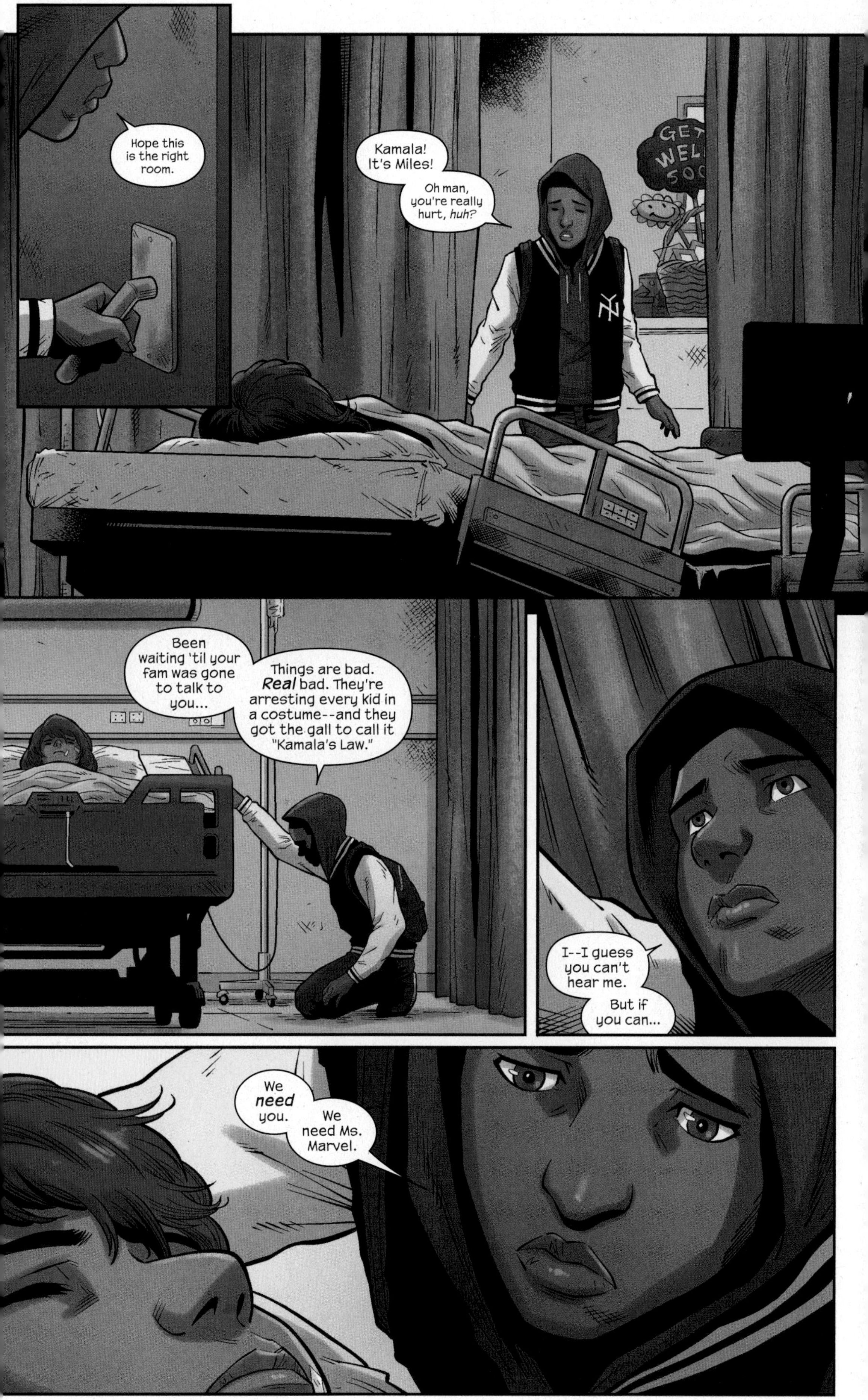
Hope this is the right room.
Kamala! It's Miles!
Oh man, you're really hurt, *huh?*
GET WELL SOO
Been waiting 'til your fam was gone to talk to you...
Things are bad. *Real* bad. They're arresting every kid in a costume--and they got the gall to call it "Kamala's Law."
I--I guess you can't hear me.
But if you can...
We *need* you.
We need Ms. Marvel.

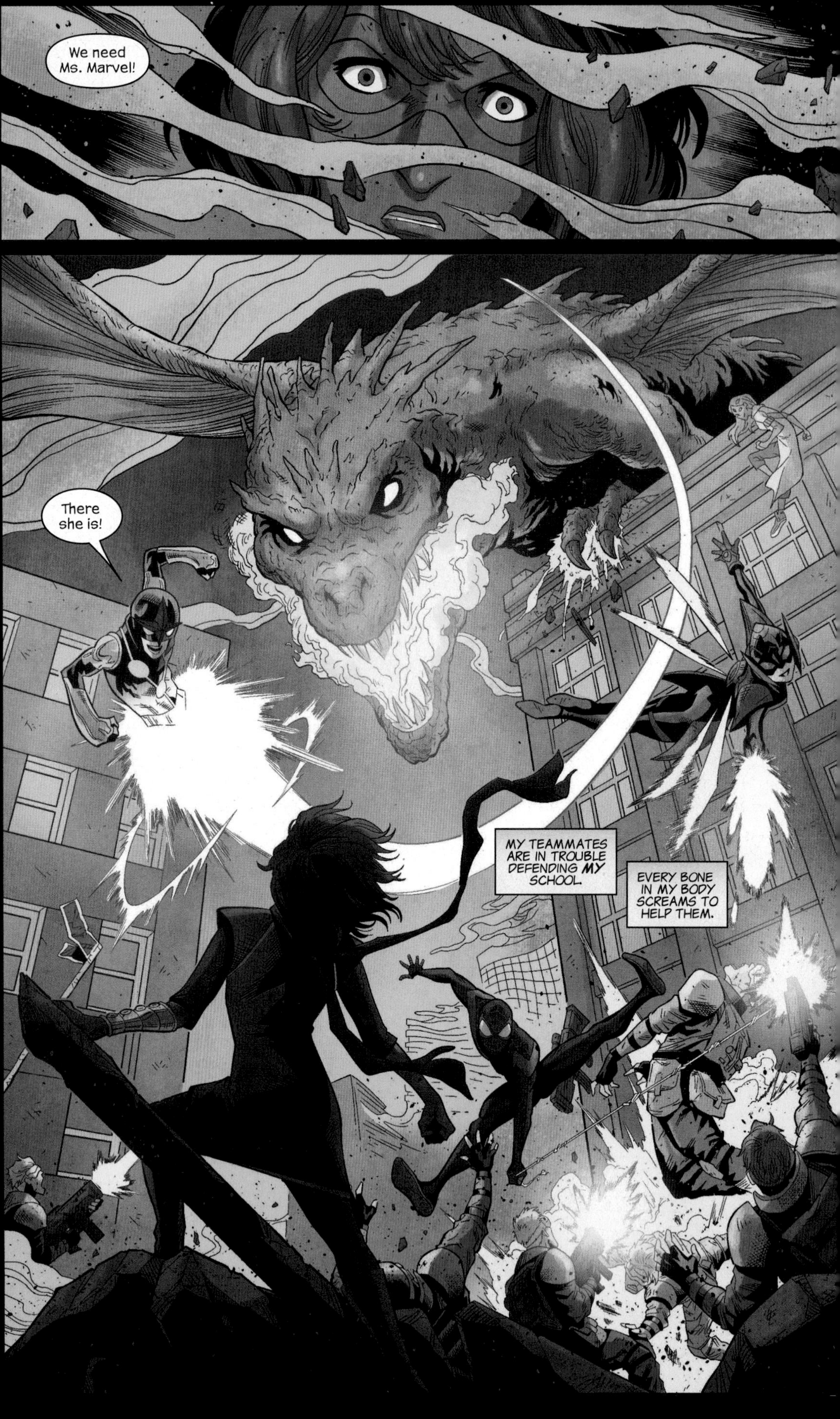

We need Ms. Marvel!
There she is!
MY TEAMMATES ARE IN TROUBLE DEFENDING **MY** SCHOOL.
EVERY BONE IN MY BODY SCREAMS TO HELP THEM.

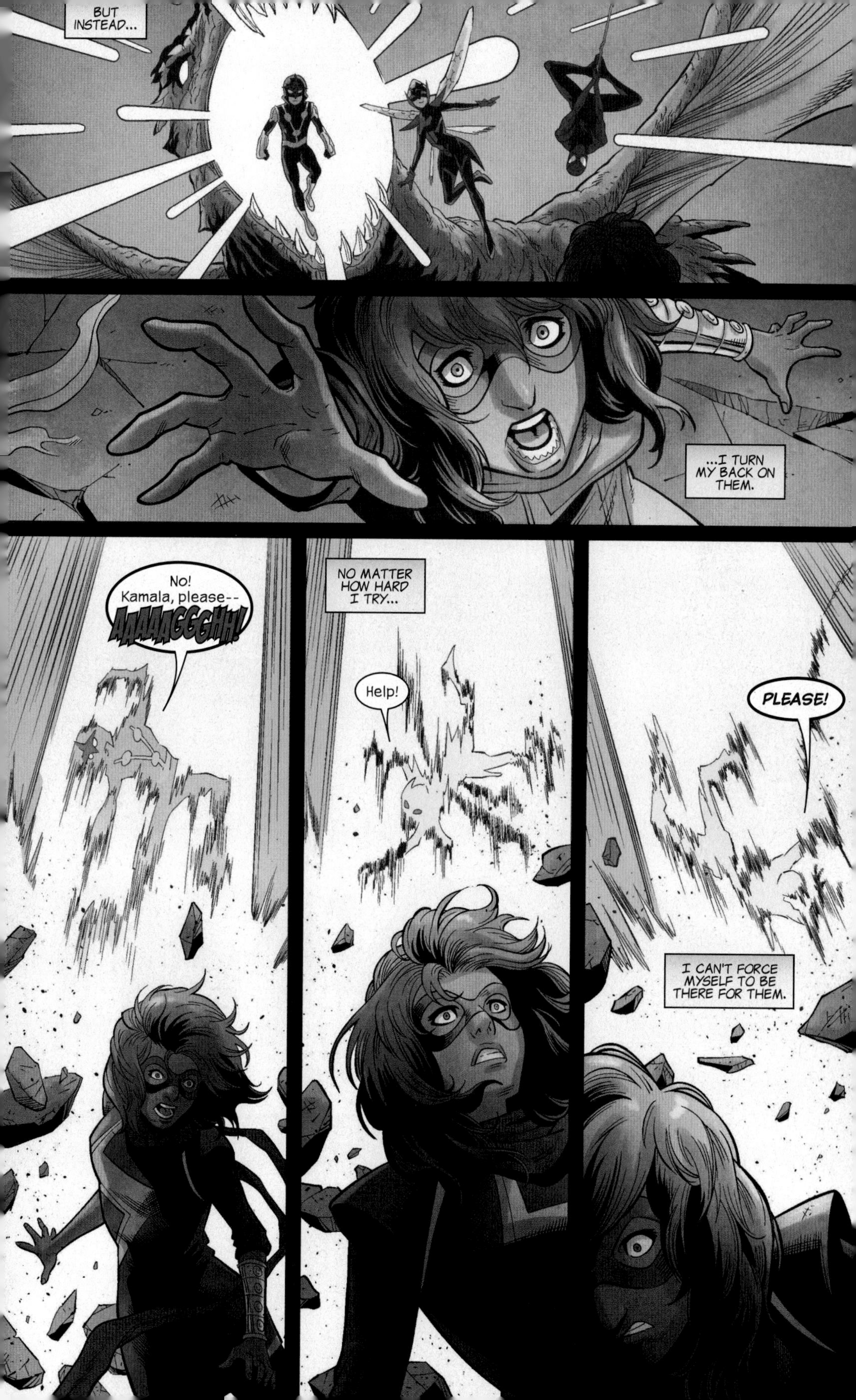
BUT INSTEAD...
...I TURN MY BACK ON THEM.
No! Kamala, please--
AAAAAGGGHH!
NO MATTER HOW HARD I TRY...
Help!
PLEASE!
I CAN'T FORCE MYSELF TO BE THERE FOR THEM.

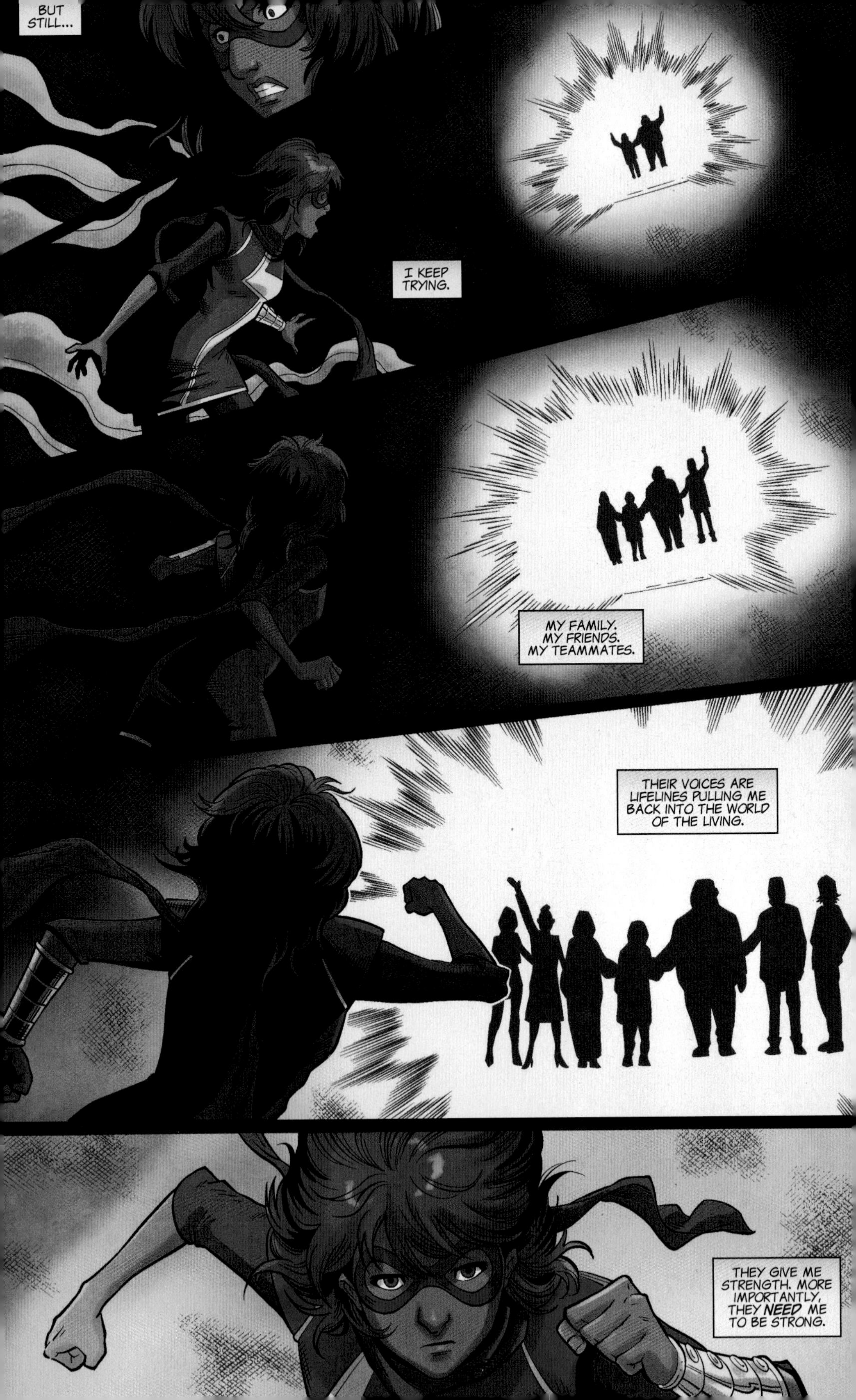
BUT STILL...
I KEEP TRYING.
MY FAMILY. MY FRIENDS. MY TEAMMATES.
THEIR VOICES ARE LIFELINES PULLING ME BACK INTO THE WORLD OF THE LIVING.
THEY GIVE ME STRENGTH. MORE IMPORTANTLY, THEY NEED ME TO BE STRONG.

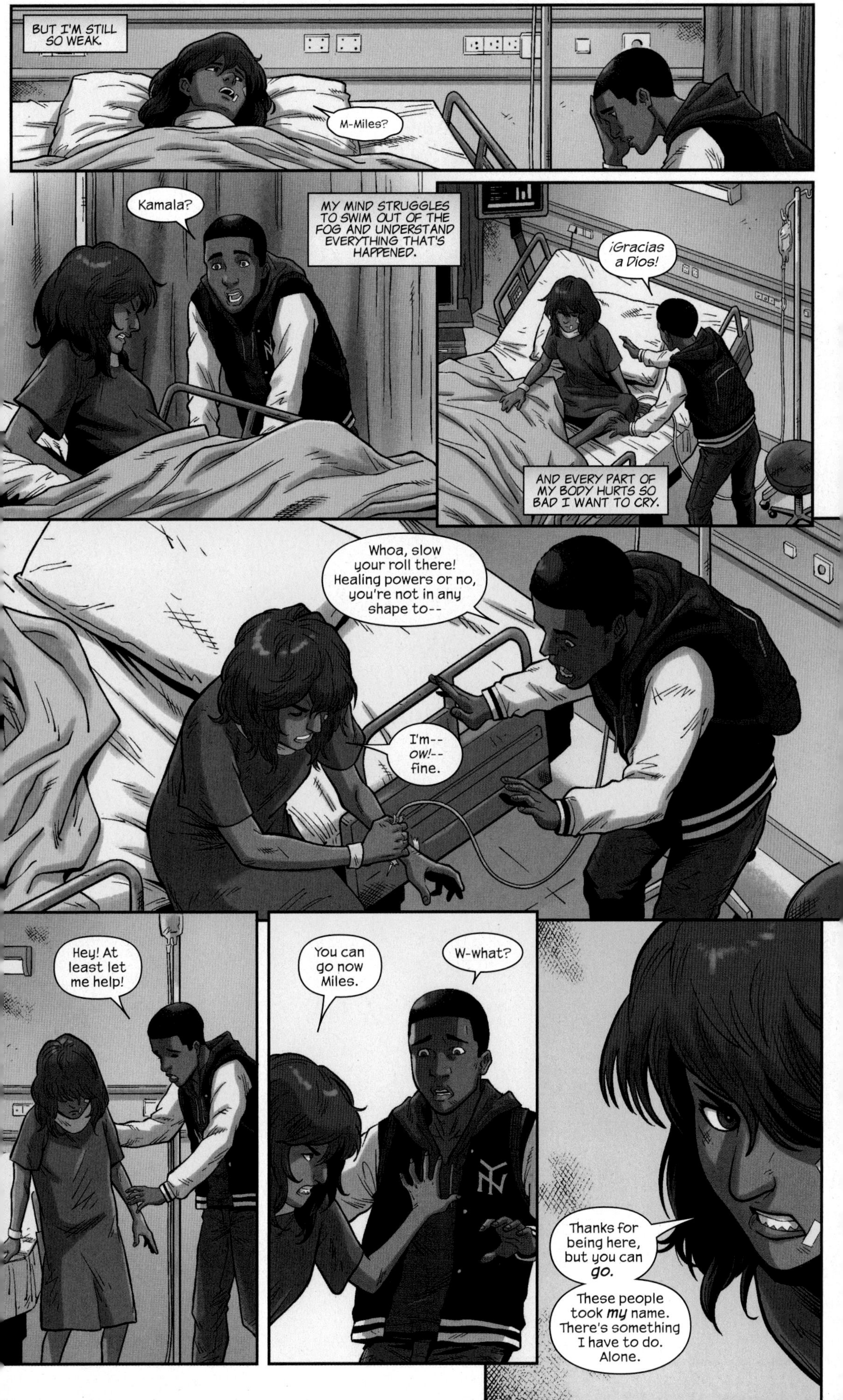
BUT I'M STILL SO WEAK.
M-Miles?
Kamala?
MY MIND STRUGGLES TO SWIM OUT OF THE FOG AND UNDERSTAND EVERYTHING THAT'S HAPPENED.
¡Gracias a Dios!
AND EVERY PART OF MY BODY HURTS SO BAD I WANT TO CRY.
Whoa, slow your roll there! Healing powers or no, you're not in any shape to--
I'm-- ow!-- fine.
Hey! At least let me help!
You can go now Miles.
W-what?
Thanks for being here, but you can *go*.
These people took *my* name. There's something I have to do. Alone.

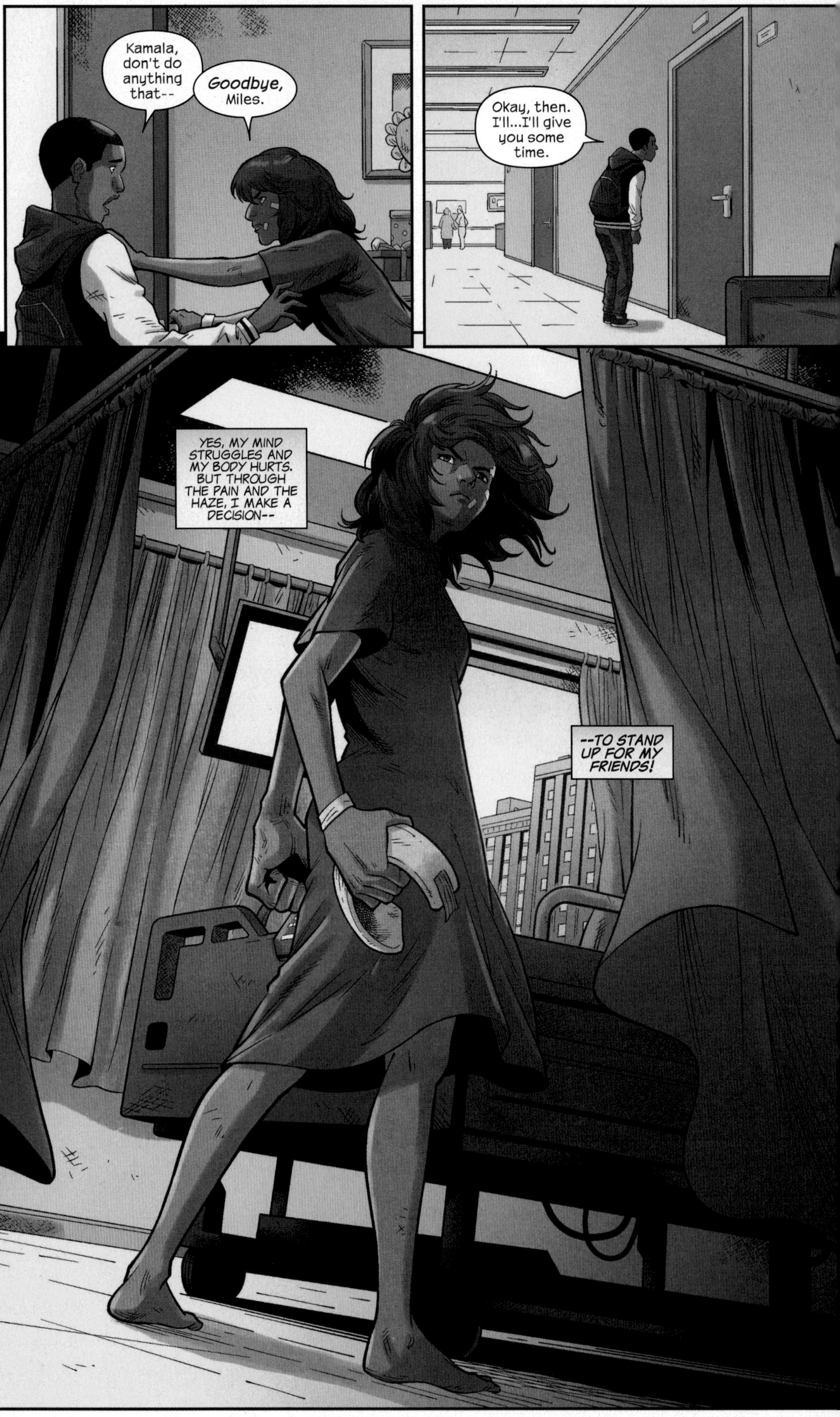

Kamala, don't do anything that--
Goodbye, Miles.
Okay, then. I'll...I'll give you some time.
YES, MY MIND STRUGGLES AND MY BODY HURTS. BUT THROUGH THE PAIN AND THE HAZE, I MAKE A DECISION--
--TO STAND UP FOR MY FRIENDS!

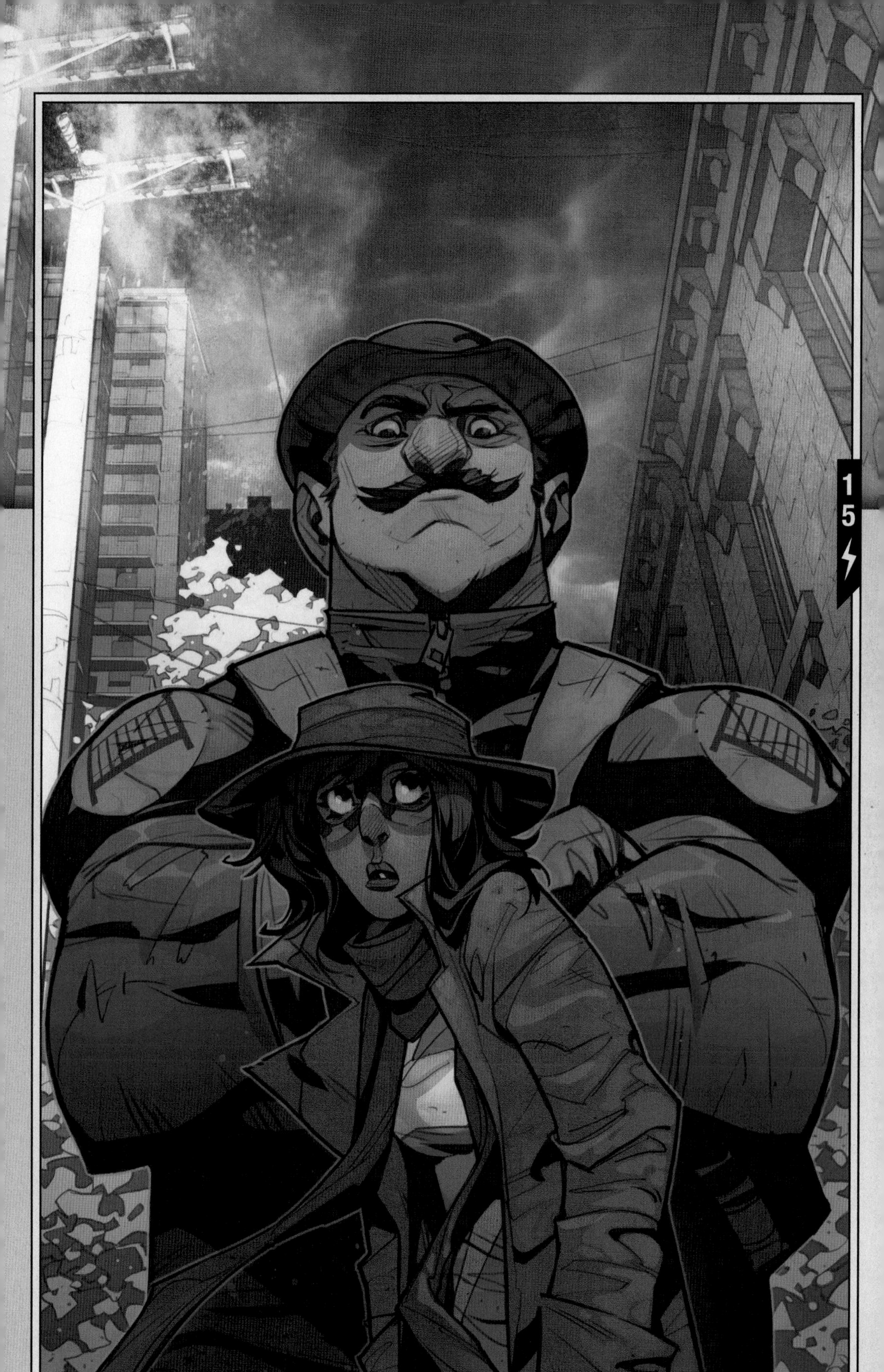
15

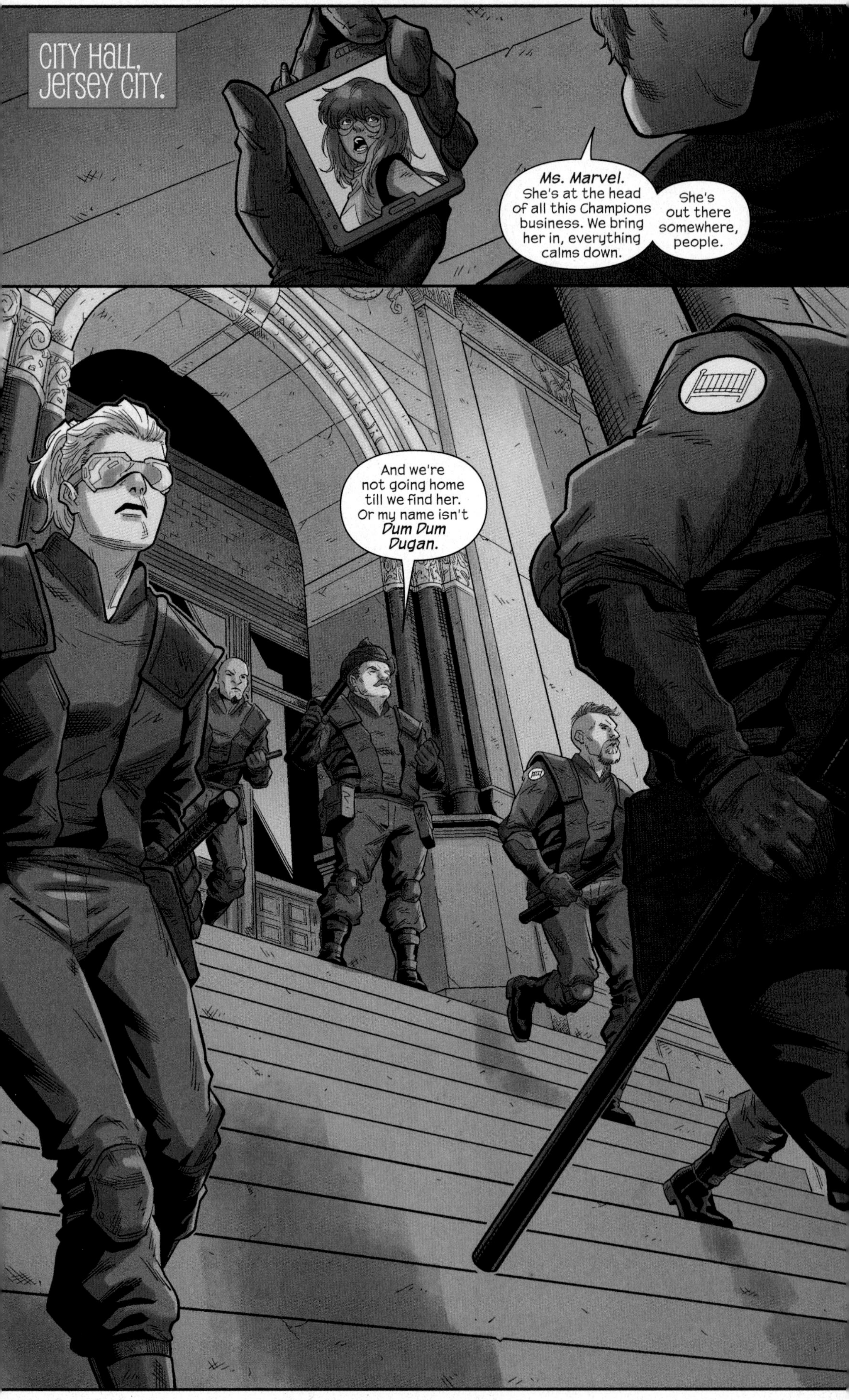
CITY HALL, JERSEY CITY.
Ms. Marvel. She's at the head of all this Champions business. We bring her in, everything calms down.
She's out there somewhere, people.
And we're not going home till we find her. Or my name isn't ***Dum Dum Dugan.***

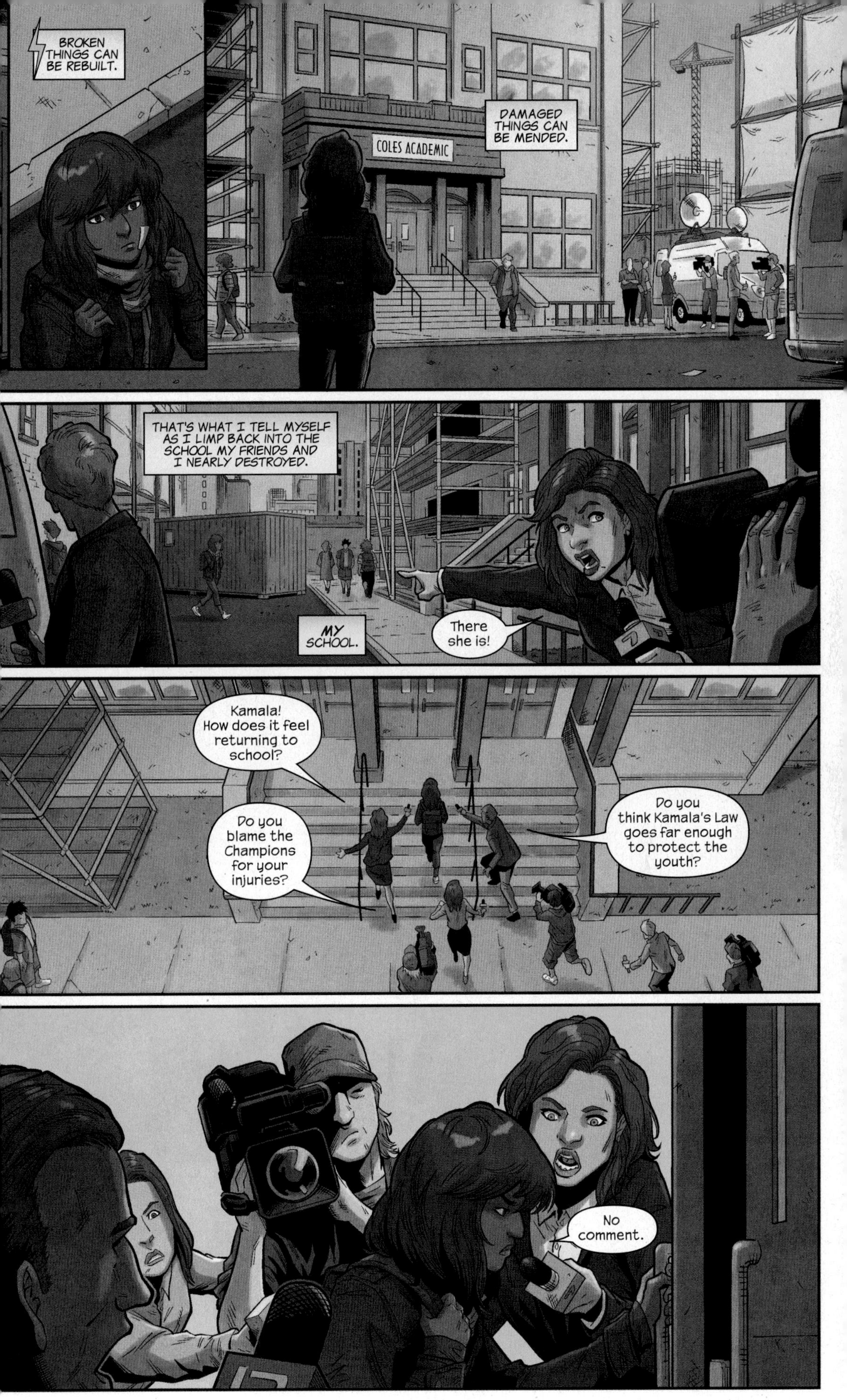

BROKEN THINGS CAN BE REBUILT.
COLES ACADEMIC
DAMAGED THINGS CAN BE MENDED.
THAT'S WHAT I TELL MYSELF AS I LIMP BACK INTO THE SCHOOL MY FRIENDS AND I NEARLY DESTROYED.
MY SCHOOL.
There she is!
Kamala! How does it feel returning to school?
Do you blame the Champions for your injuries?
Do you think Kamala's Law goes far enough to protect the youth?
No comment.

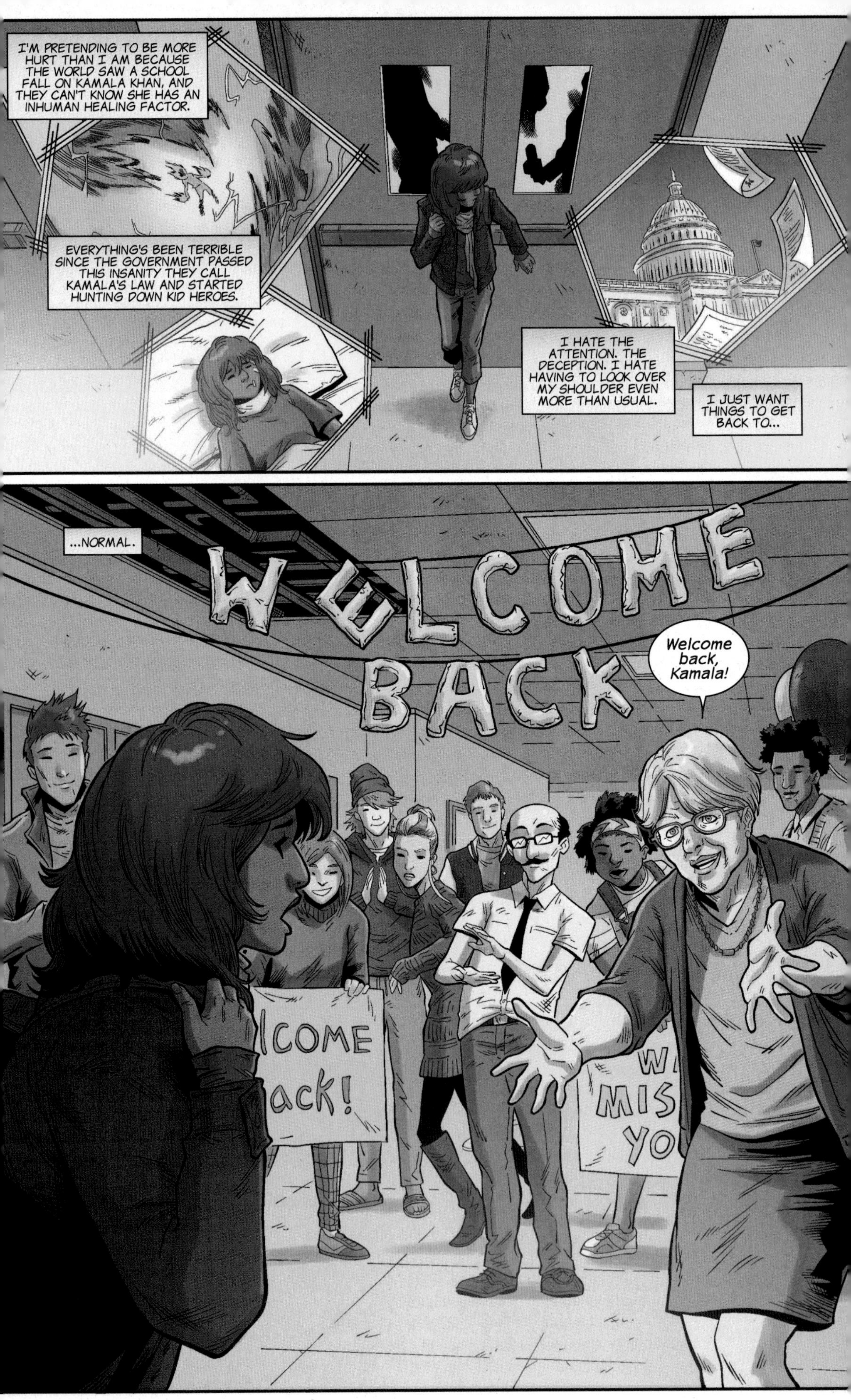
I'M PRETENDING TO BE MORE HURT THAN I AM BECAUSE THE WORLD SAW A SCHOOL FALL ON KAMALA KHAN, AND THEY CAN'T KNOW SHE HAS AN INHUMAN HEALING FACTOR.
EVERYTHING'S BEEN TERRIBLE SINCE THE GOVERNMENT PASSED THIS INSANITY THEY CALL KAMALA'S LAW AND STARTED HUNTING DOWN KID HEROES.
I HATE THE ATTENTION. THE DECEPTION. I HATE HAVING TO LOOK OVER MY SHOULDER EVEN MORE THAN USUAL.
I JUST WANT THINGS TO GET BACK TO...
...NORMAL.
WELCOME BACK
Welcome back, Kamala!
lCOME ack!
W MIS YO

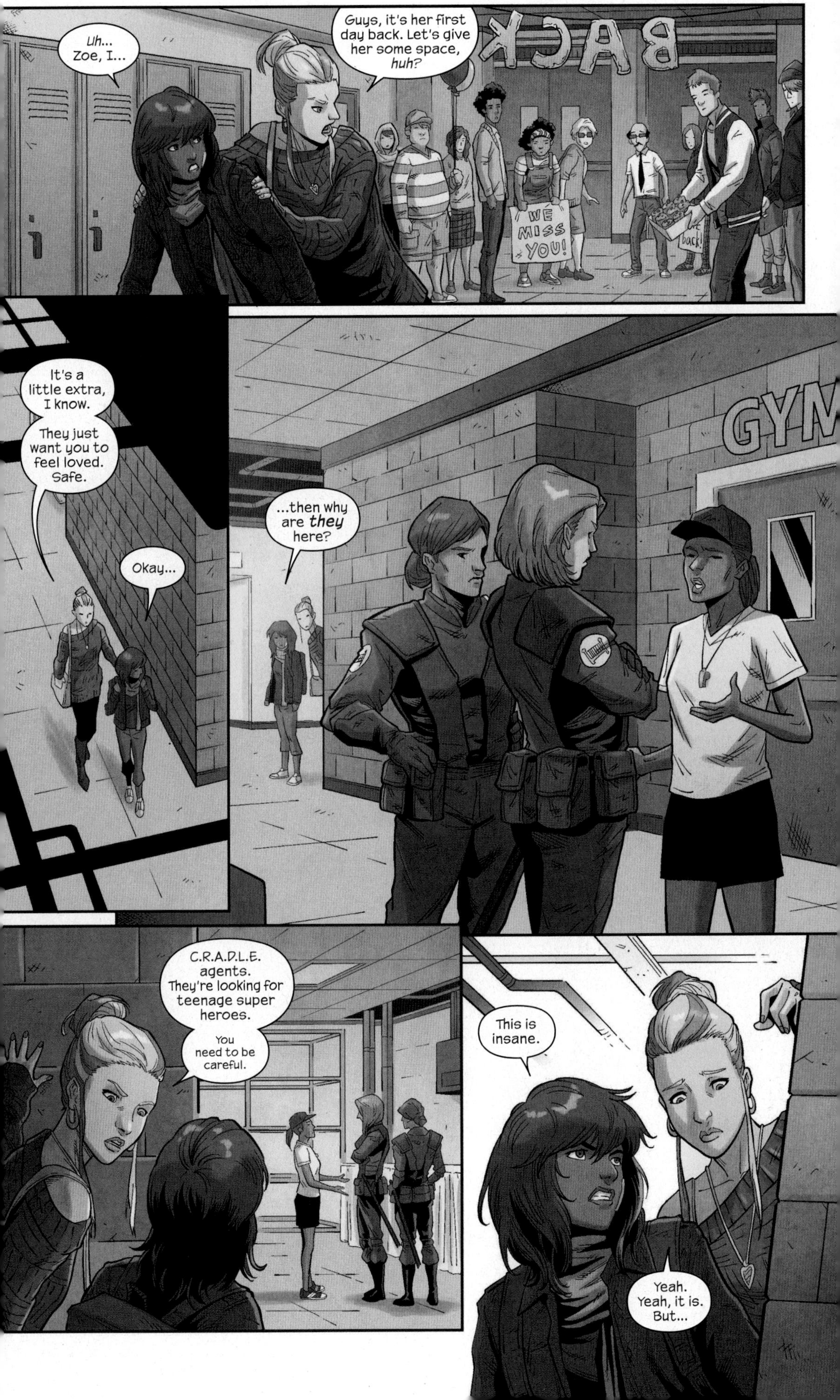

Uh... Zoe, I...
Guys, it's her first day back. Let's give her some space, *huh?*
BACK
WE MISS YOU!
back!
It's a little extra, I know.
They just want you to feel loved. Safe.
Okay...
...then why are ***they*** here?
GYM
C.R.A.D.L.E. agents. They're looking for teenage super heroes.
You need to be careful.
This is insane.
Yeah. Yeah, it is. But...

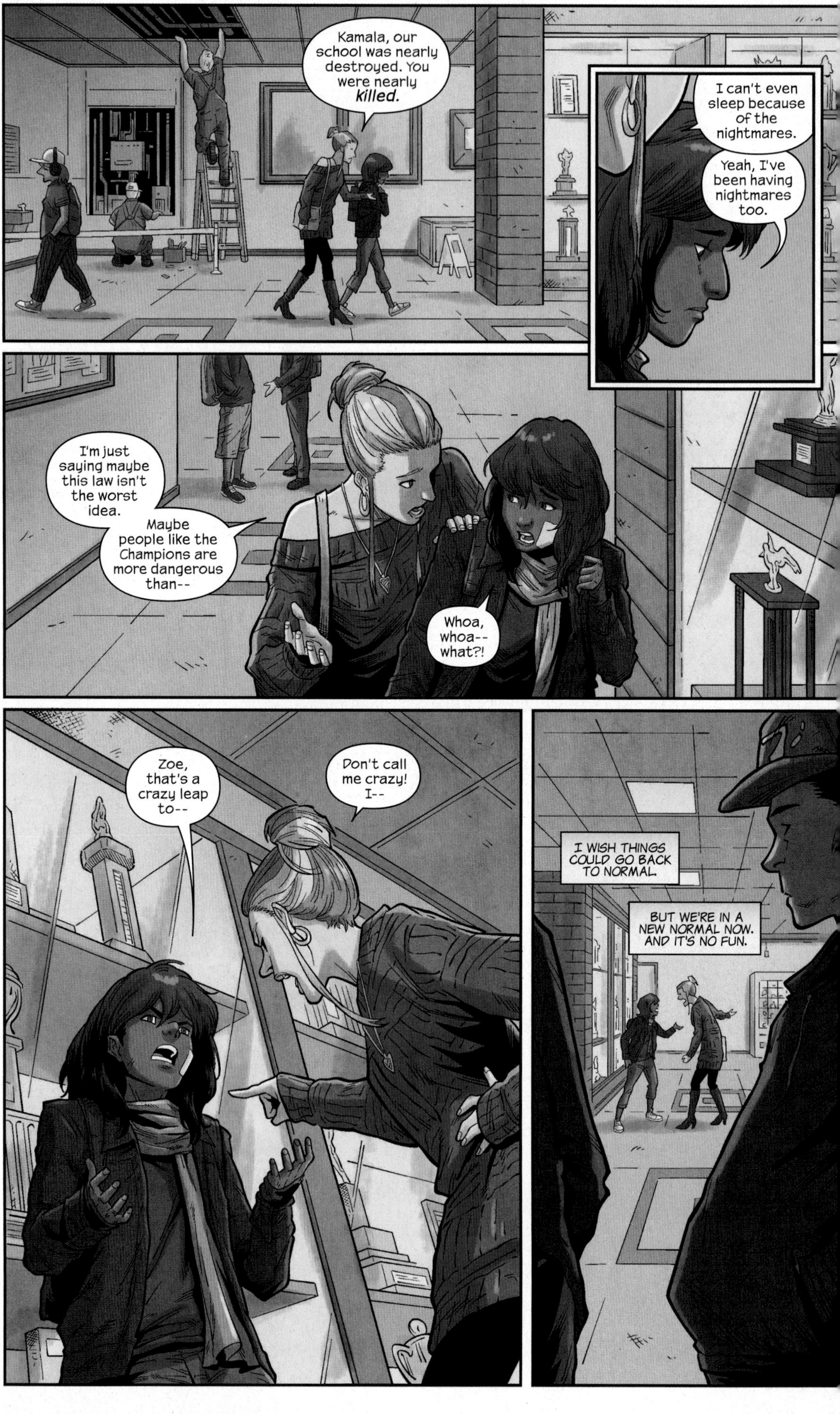

Kamala, our school was nearly destroyed. You were nearly *killed.*
I can't even sleep because of the nightmares.
Yeah, I've been having nightmares too.
I'm just saying maybe this law isn't the worst idea.
Maybe people like the Champions are more dangerous than--
Whoa, whoa-- what?!
Zoe, that's a crazy leap to--
Don't call me crazy! I--
I WISH THINGS COULD GO BACK TO NORMAL.
BUT WE'RE IN A NEW NORMAL NOW. AND IT'S NO FUN.

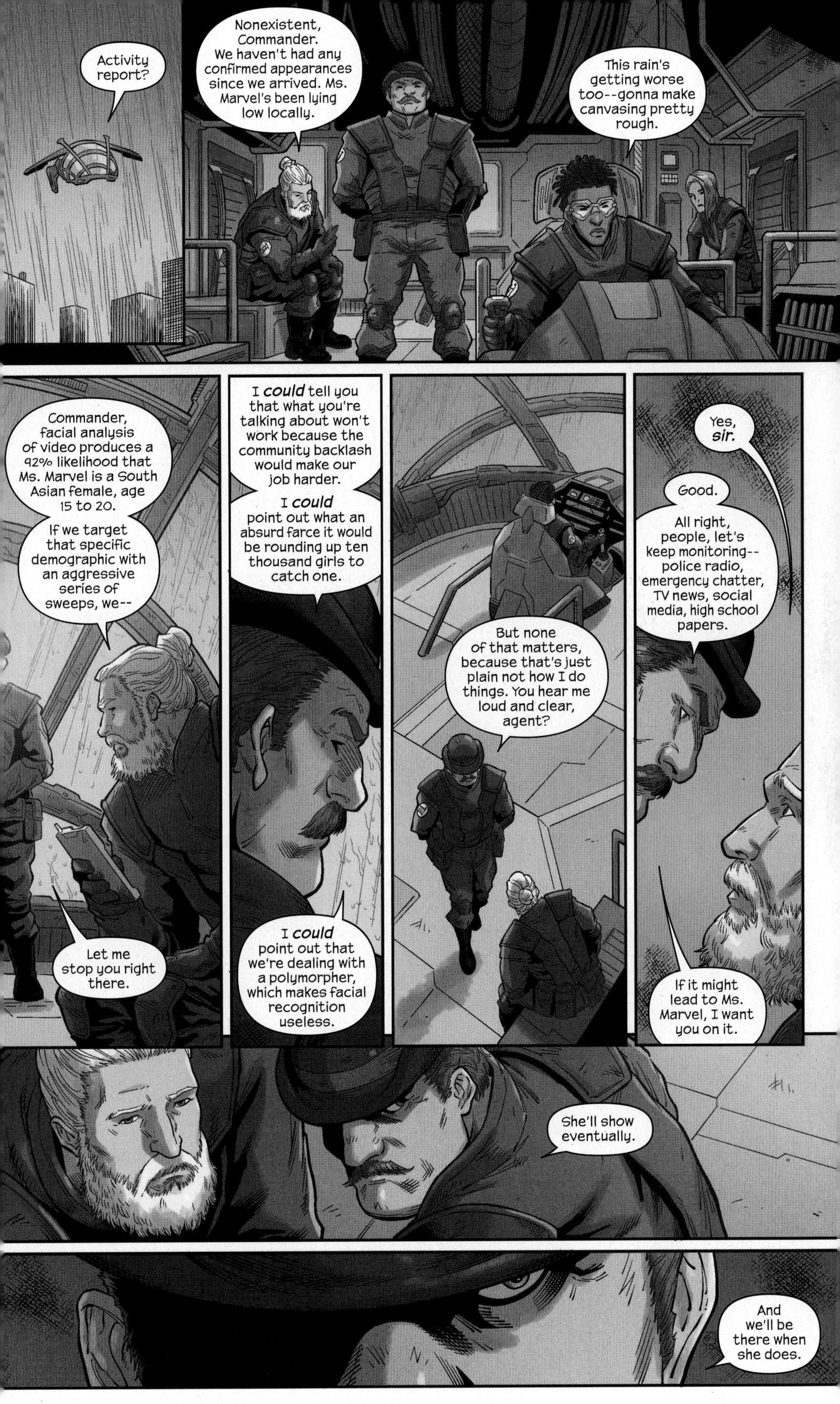
Activity report?
Nonexistent, Commander. We haven't had any confirmed appearances since we arrived. Ms. Marvel's been lying low locally.
This rain's getting worse too--gonna make canvasing pretty rough.
Commander, facial analysis of video produces a 92% likelihood that Ms. Marvel is a South Asian female, age 15 to 20.
If we target that specific demographic with an aggressive series of sweeps, we--
Let me stop you right there.
I could tell you that what you're talking about won't work because the community backlash would make our job harder.
I could point out what an absurd farce it would be rounding up ten thousand girls to catch one.
I could point out that we're dealing with a polymorpher, which makes facial recognition useless.
But none of that matters, because that's just plain not how I do things. You hear me loud and clear, agent?
Yes, sir.
Good.
All right, people, let's keep monitoring--police radio, emergency chatter, TV news, social media, high school papers.
If it might lead to Ms. Marvel, I want you on it.
She'll show eventually.
And we'll be there when she does.

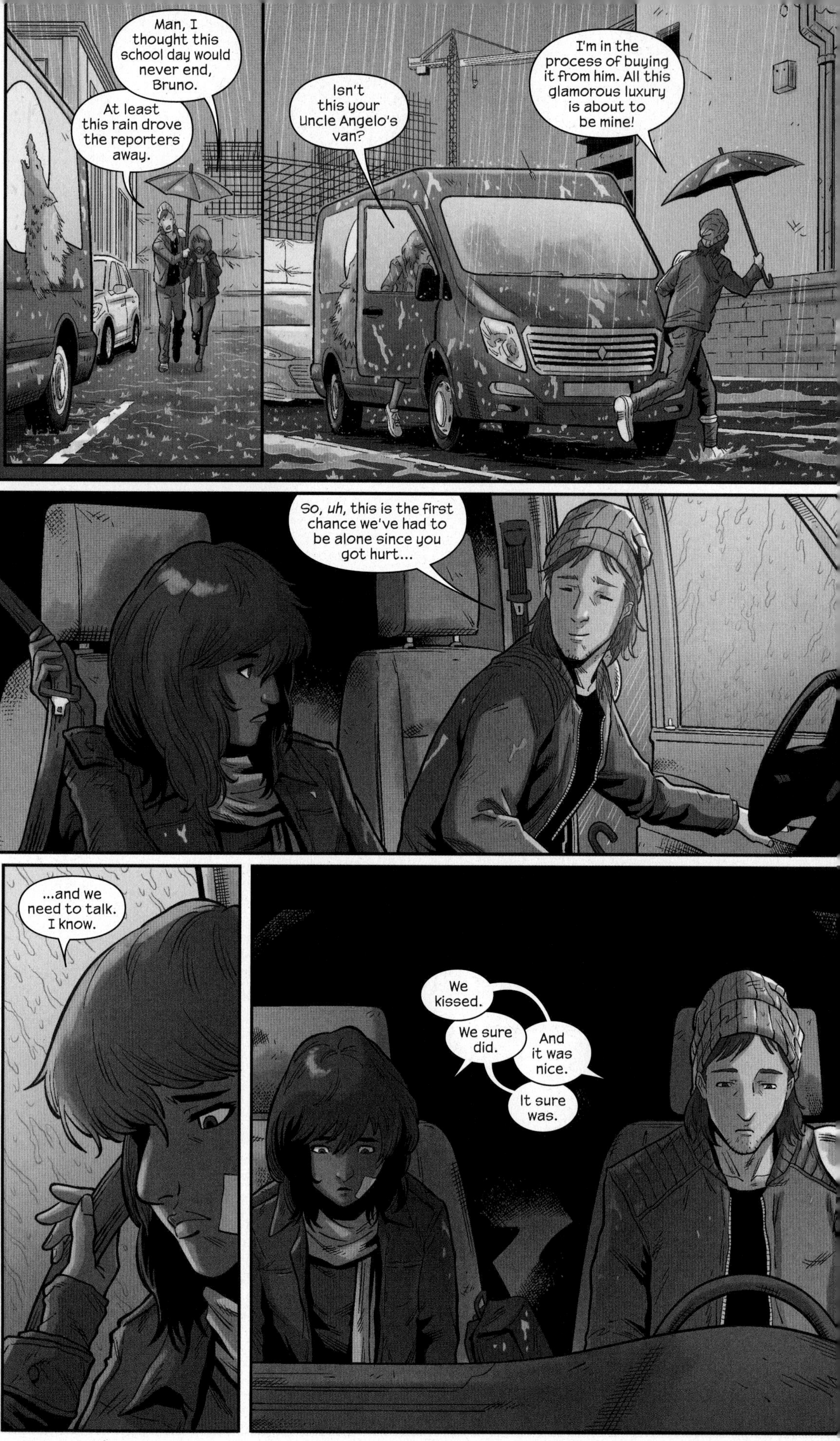
Man, I thought this school day would never end, Bruno.
At least this rain drove the reporters away.
Isn't this your Uncle Angelo's van?
I'm in the process of buying it from him. All this glamorous luxury is about to be mine!
So, *uh*, this is the first chance we've had to be alone since you got hurt...
...and we need to talk. I know.
We kissed.
We sure did.
And it was nice.
It sure was.

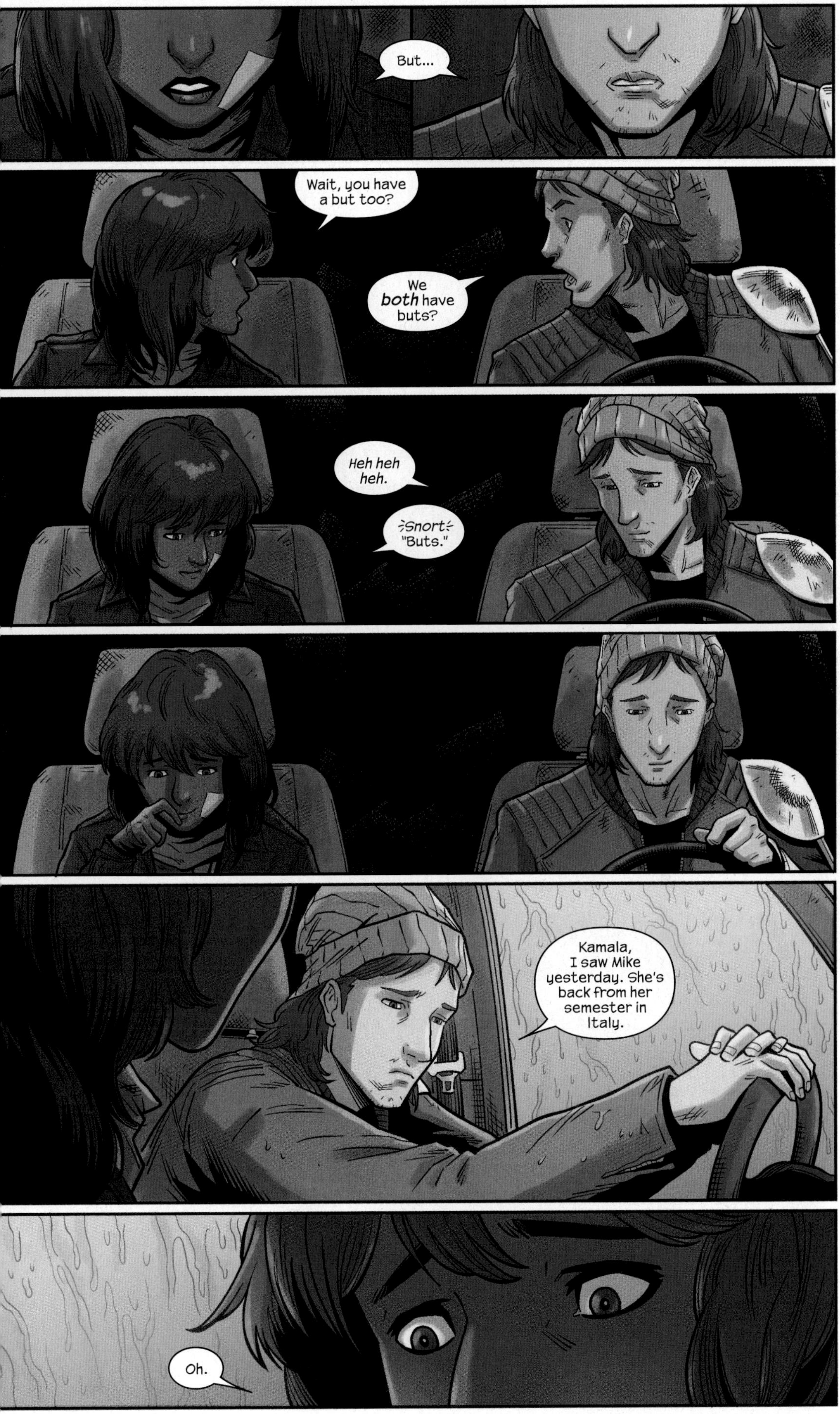
But...
Wait, you have a but too?
We *both* have buts?
Heh heh heh.
Snort "Buts."
Kamala, I saw Mike yesterday. She's back from her semester in Italy.
Oh.

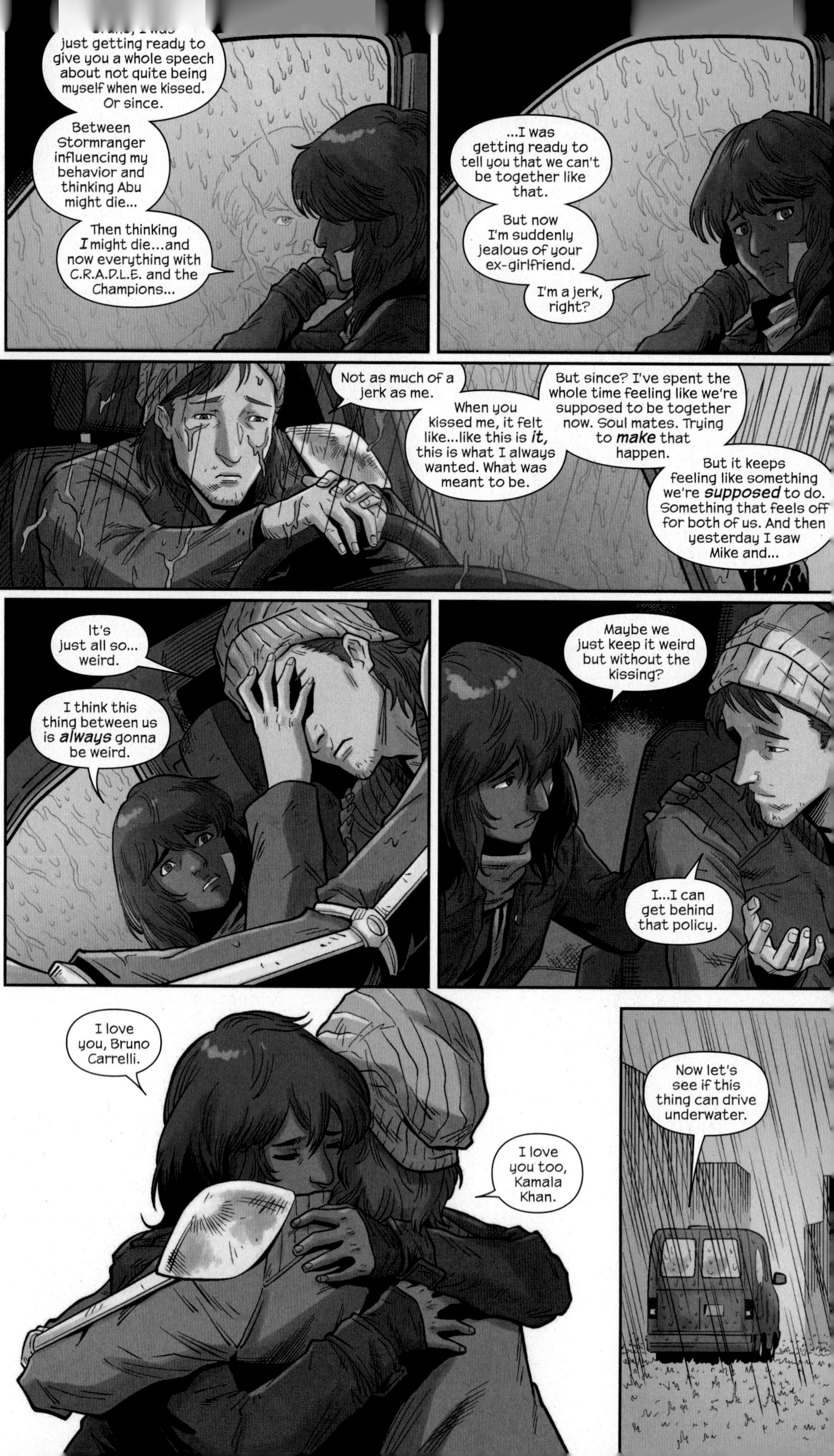
just getting ready to give you a whole speech about not quite being myself when we kissed. Or since.
Between Stormranger influencing my behavior and thinking Abu might die...
Then thinking *I* might die...and now everything with C.R.A.D.L.E. and the Champions...
...I was getting ready to tell you that we can't be together like that.
But now I'm suddenly jealous of your ex-girlfriend.
I'm a jerk, right?
Not as much of a jerk as me.
When you kissed me, it felt like...like this is *it,* this is what I always wanted. What was meant to be.
But since? I've spent the whole time feeling like we're supposed to be together now. Soul mates. Trying to ***make*** that happen.
But it keeps feeling like something we're ***supposed*** to do. Something that feels off for both of us. And then yesterday I saw Mike and...
It's just all so... weird.
I think this thing between us is ***always*** gonna be weird.
Maybe we just keep it weird but without the kissing?
I...I can get behind that policy.
I love you, Bruno Carrelli.
I love you too, Kamala Khan.
Now let's see if this thing can drive underwater.

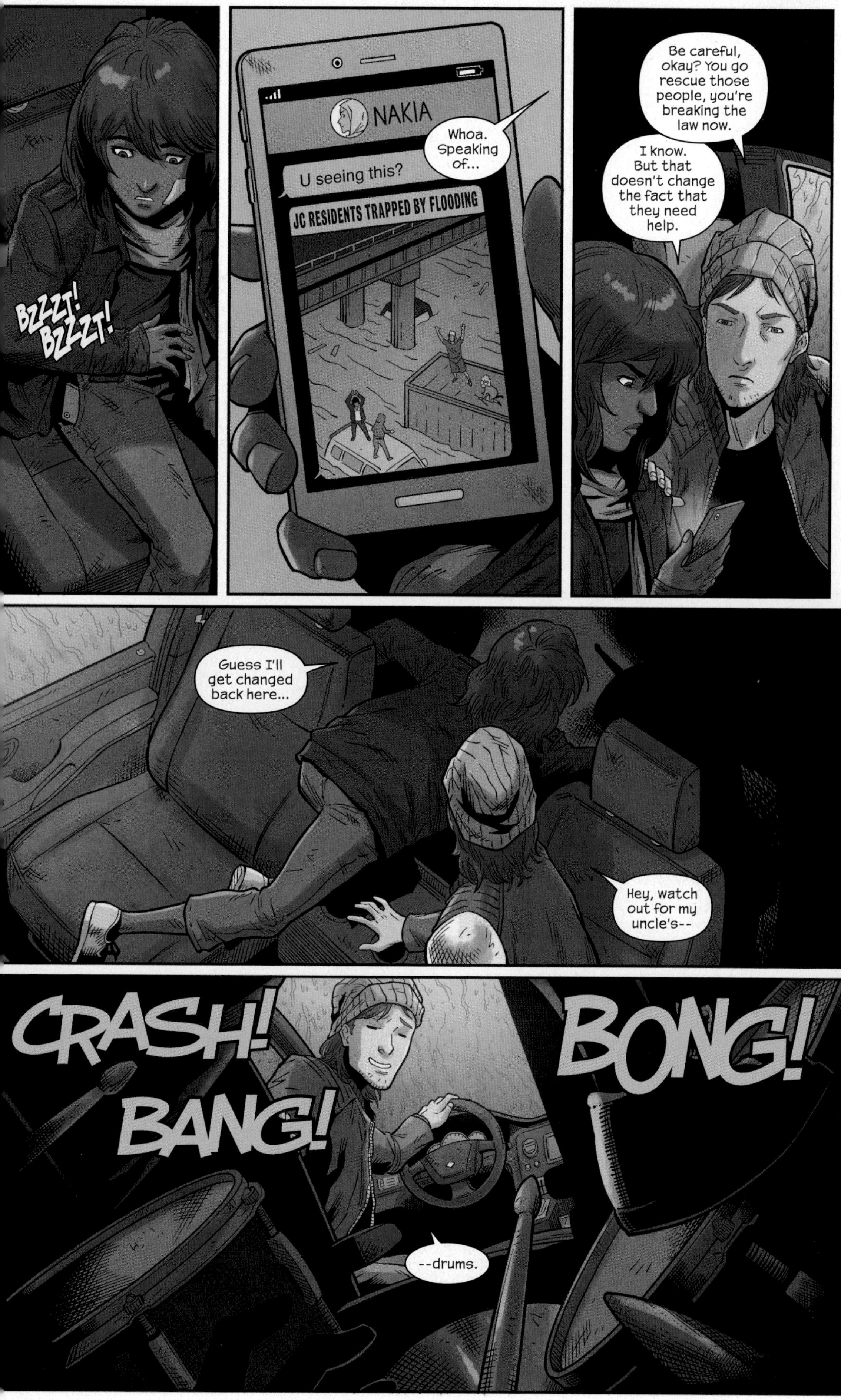
BZZZT! BZZZT!
NAKIA
U seeing this?
JC RESIDENTS TRAPPED BY FLOODING
Whoa. Speaking of...
Be careful, okay? You go rescue those people, you're breaking the law now.
I know. But that doesn't change the fact that they need help.
Guess I'll get changed back here...
Hey, watch out for my uncle's--
CRASH!
BANG!
BONG!
--drums.

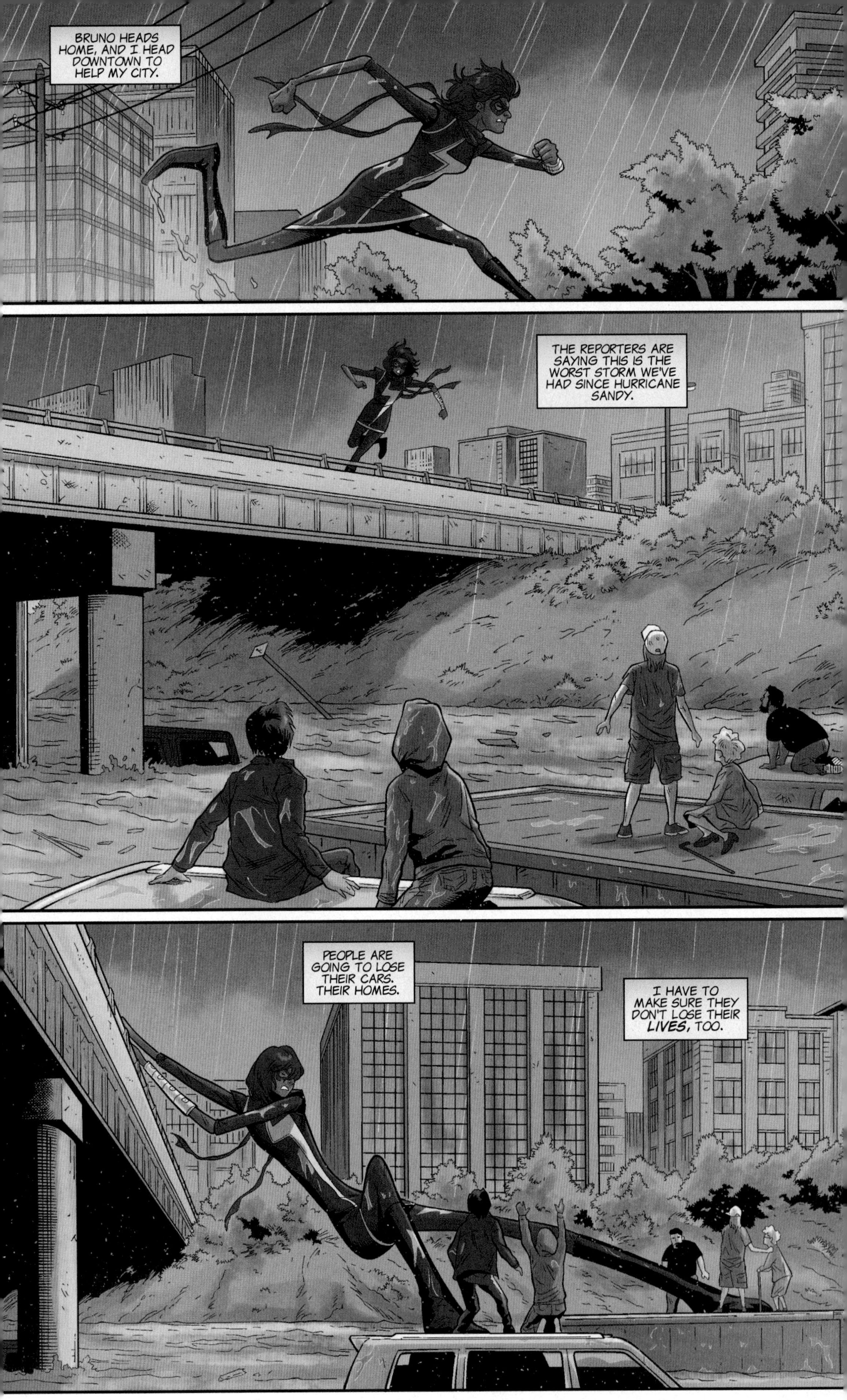
BRUNO HEADS HOME, AND I HEAD DOWNTOWN TO HELP MY CITY.
THE REPORTERS ARE SAYING THIS IS THE WORST STORM WE'VE HAD SINCE HURRICANE SANDY.
PEOPLE ARE GOING TO LOSE THEIR CARS. THEIR HOMES.
I HAVE TO MAKE SURE THEY DON'T LOSE THEIR ***LIVES***, TOO.

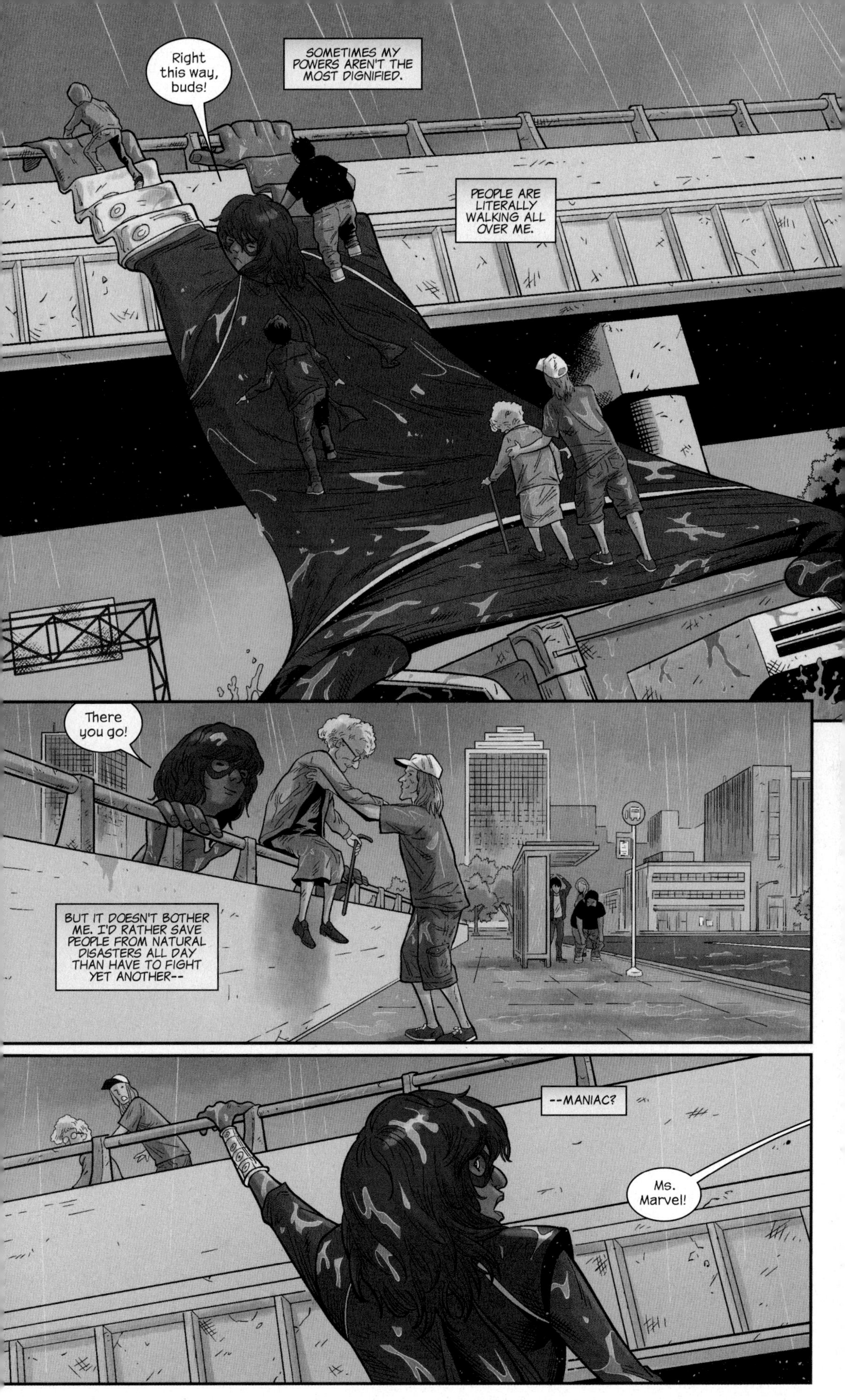

SOMETIMES MY POWERS AREN'T THE MOST DIGNIFIED.
Right this way, buds!
PEOPLE ARE LITERALLY WALKING ALL OVER ME.
There you go!
BUT IT DOESN'T BOTHER ME. I'D RATHER SAVE PEOPLE FROM NATURAL DISASTERS ALL DAY THAN HAVE TO FIGHT YET ANOTHER--
--MANIAC?
Ms. Marvel!

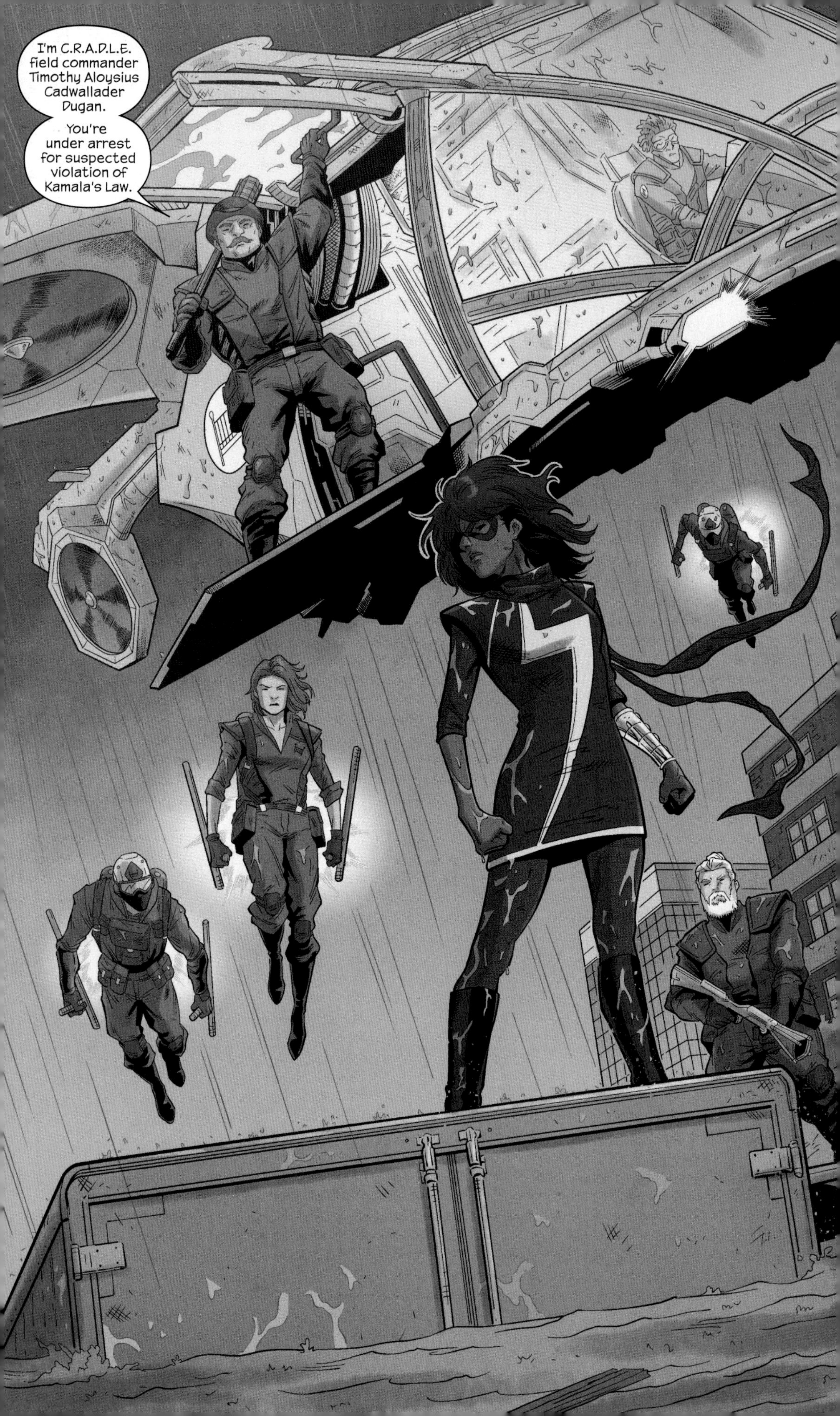
I'm C.R.A.D.L.E. field commander Timothy Aloysius Cadwallader Dugan.
You're under arrest for suspected violation of Kamala's Law.

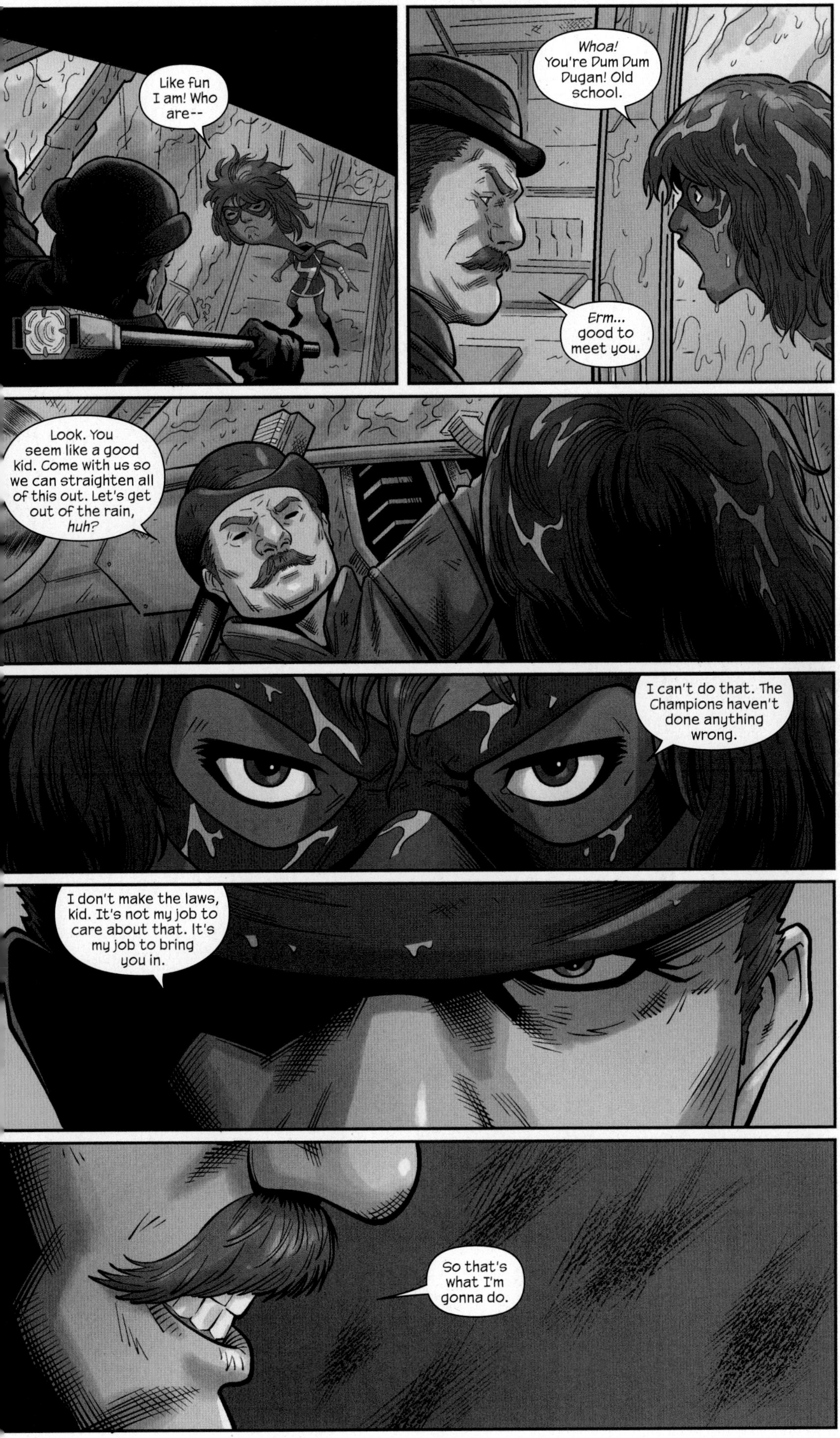
Like fun I am! Who are--
Whoa! You're Dum Dum Dugan! Old school.
Erm... good to meet you.
Look. You seem like a good kid. Come with us so we can straighten all of this out. Let's get out of the rain, huh?
I can't do that. The Champions haven't done anything wrong.
I don't make the laws, kid. It's not my job to care about that. It's my job to bring you in.
So that's what I'm gonna do.

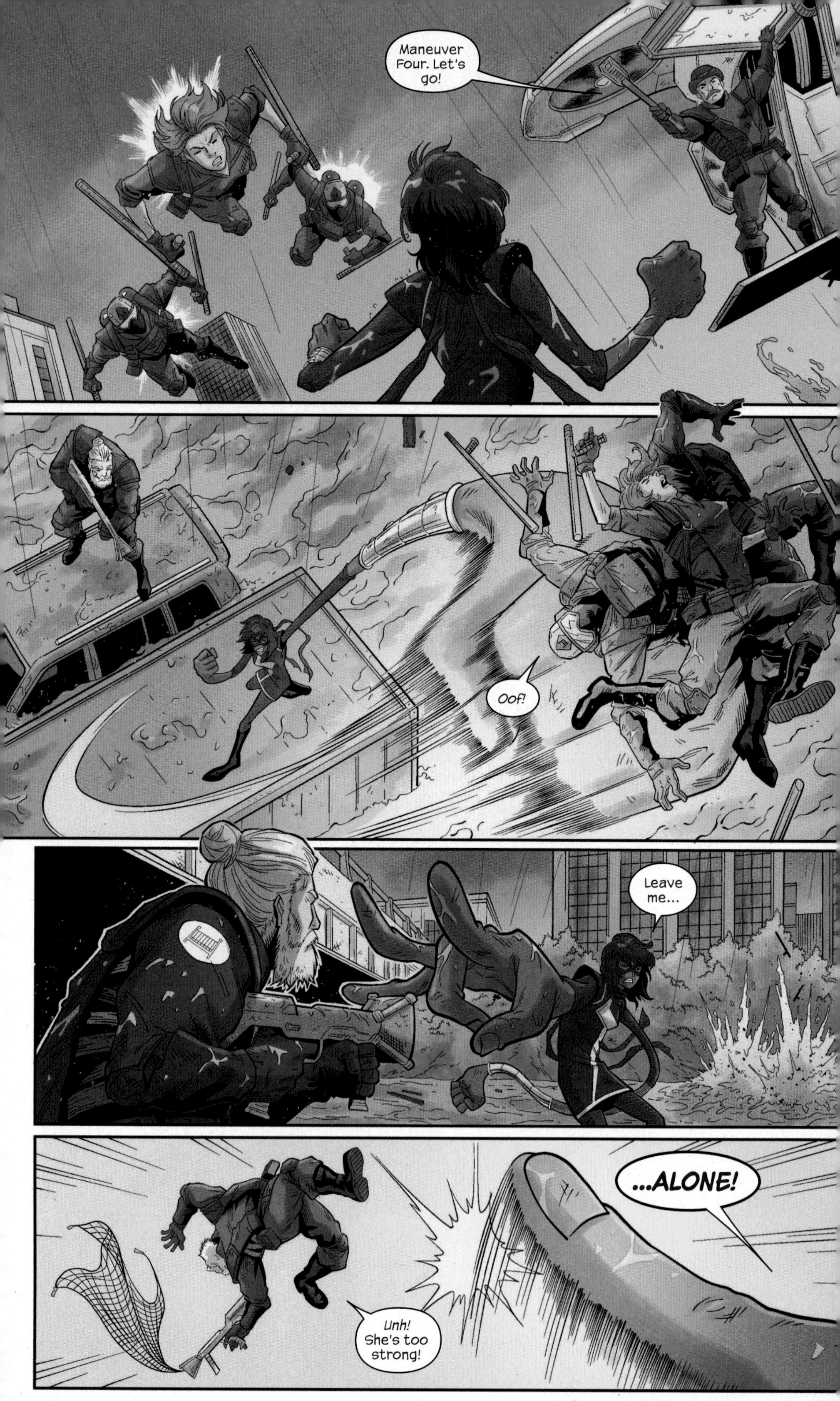
Maneuver Four. Let's go!
Oof!
Leave me...
...ALONE!
Unh! She's too strong!

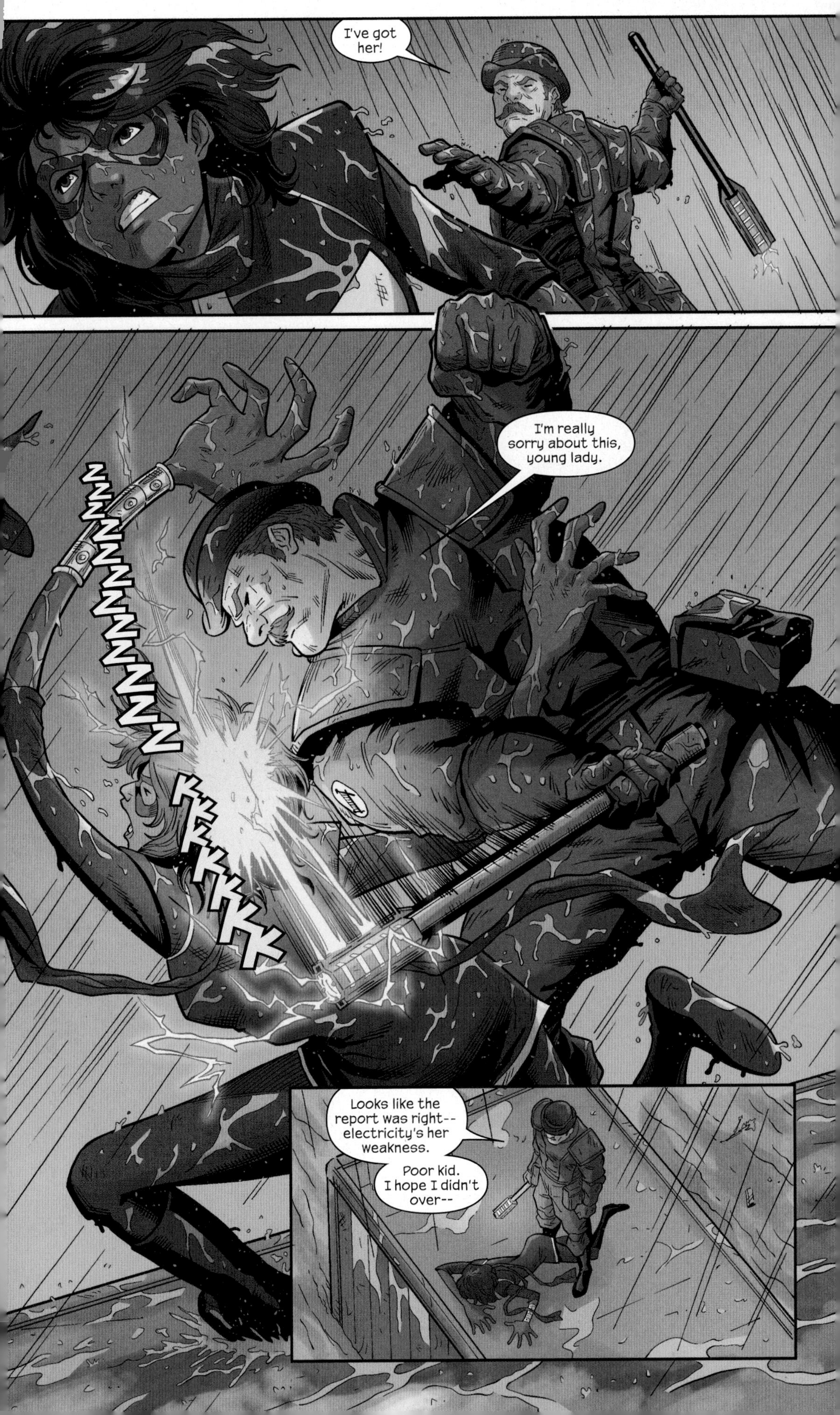
I've got her!
I'm really sorry about this, young lady.
ZZZZZZZZZZZZZ
KKKKKKKKK
Looks like the report was right-- electricity's her weakness.
Poor kid. I hope I didn't over--

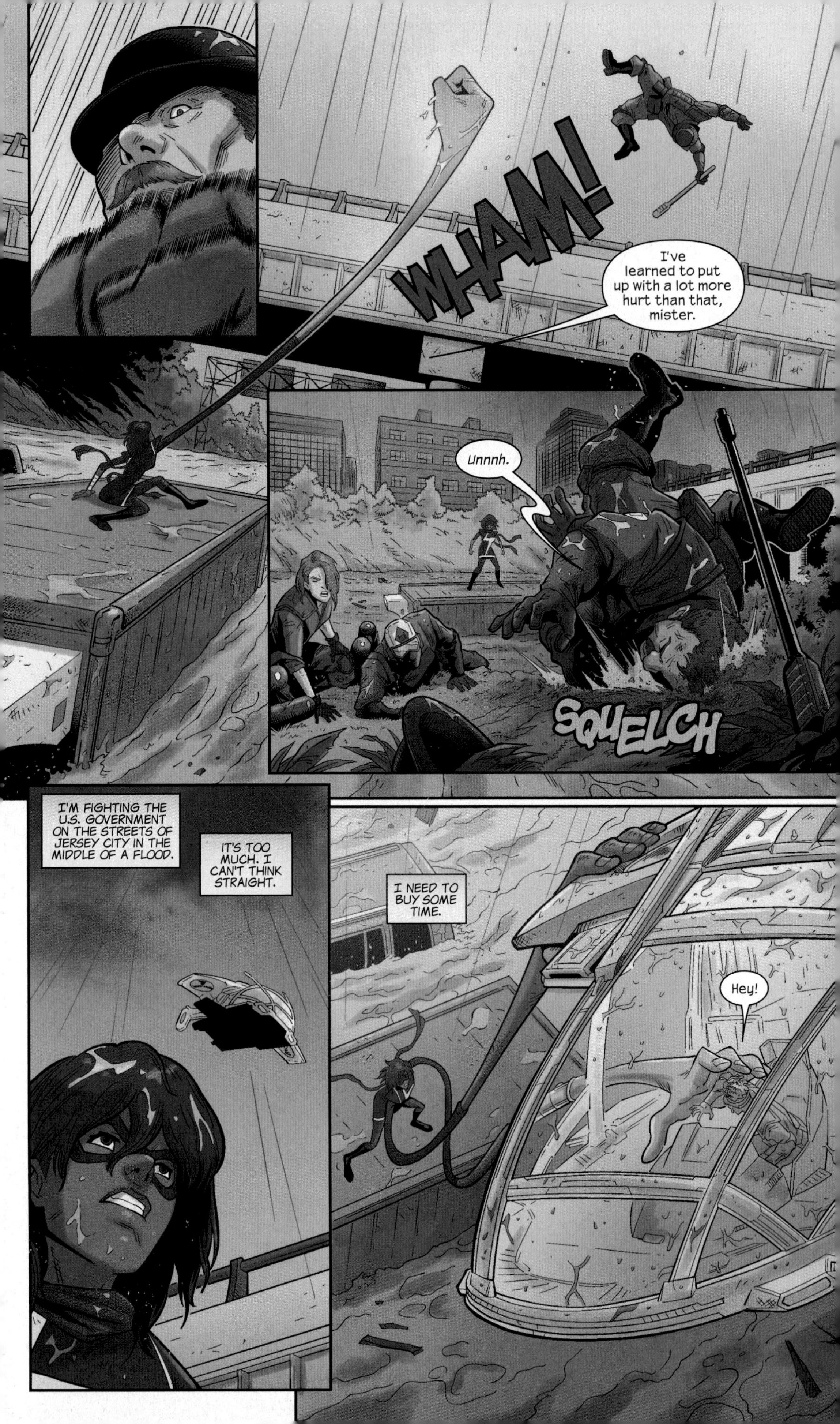
WHAM!
I've learned to put up with a lot more hurt than that, mister.
Unnnh.
SQUELCH
I'M FIGHTING THE U.S. GOVERNMENT ON THE STREETS OF JERSEY CITY IN THE MIDDLE OF A FLOOD.
IT'S TOO MUCH. I CAN'T THINK STRAIGHT.
I NEED TO BUY SOME TIME.
Hey!

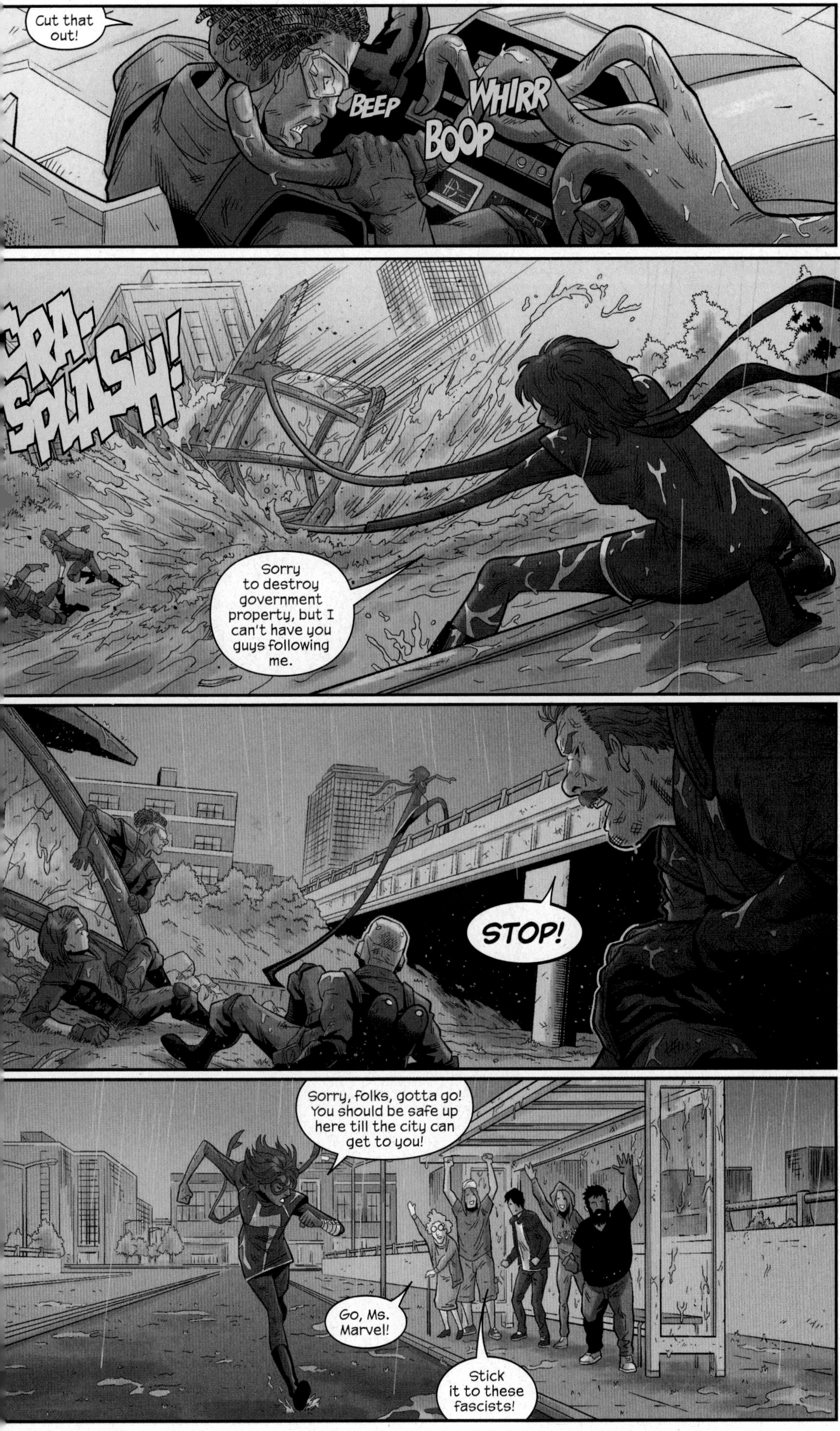
Cut that out!
BEEP
WHIRR
BOOP
CRA-SPLASH!
Sorry to destroy government property, but I can't have you guys following me.
STOP!
Sorry, folks, gotta go! You should be safe up here till the city can get to you!
Go, Ms. Marvel!
Stick it to these fascists!

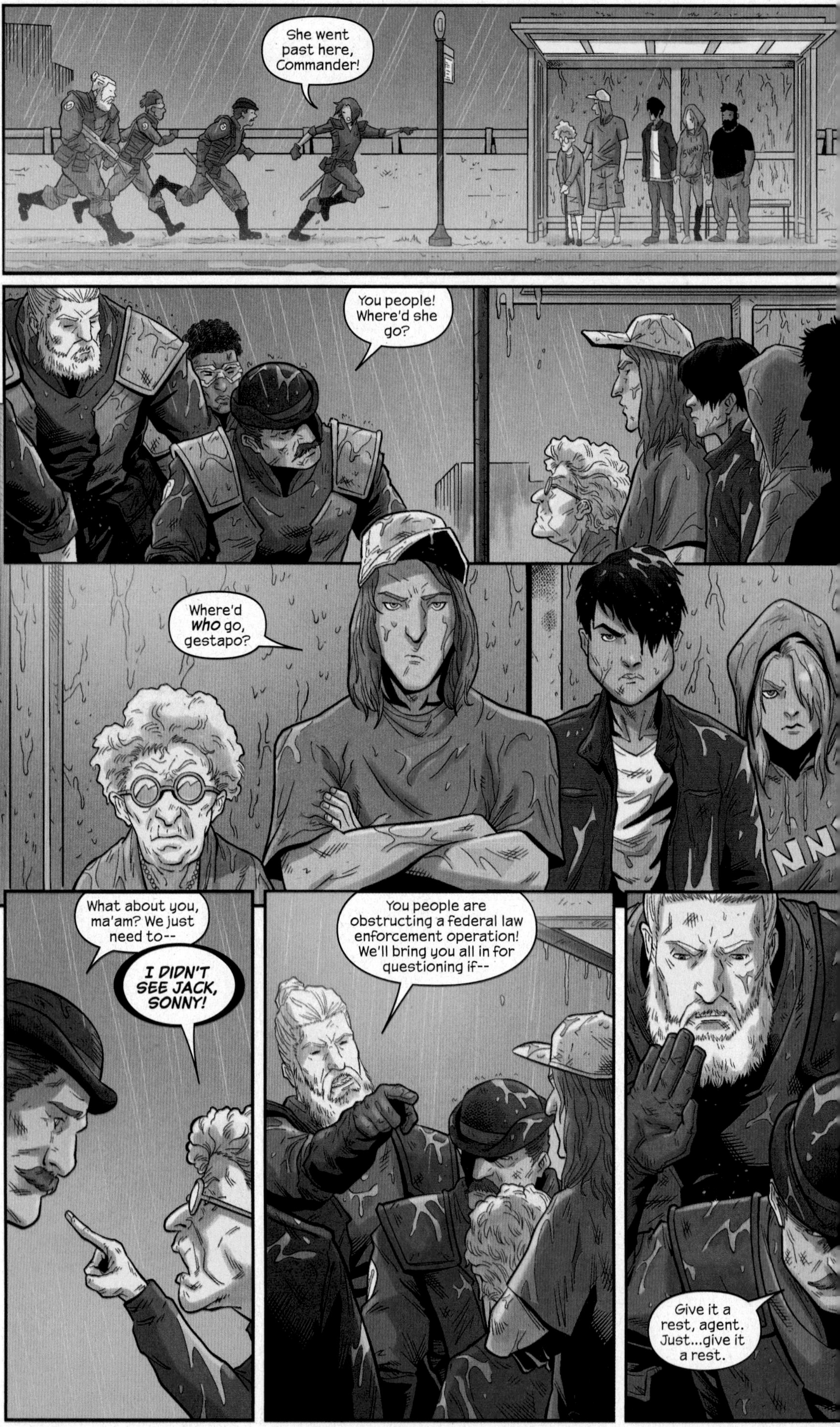
She went past here, Commander!
You people! Where'd she go?
Where'd *WHO* go, gestapo?
What about you, ma'am? We just need to--
I DIDN'T SEE JACK, SONNY!
You people are obstructing a federal law enforcement operation! We'll bring you all in for questioning if--
Give it a rest, agent. Just...give it a rest.

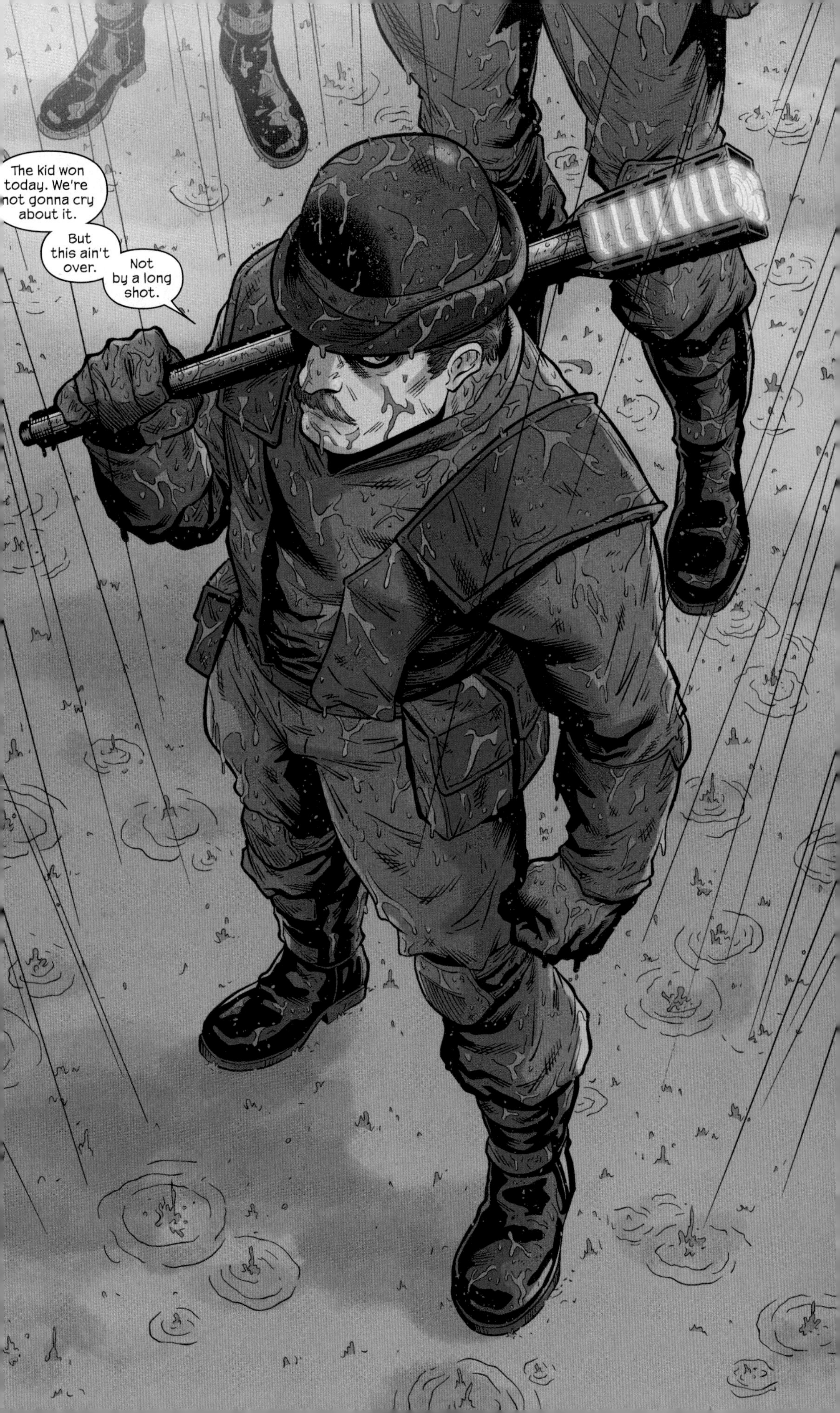
The kid won today. We're not gonna cry about it.
But this ain't over.
Not by a long shot.

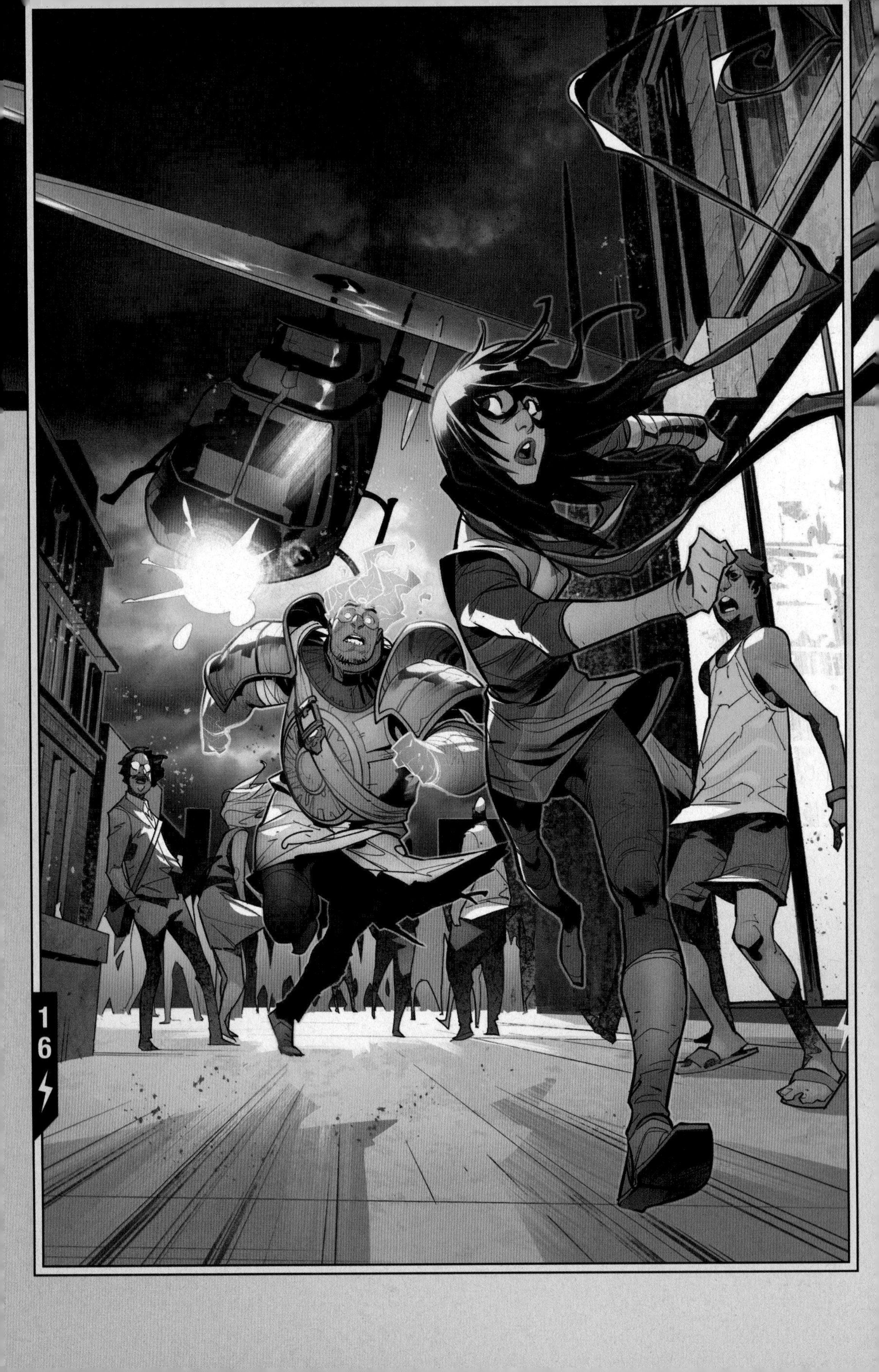
16

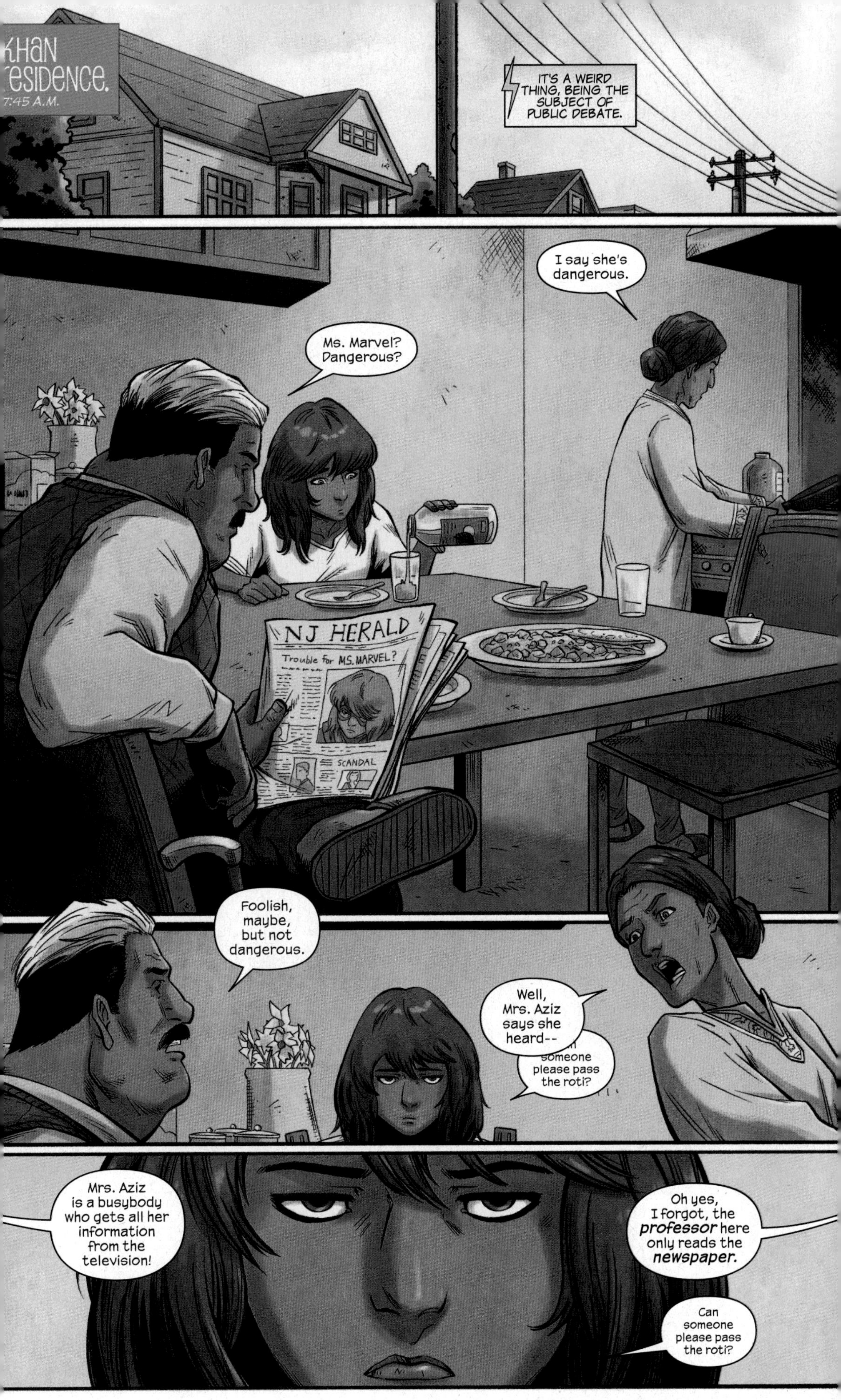

KHAN RESIDENCE.
7:45 A.M.
IT'S A WEIRD THING, BEING THE SUBJECT OF PUBLIC DEBATE.
I say she's dangerous.
Ms. Marvel? Dangerous?
NJ HERALD
Trouble for MS. MARVEL?
SCANDAL
Foolish, maybe, but not dangerous.
Well, Mrs. Aziz says she heard--
someone please pass the roti?
Mrs. Aziz is a busybody who gets all her information from the television!
Oh yes, I forgot, the *professor* here only reads the *newspaper*.
Can someone please pass the roti?

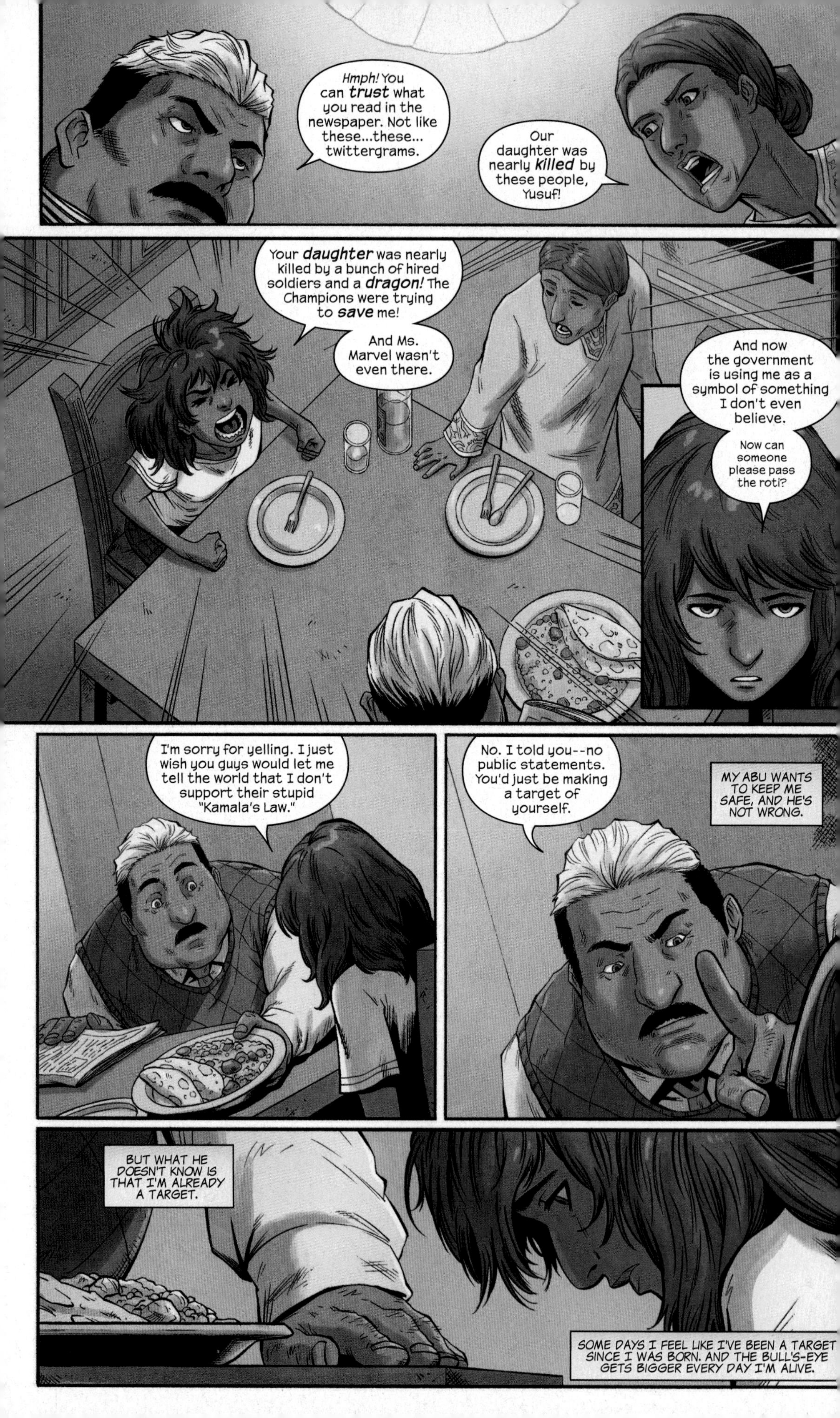

Hmph! You can trust what you read in the newspaper. Not like these...these... twittergrams.
Our daughter was nearly killed by these people, Yusuf!
Your daughter was nearly killed by a bunch of hired soldiers and a dragon! The Champions were trying to save me!
And Ms. Marvel wasn't even there.
And now the government is using me as a symbol of something I don't even believe.
Now can someone please pass the roti?
I'm sorry for yelling. I just wish you guys would let me tell the world that I don't support their stupid "Kamala's Law."
No. I told you--no public statements. You'd just be making a target of yourself.
MY ABU WANTS TO KEEP ME SAFE, AND HE'S NOT WRONG.
BUT WHAT HE DOESN'T KNOW IS THAT I'M ALREADY A TARGET.
SOME DAYS I FEEL LIKE I'VE BEEN A TARGET SINCE I WAS BORN. AND THE BULL'S-EYE GETS BIGGER EVERY DAY I'M ALIVE.

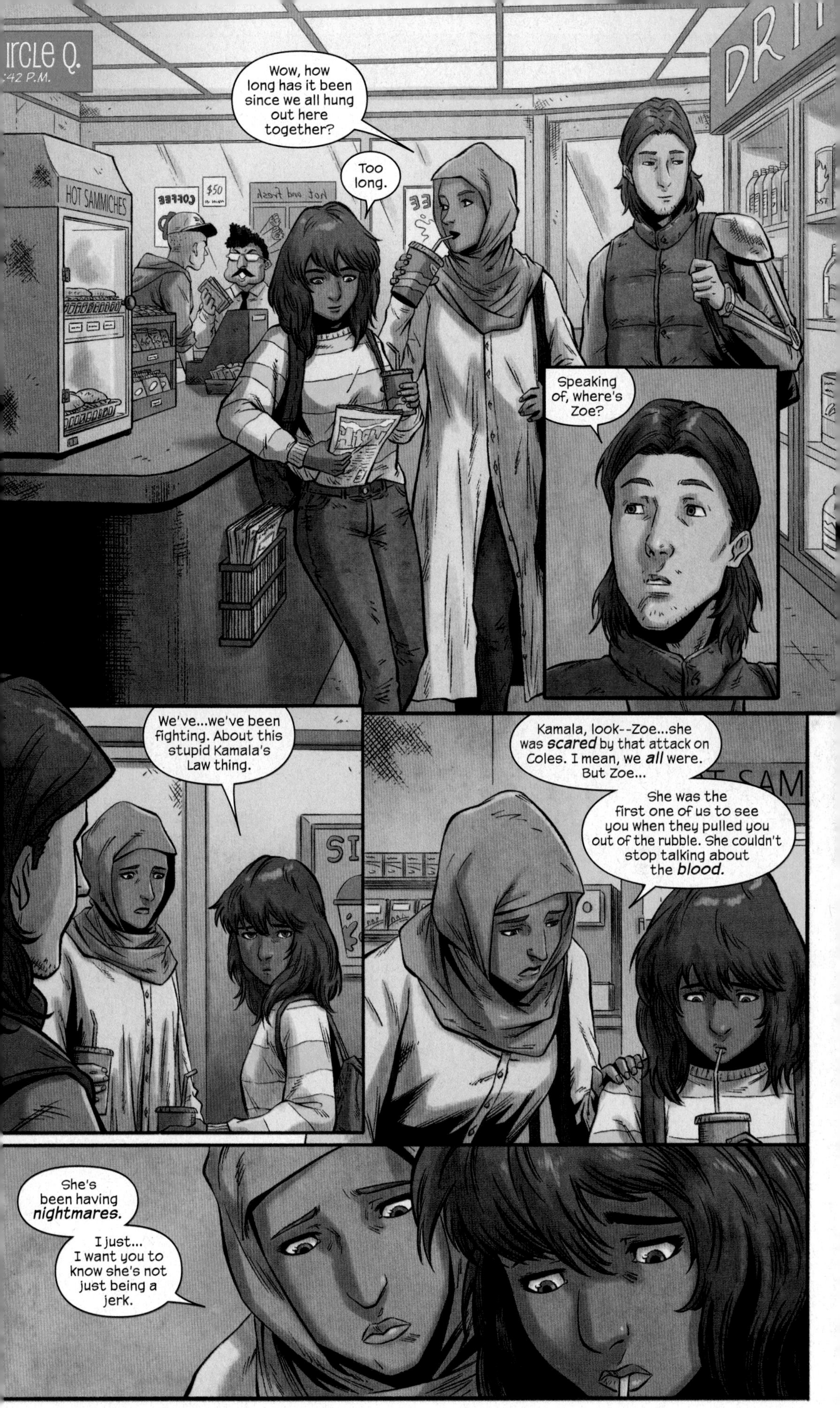

IRCLE Q.
:42 P.M.
Wow, how long has it been since we all hung out here together?
Too long.
Speaking of, where's Zoe?
We've...we've been fighting. About this stupid Kamala's Law thing.
Kamala, look--Zoe...she was *scared* by that attack on Coles. I mean, we *all* were. But Zoe...
She was the first one of us to see you when they pulled you out of the rubble. She couldn't stop talking about the *blood.*
She's been having *nightmares.*
I just... I want you to know she's not just being a jerk.

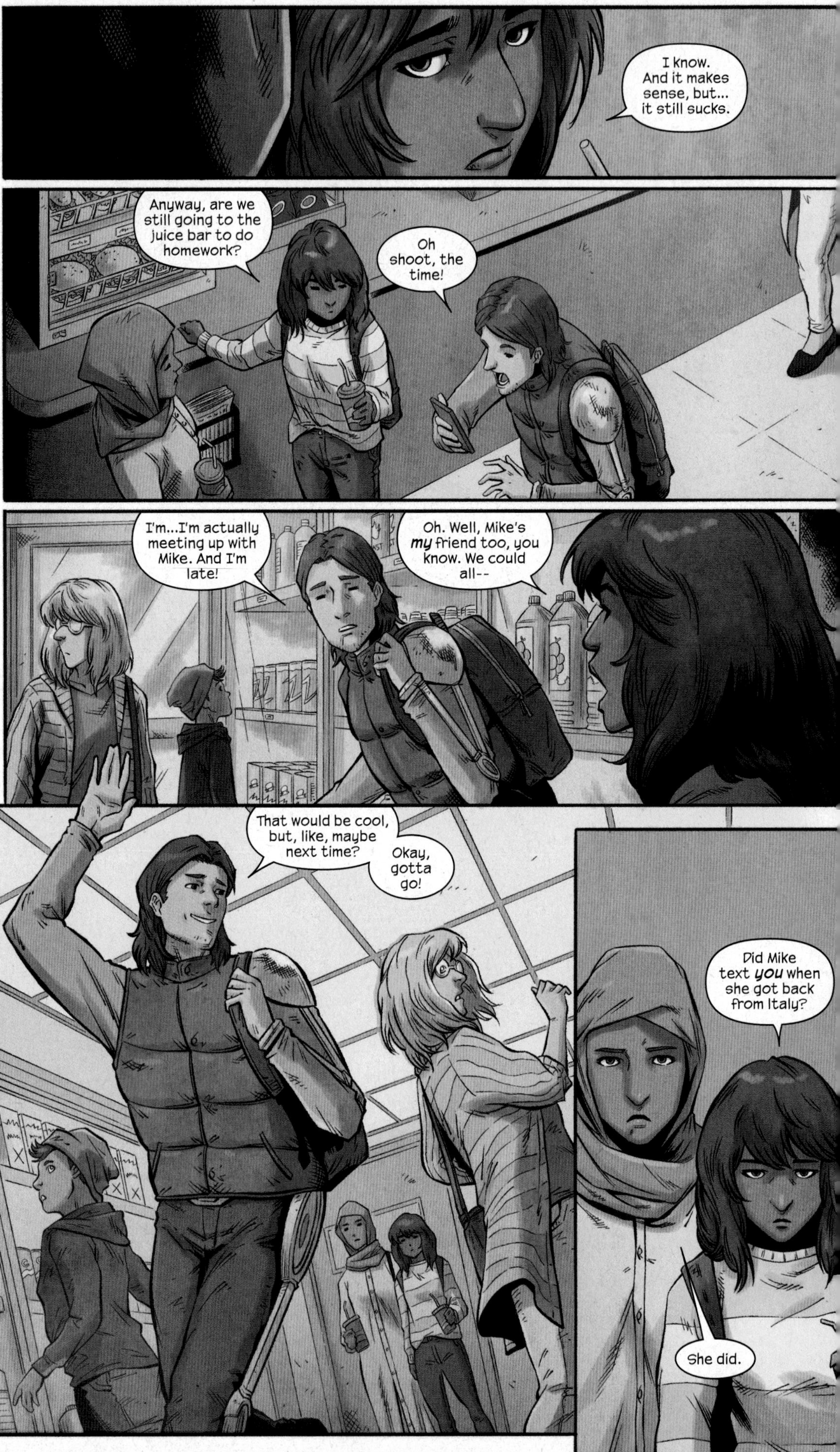
I know. And it makes sense, but... it still sucks.
Anyway, are we still going to the juice bar to do homework?
Oh shoot, the time!
I'm...I'm actually meeting up with Mike. And I'm late!
Oh. Well, Mike's *my* friend too, you know. We could all--
That would be cool, but, like, maybe next time?
Okay, gotta go!
Did Mike text *you* when she got back from Italy?
She did.

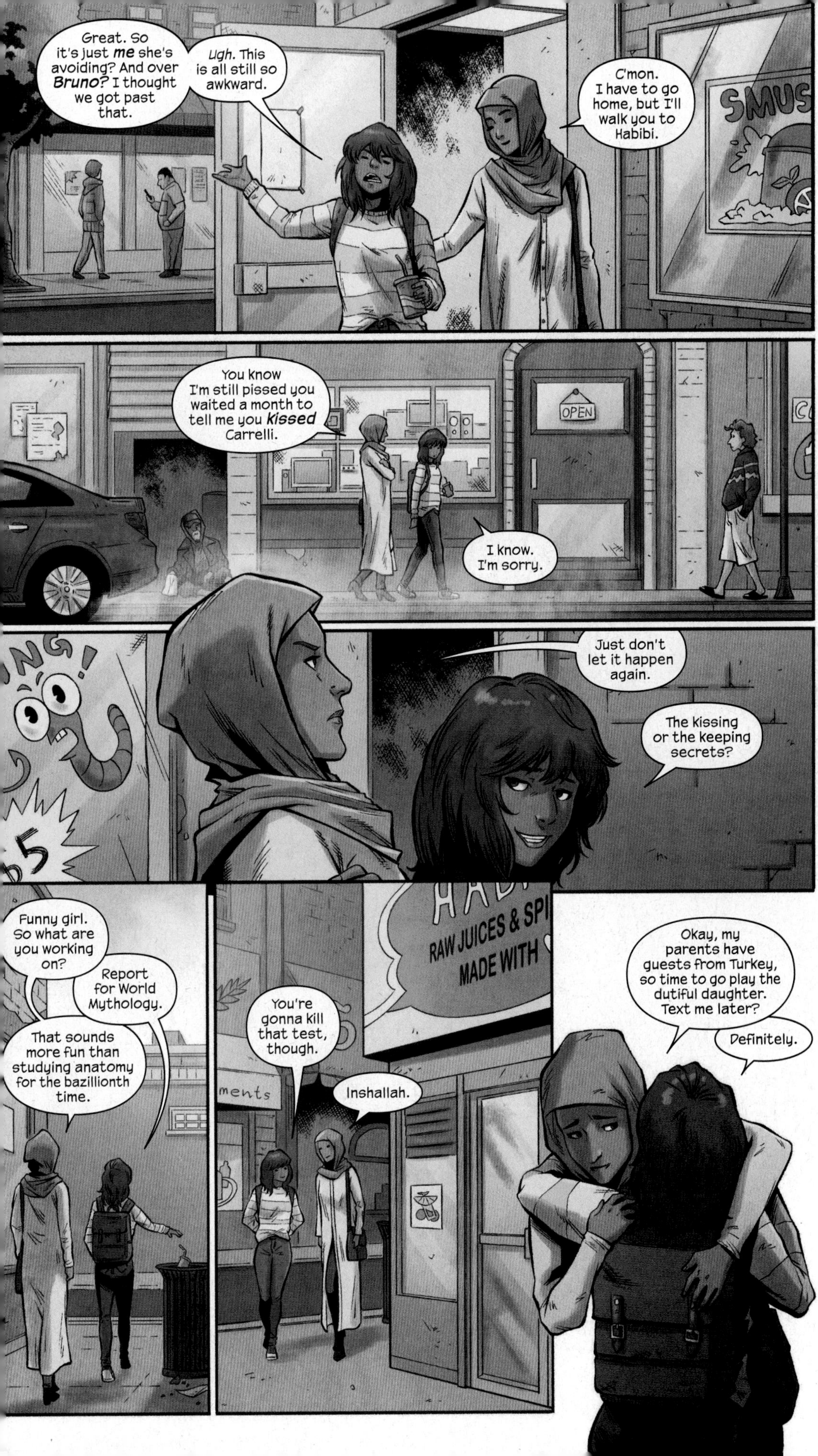
Great. So it's just *me* she's avoiding? And over *Bruno?* I thought we got past that.
Ugh. This is all still so awkward.
C'mon. I have to go home, but I'll walk you to Habibi.
SMUS
You know I'm still pissed you waited a month to tell me you *kissed* Carrelli.
OPEN
I know. I'm sorry.
Just don't let it happen again.
The kissing or the keeping secrets?
Funny girl. So what are you working on?
Report for World Mythology.
That sounds more fun than studying anatomy for the bazillionth time.
You're gonna kill that test, though.
Inshallah.
RAW JUICES & SPI
MADE WITH
Okay, my parents have guests from Turkey, so time to go play the dutiful daughter. Text me later?
Definitely.

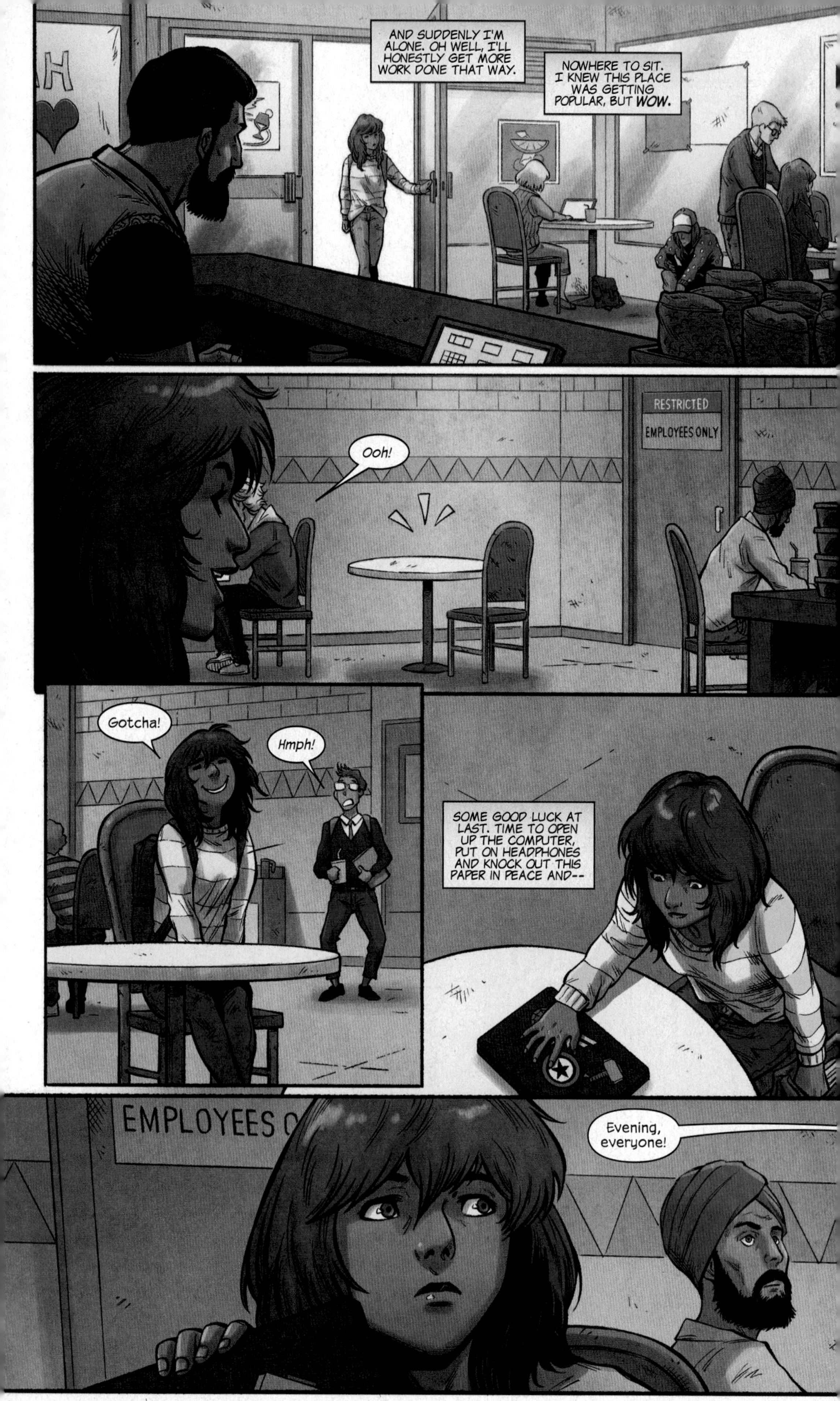
AND SUDDENLY I'M ALONE. OH WELL, I'LL HONESTLY GET MORE WORK DONE THAT WAY.
NOWHERE TO SIT. I KNEW THIS PLACE WAS GETTING POPULAR, BUT **WOW**.
RESTRICTED
EMPLOYEES ONLY
Ooh!
Gotcha!
Hmph!
SOME GOOD LUCK AT LAST. TIME TO OPEN UP THE COMPUTER, PUT ON HEADPHONES AND KNOCK OUT THIS PAPER IN PEACE AND--
Evening, everyone!

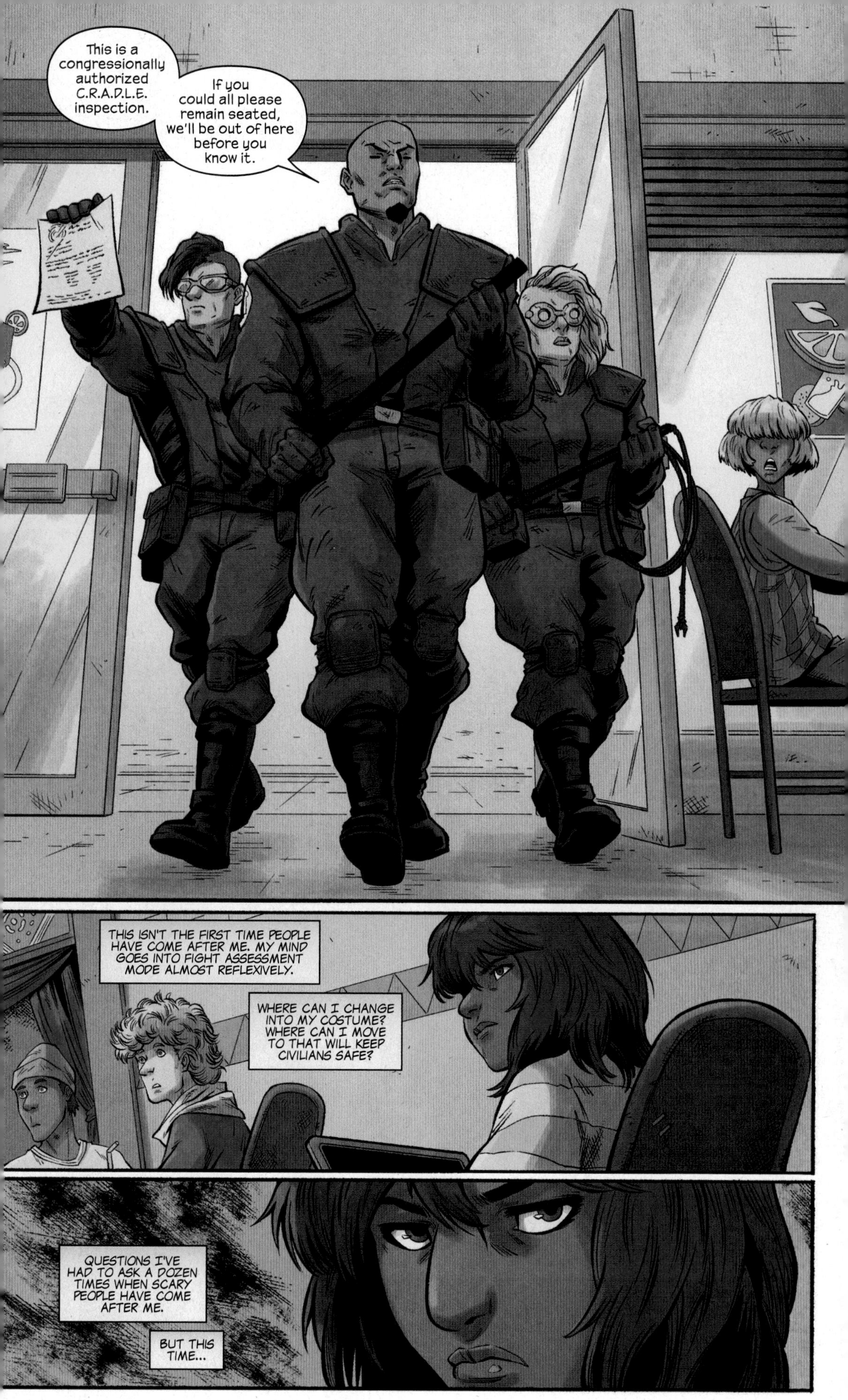
This is a congressionally authorized C.R.A.D.L.E. inspection.
If you could all please remain seated, we'll be out of here before you know it.
THIS ISN'T THE FIRST TIME PEOPLE HAVE COME AFTER ME. MY MIND GOES INTO FIGHT ASSESSMENT MODE ALMOST REFLEXIVELY.
WHERE CAN I CHANGE INTO MY COSTUME? WHERE CAN I MOVE TO THAT WILL KEEP CIVILIANS SAFE?
QUESTIONS I'VE HAD TO ASK A DOZEN TIMES WHEN SCARY PEOPLE HAVE COME AFTER ME.
BUT THIS TIME...

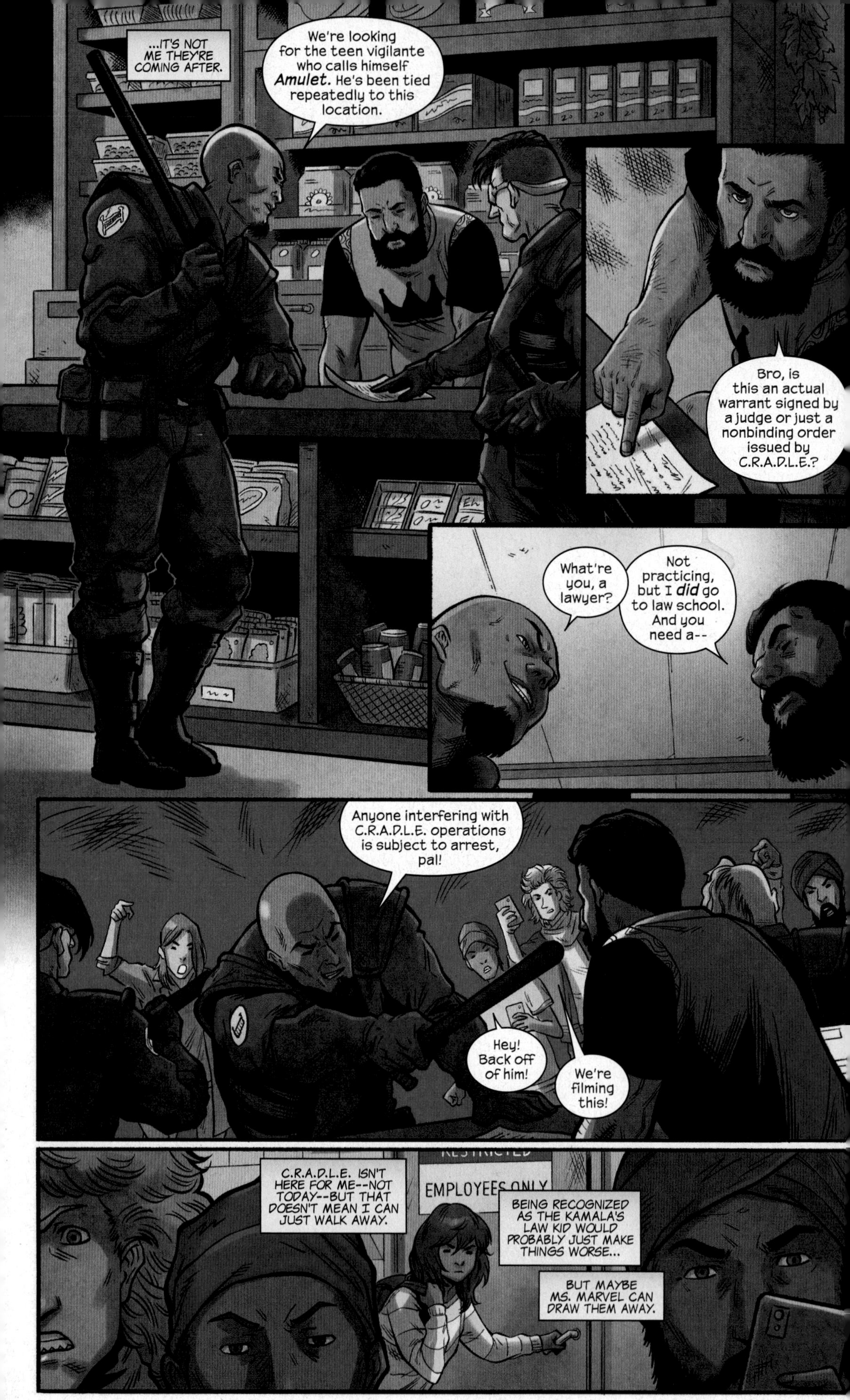
...IT'S NOT ME THEY'RE COMING AFTER.
We're looking for the teen vigilante who calls himself *Amulet*. He's been tied repeatedly to this location.
Bro, is this an actual warrant signed by a judge or just a nonbinding order issued by C.R.A.D.L.E.?
What're you, a lawyer?
Not practicing, but I *did* go to law school. And you need a--
Anyone interfering with C.R.A.D.L.E. operations is subject to arrest, pal!
Hey! Back off of him!
We're filming this!
EMPLOYEES ONLY
C.R.A.D.L.E. ISN'T HERE FOR ME--NOT TODAY--BUT THAT DOESN'T MEAN I CAN JUST WALK AWAY.
BEING RECOGNIZED AS THE KAMALA'S LAW KID WOULD PROBABLY JUST MAKE THINGS WORSE...
BUT MAYBE MS. MARVEL CAN DRAW THEM AWAY.

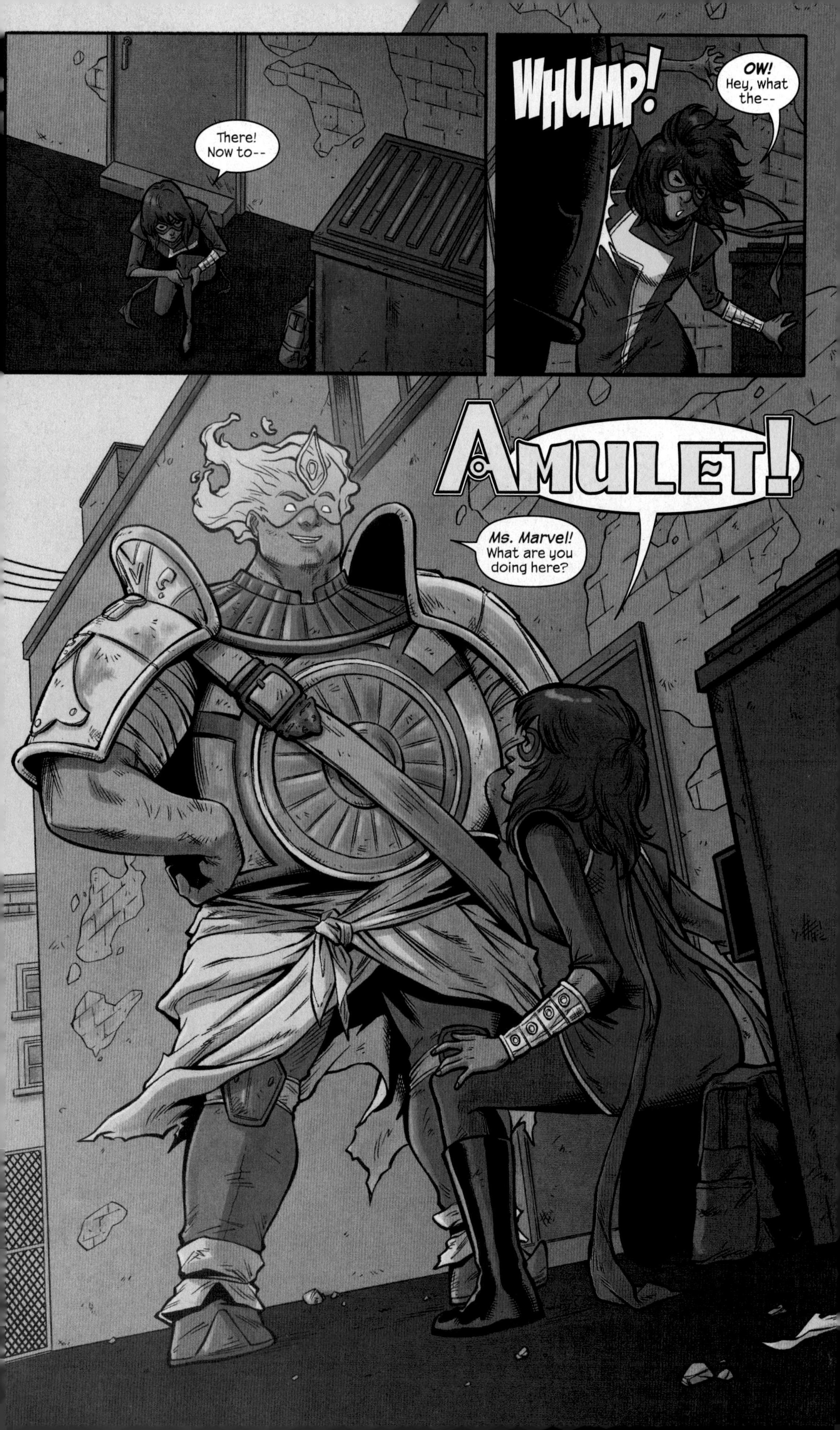
There! Now to--
WHUMP!
OW! Hey, what the--
AMULET!
Ms. Marvel! What are you doing here?

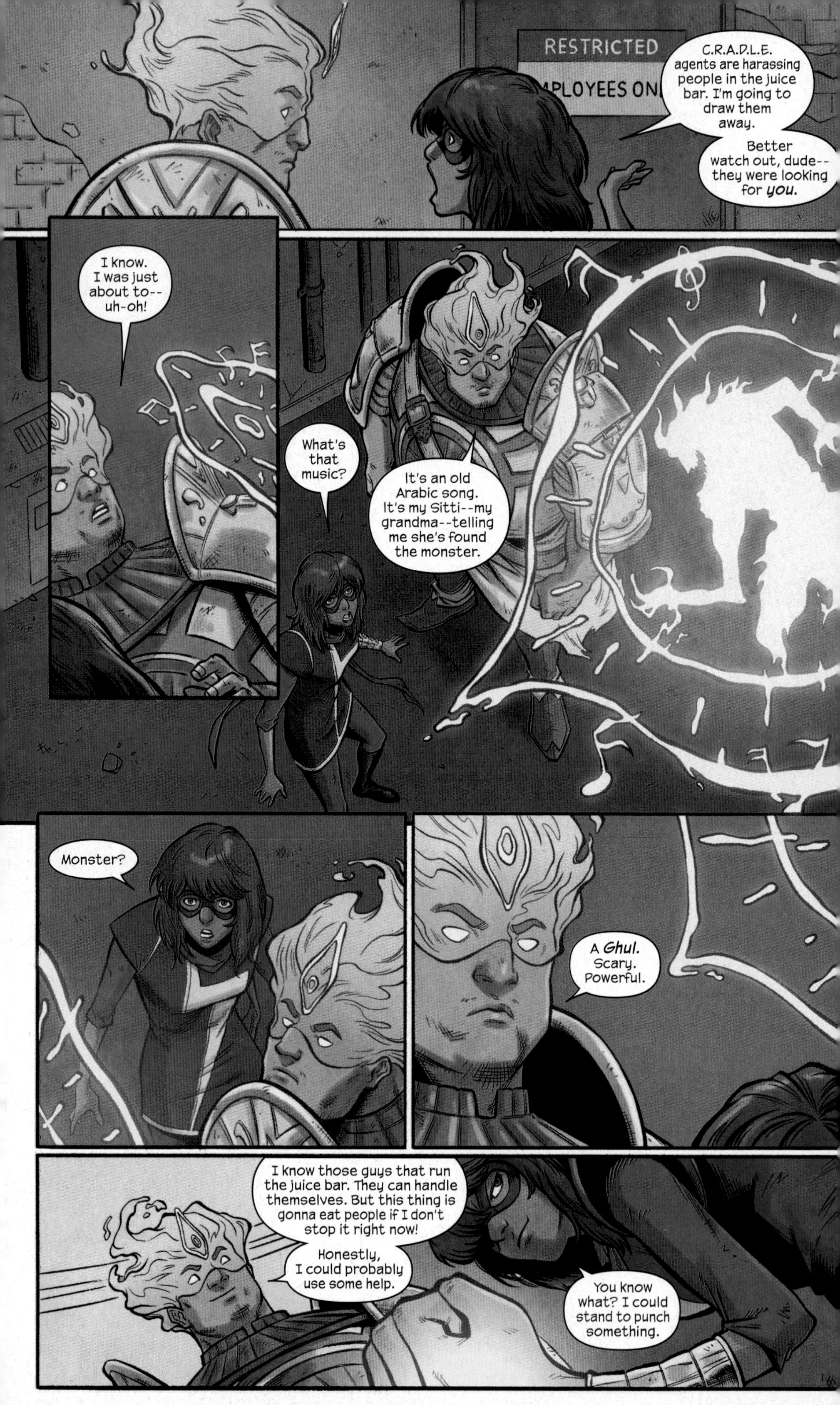
RESTRICTED
MPLOYEES ON
C.R.A.D.L.E. agents are harassing people in the juice bar. I'm going to draw them away.
Better watch out, dude--they were looking for *you.*
I know. I was just about to--uh-oh!
What's that music?
It's an old Arabic song. It's my Sitti--my grandma--telling me she's found the monster.
Monster?
A *Ghul.* Scary. Powerful.
I know those guys that run the juice bar. They can handle themselves. But this thing is gonna eat people if I don't stop it right now!
Honestly, I could probably use some help.
You know what? I could stand to punch something.

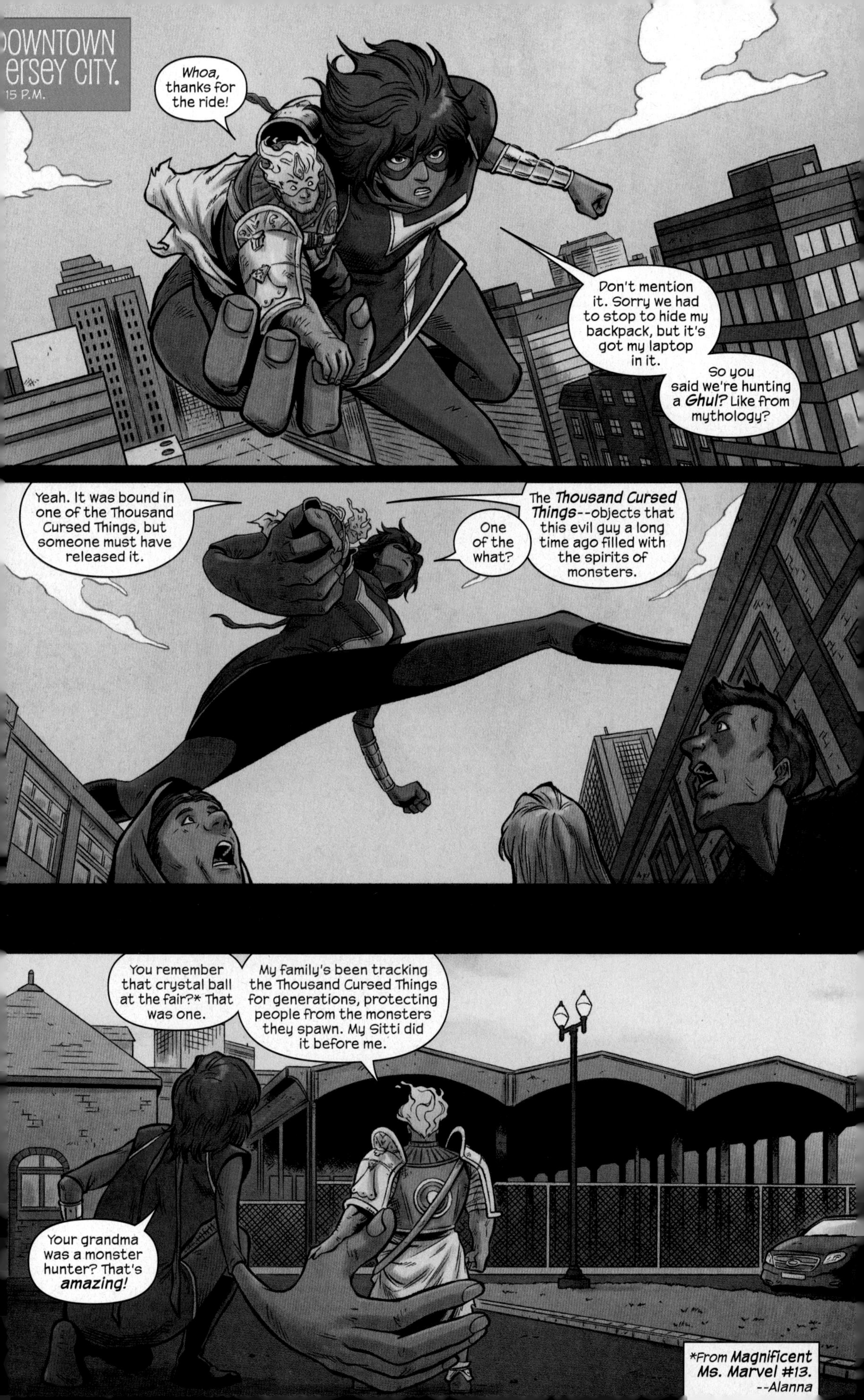

OWNTOWN ersey City.
15 P.M.
Whoa, thanks for the ride!
Don't mention it. Sorry we had to stop to hide my backpack, but it's got my laptop in it.
So you said we're hunting a *Ghul?* Like from mythology?
Yeah. It was bound in one of the Thousand Cursed Things, but someone must have released it.
One of the what?
The *Thousand Cursed Things*--objects that this evil guy a long time ago filled with the spirits of monsters.
You remember that crystal ball at the fair?* That was one.
My family's been tracking the Thousand Cursed Things for generations, protecting people from the monsters they spawn. My Sitti did it before me.
Your grandma was a monster hunter? That's *amazing!*
*From *Magnificent Ms. Marvel #13.* --Alanna

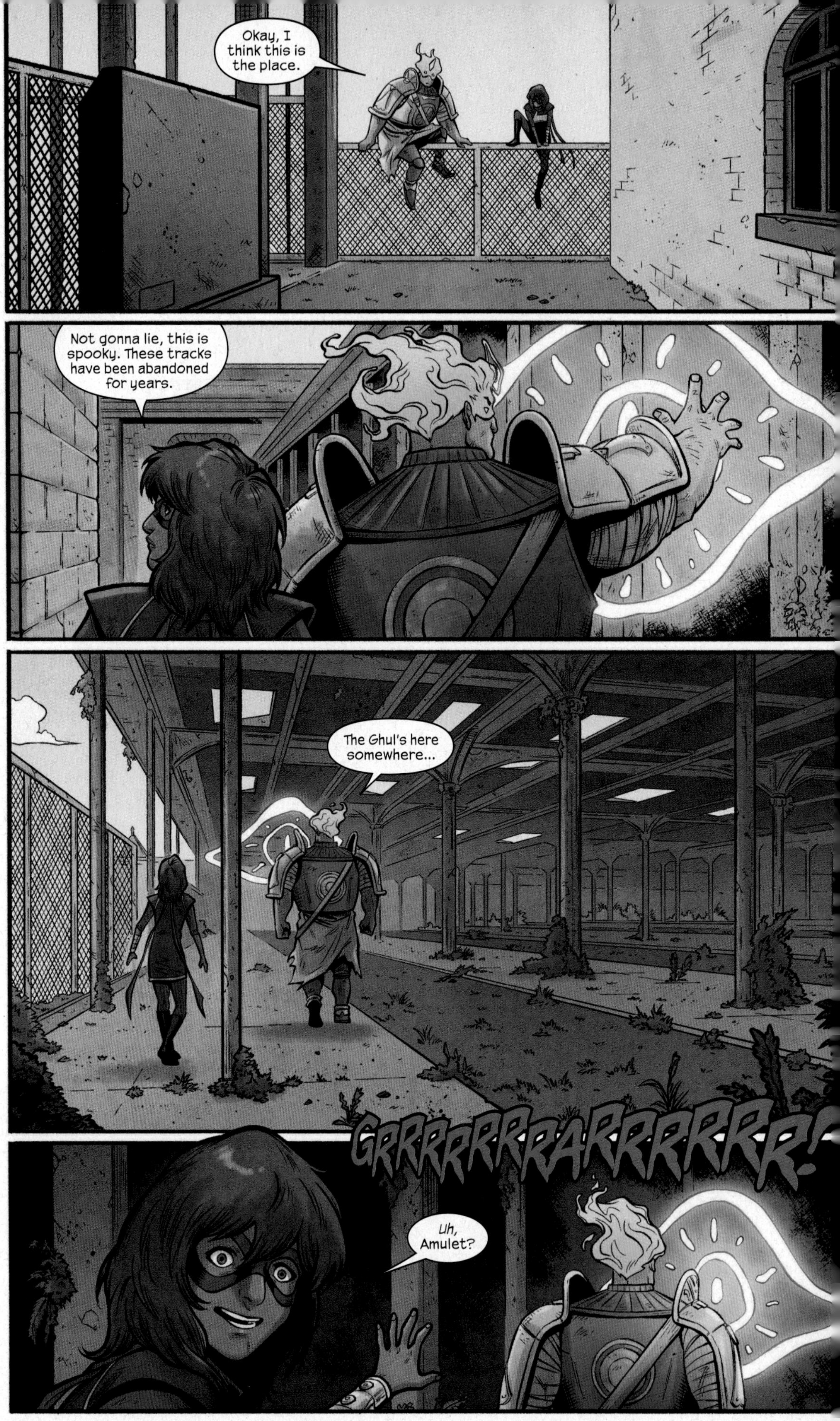
Okay, I think this is the place.
Not gonna lie, this is spooky. These tracks have been abandoned for years.
The Ghul's here somewhere...
GRRRRRRRARRRRRRR!
Uh, Amulet?

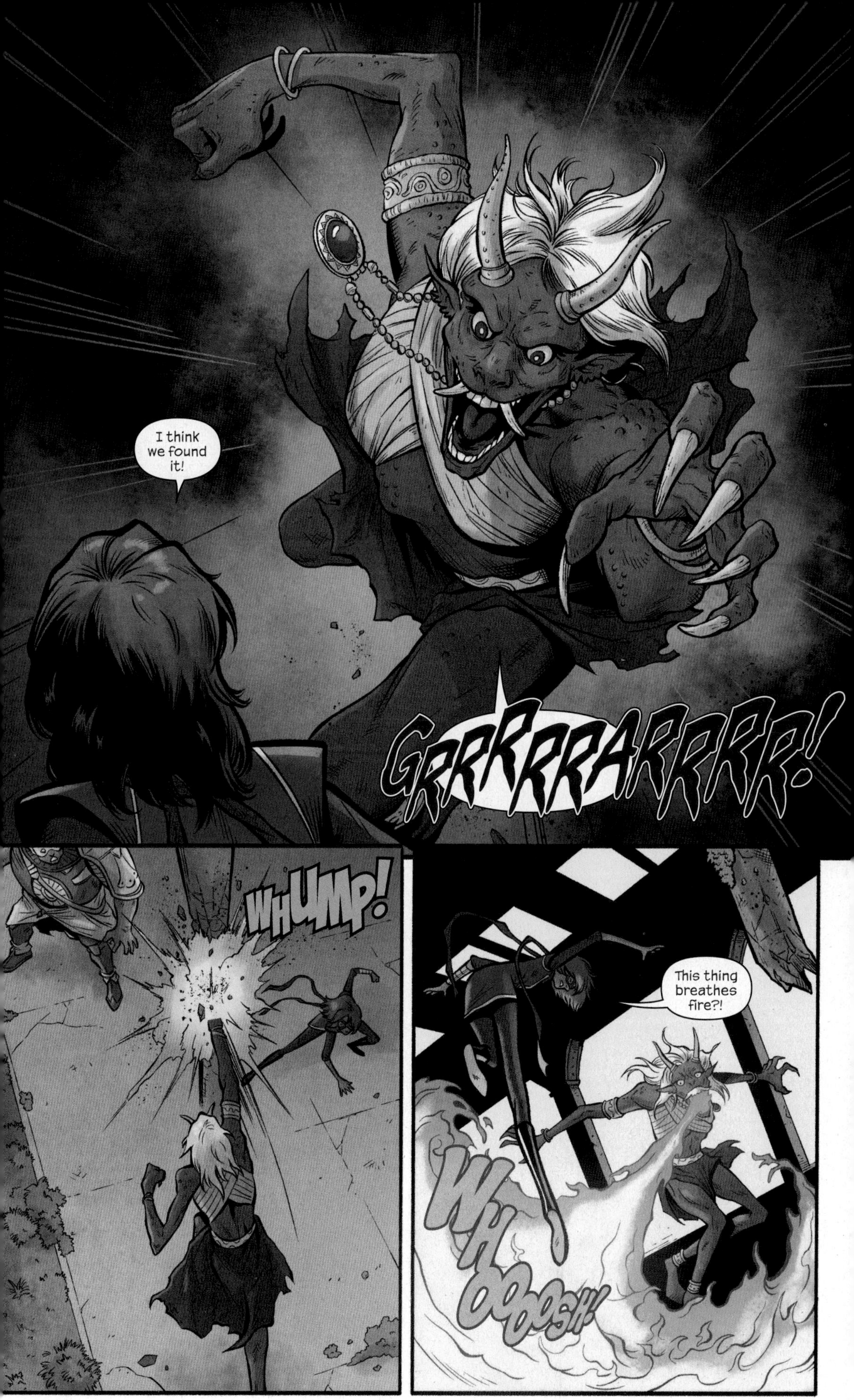
I think we found it!
GRRRRRARRRR!
WHUMP!
This thing breathes fire?!
WHOOOOSH!

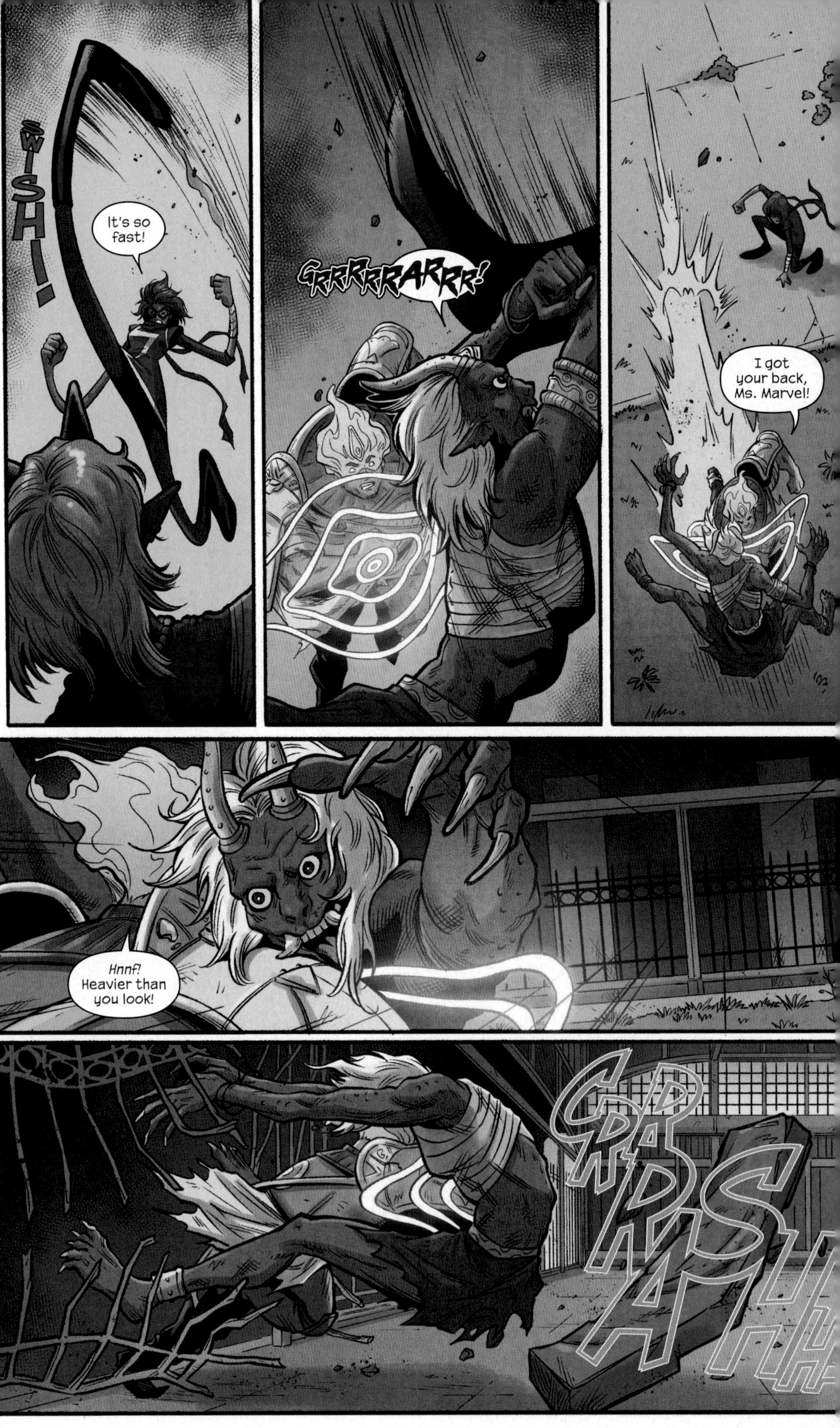
SWISH!
It's so fast!
GRRRRRRARRR!
I got your back, Ms. Marvel!
Hnnf! Heavier than you look!
CRASH

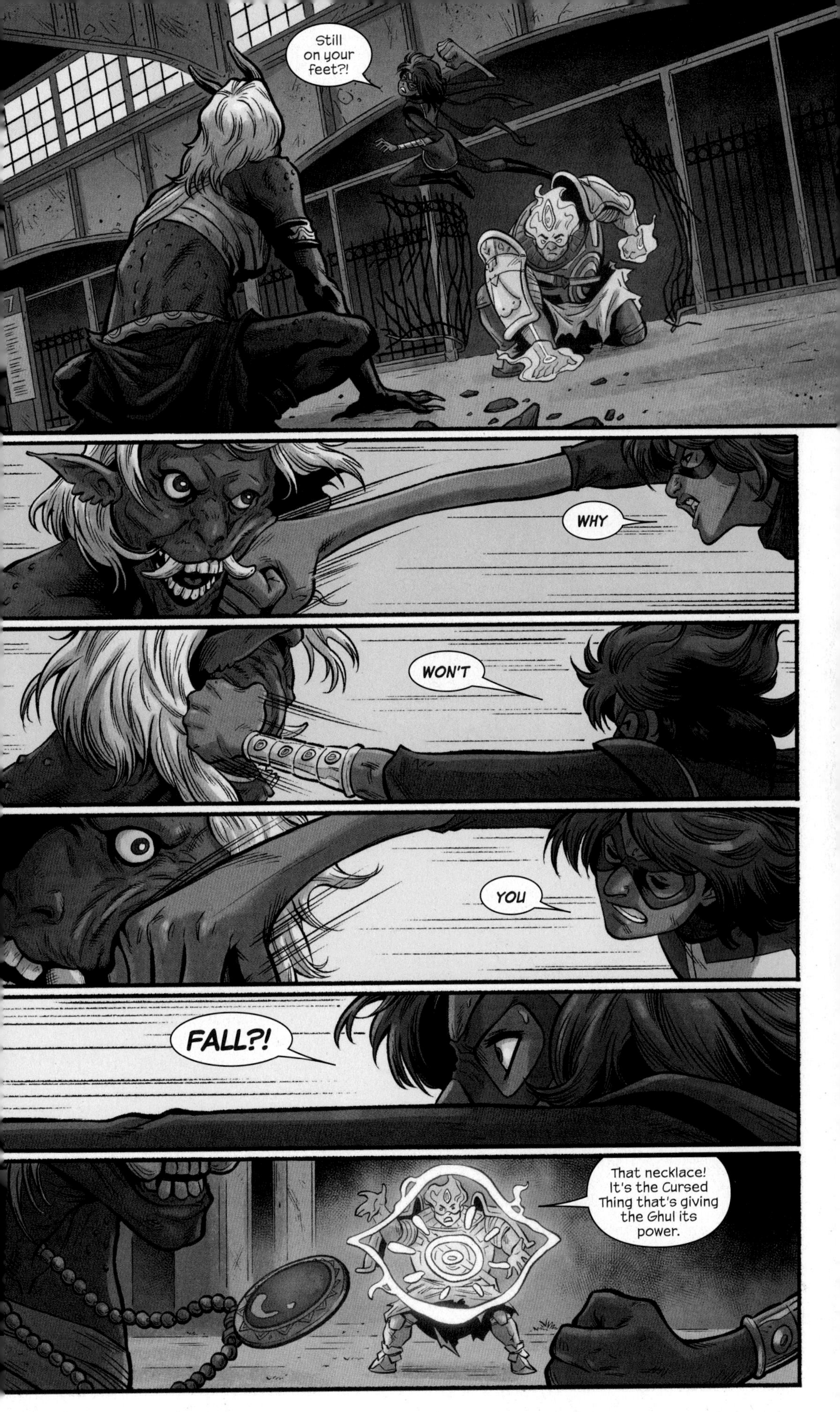
Still on your feet?!
WHY
WON'T
YOU
FALL?!
That necklace! It's the Cursed Thing that's giving the Ghul its power.

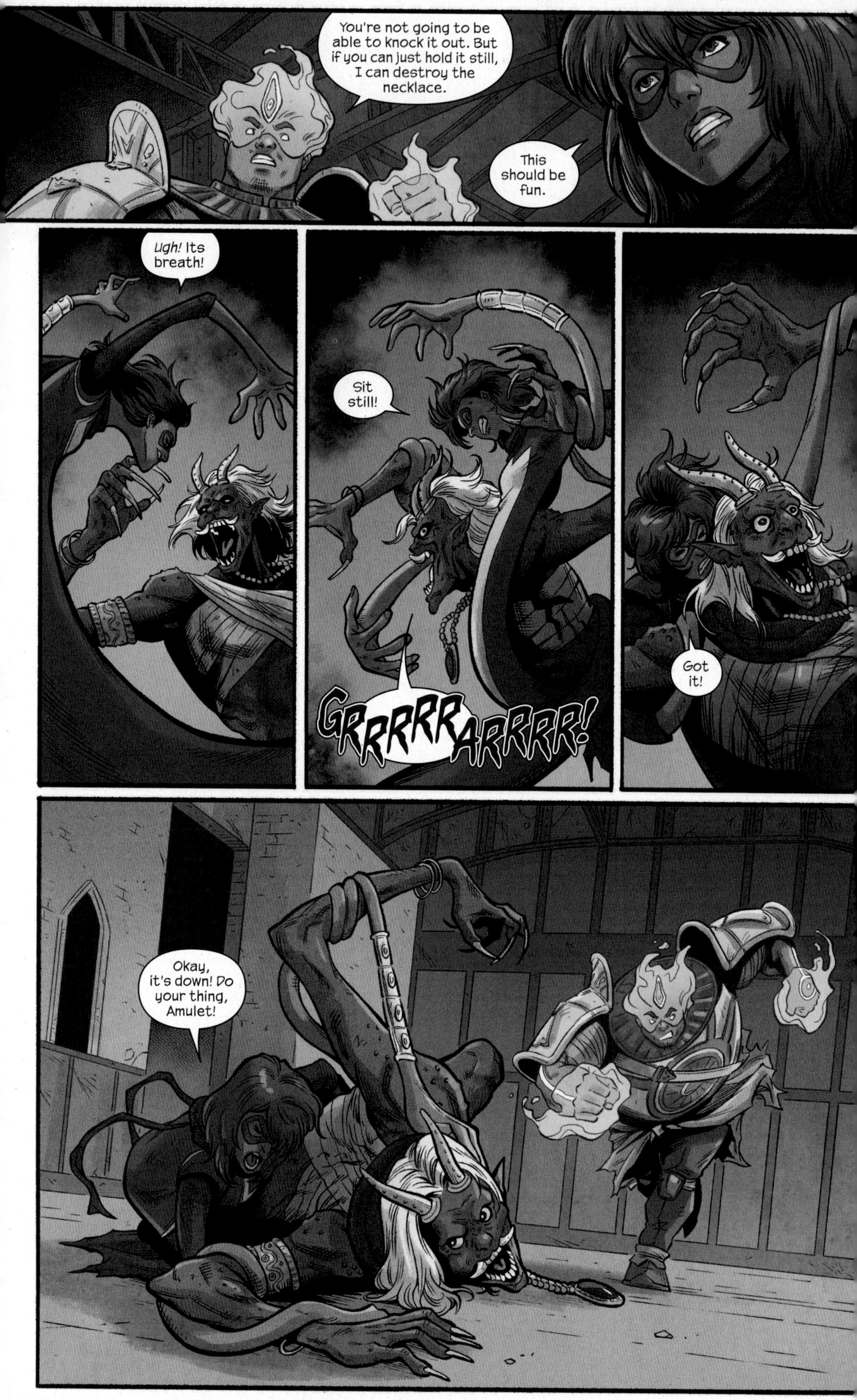
You're not going to be able to knock it out. But if you can just hold it still, I can destroy the necklace.
This should be fun.
Ugh! Its breath!
Sit still!
GRRRRRARRRRR!
Got it!
Okay, it's down! Do your thing, Amulet!

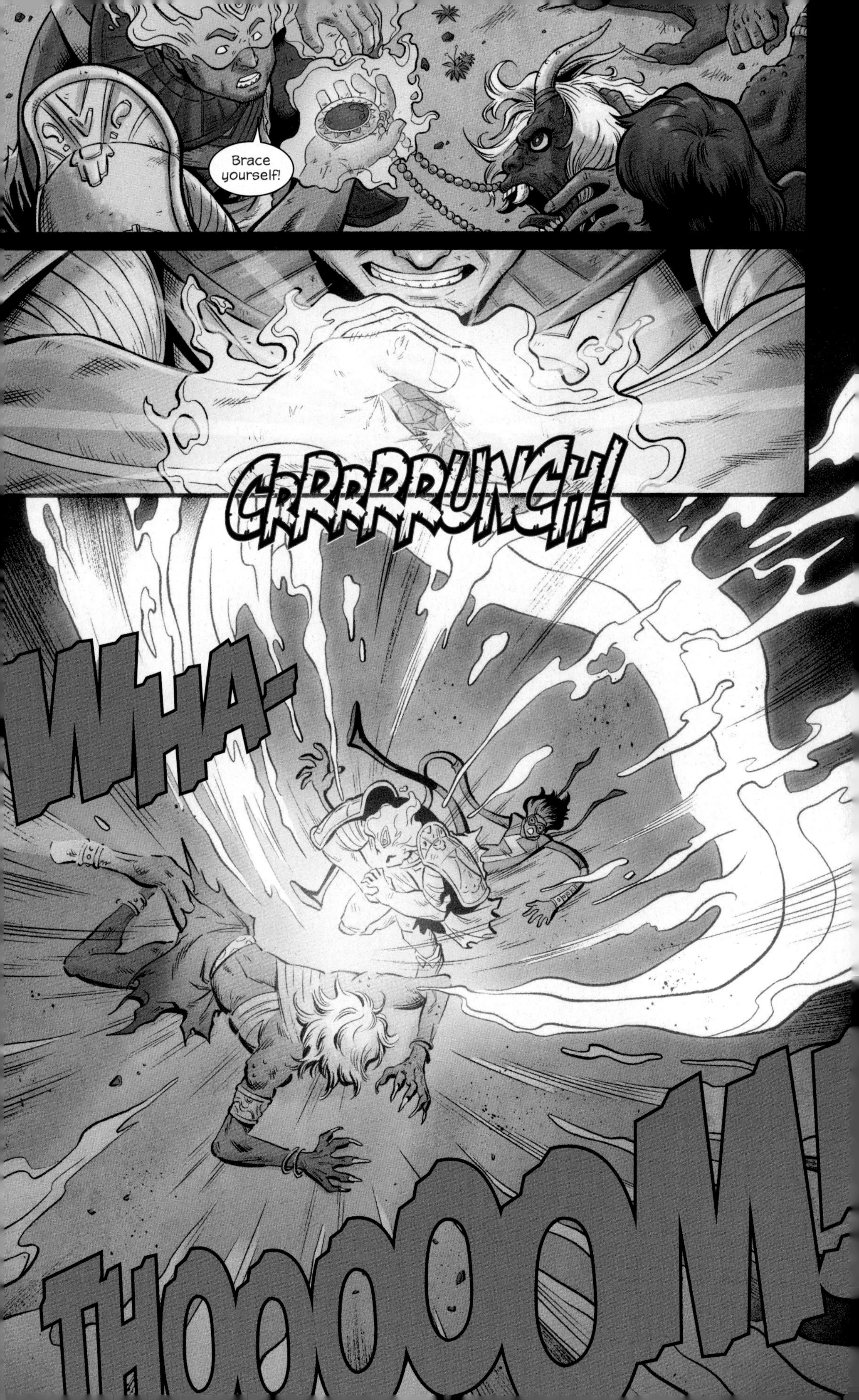
Brace yourself!
CRRRRRUNCH!
WHA-
THOOOOM!

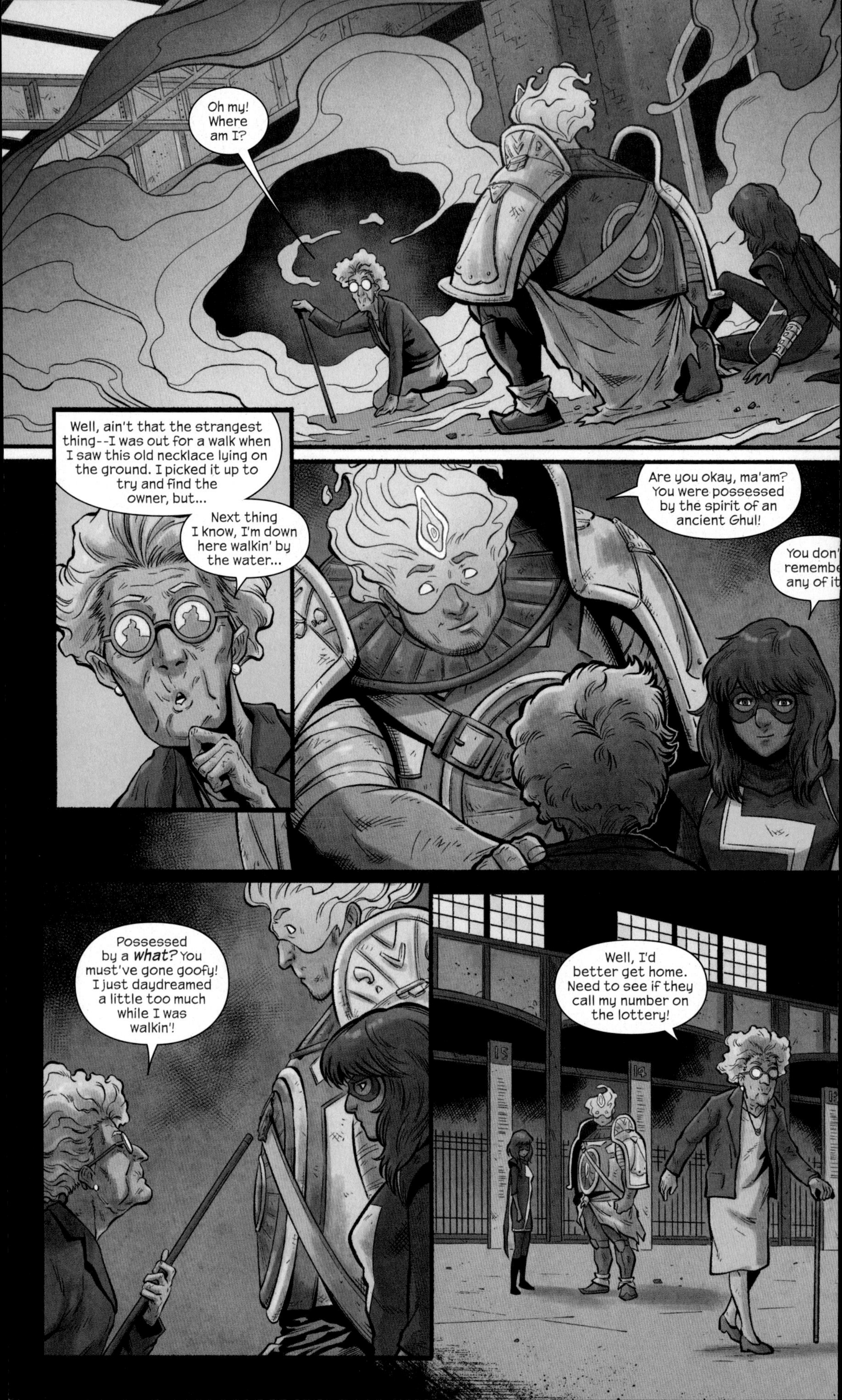
Oh my! Where am I?
Well, ain't that the strangest thing--I was out for a walk when I saw this old necklace lying on the ground. I picked it up to try and find the owner, but...
Next thing I know, I'm down here walkin' by the water...
Are you okay, ma'am? You were possessed by the spirit of an ancient Ghul!
Possessed by a *what?* You must've gone goofy! I just daydreamed a little too much while I was walkin'!
Well, I'd better get home. Need to see if they call my number on the lottery!
15
14

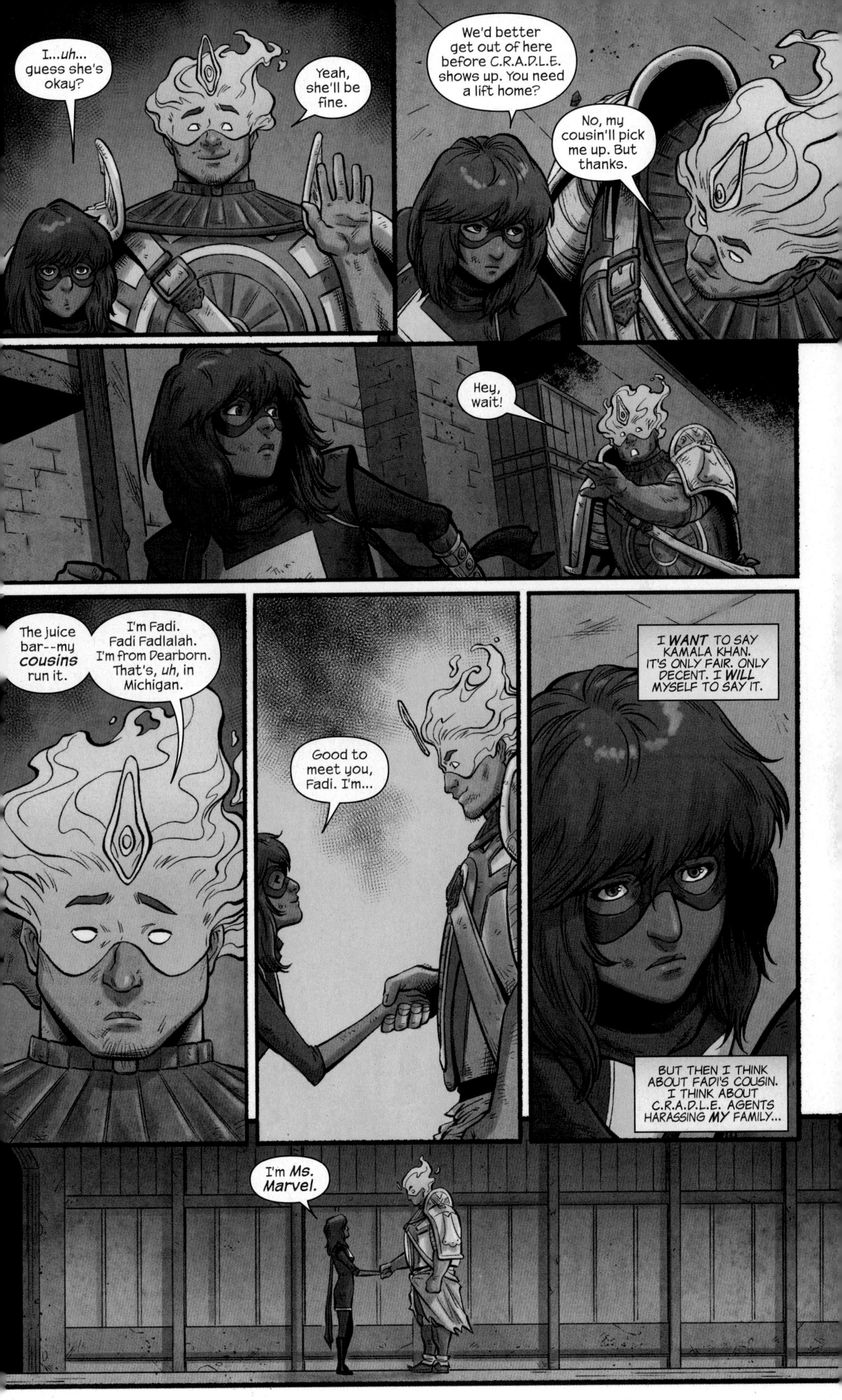
I...*uh*... guess she's okay?
Yeah, she'll be fine.
We'd better get out of here before C.R.A.D.L.E. shows up. You need a lift home?
No, my cousin'll pick me up. But thanks.
Hey, wait!
The juice bar--my ***cousins*** run it.
I'm Fadi. Fadi Fadlalah. I'm from Dearborn. That's, *uh*, in Michigan.
Good to meet you, Fadi. I'm...
I ***WANT*** TO SAY KAMALA KHAN. IT'S ONLY FAIR. ONLY DECENT. I ***WILL*** MYSELF TO SAY IT.
BUT THEN I THINK ABOUT FADI'S COUSIN. I THINK ABOUT C.R.A.D.L.E. AGENTS HARASSING ***MY*** FAMILY...
I'm ***Ms. Marvel.***

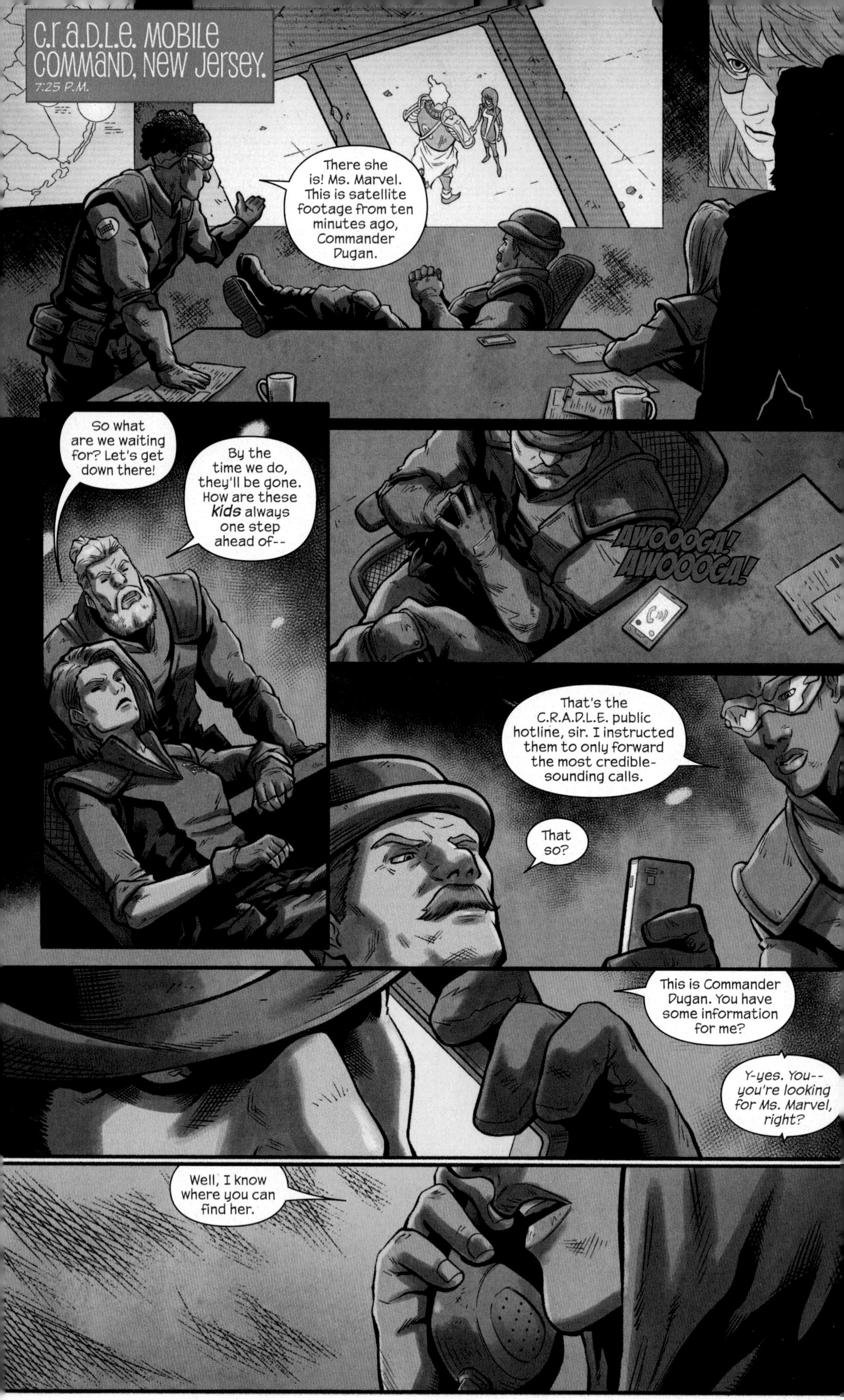
C.R.A.D.L.E. MOBILE COMMAND, NEW JERSEY.
7:25 P.M.
There she is! Ms. Marvel. This is satellite footage from ten minutes ago, Commander Dugan.
So what are we waiting for? Let's get down there!
By the time we do, they'll be gone. How are these *kids* always one step ahead of--
AWOOOGA! AWOOOGA!
That's the C.R.A.D.L.E. public hotline, sir. I instructed them to only forward the most credible-sounding calls.
That so?
This is Commander Dugan. You have some information for me?
Y-yes. You-- you're looking for Ms. Marvel, right?
Well, I know where you can find her.

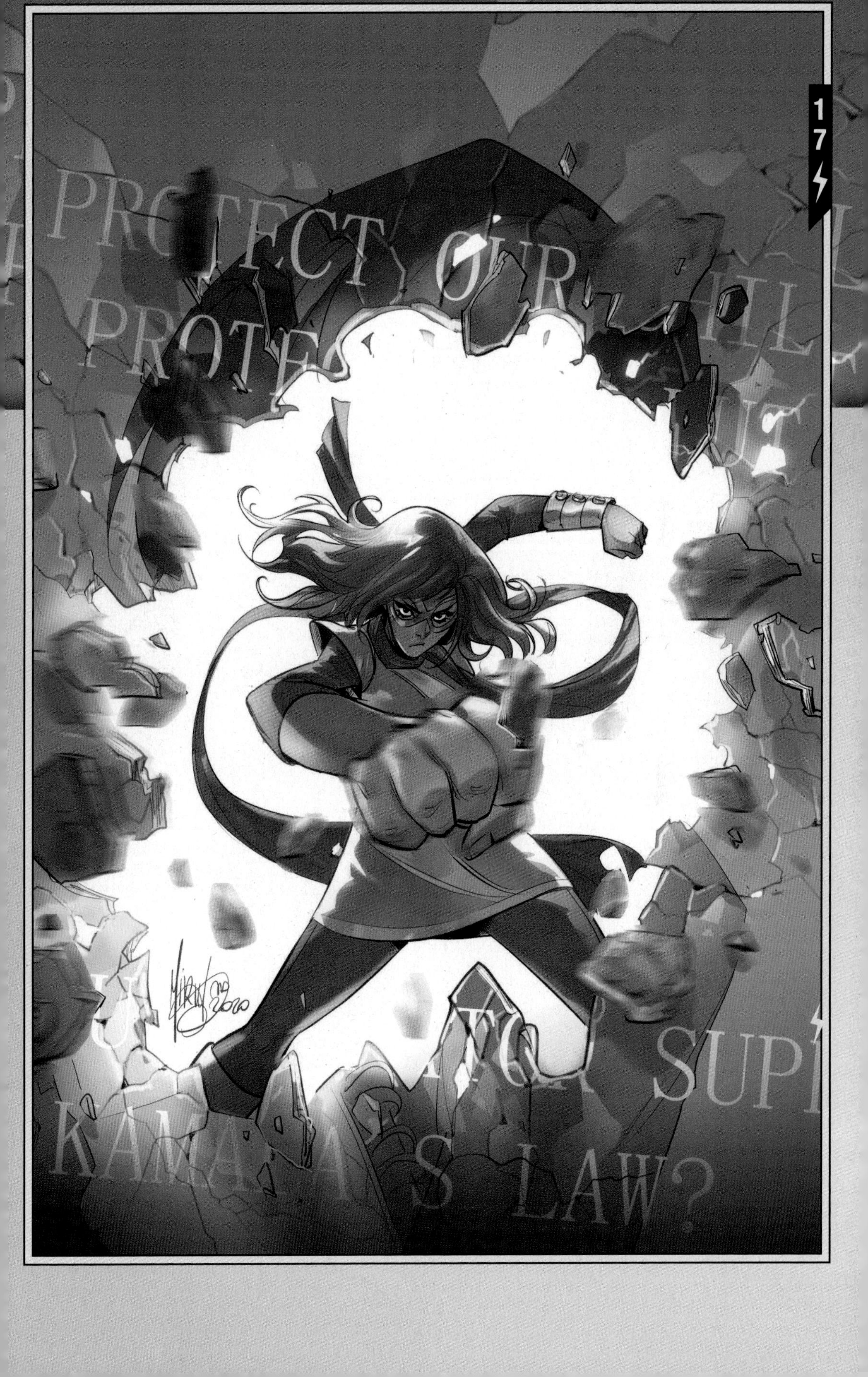
LAW?

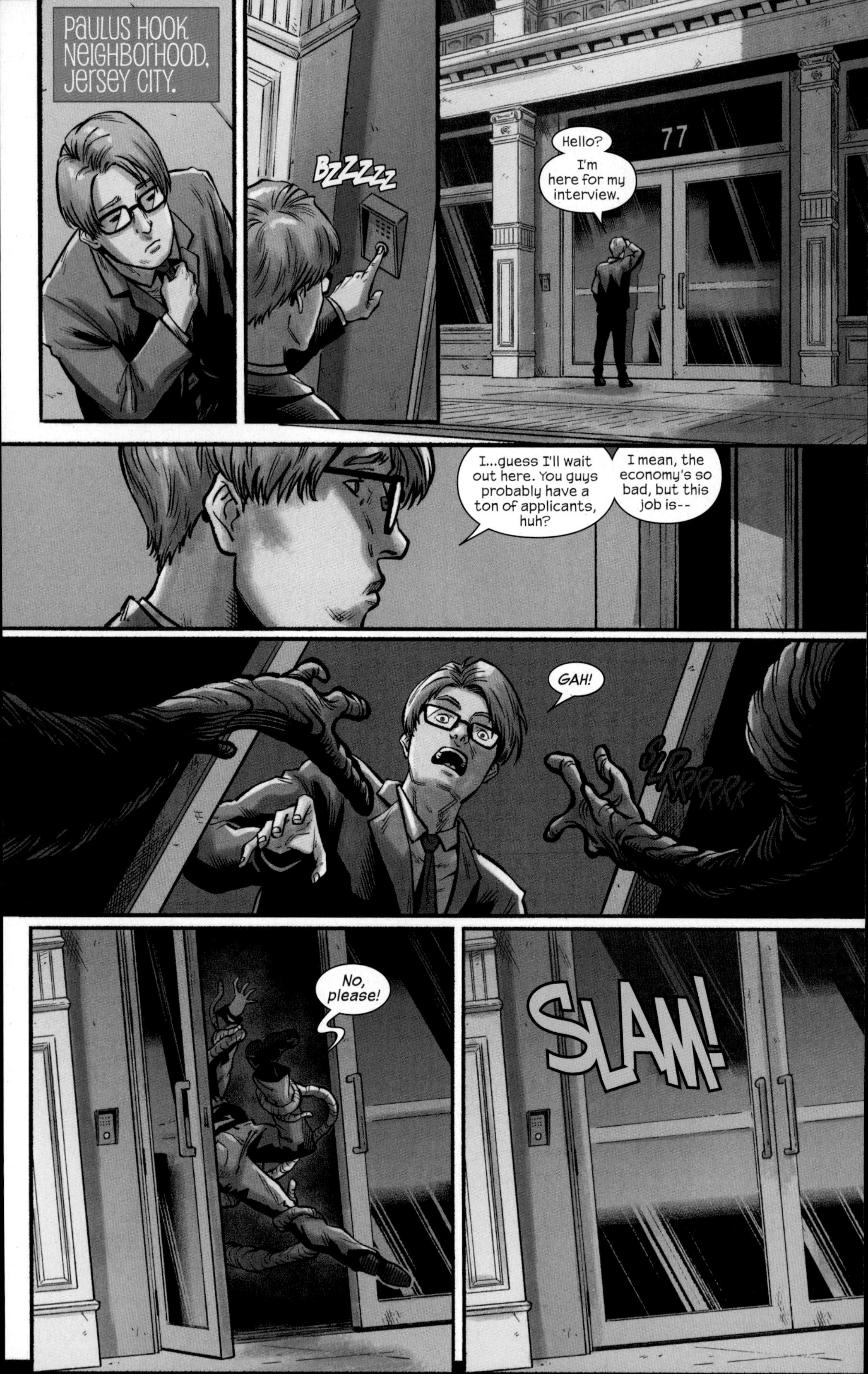

Paulus Hook Neighborhood, Jersey City.
BZZZZZZ
Hello?
I'm here for my interview.
I...guess I'll wait out here. You guys probably have a ton of applicants, huh?
I mean, the economy's so bad, but this job is--
GAH!
SLRRRRRK
No, please!
SLAM!

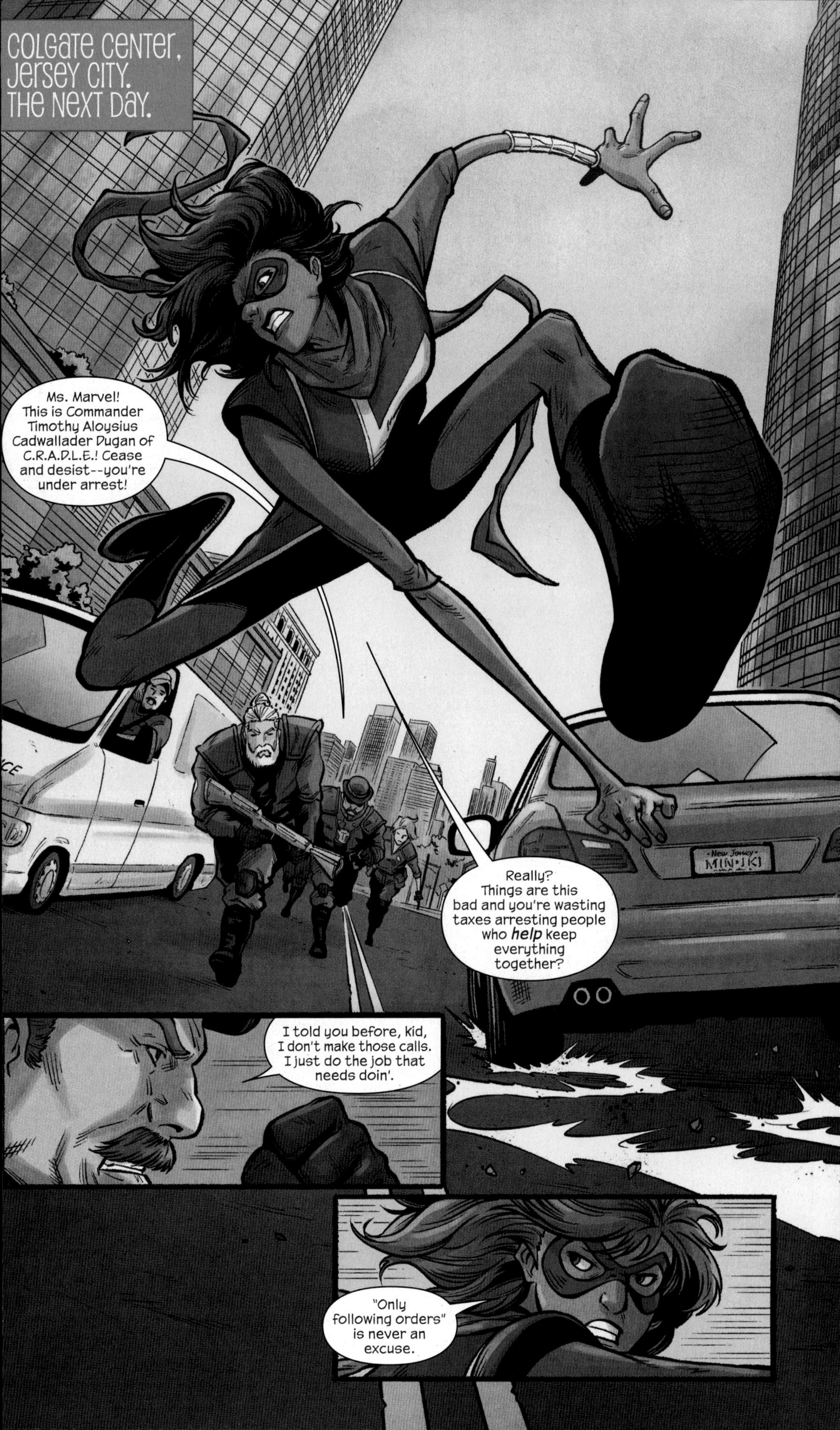

Colgate Center, Jersey City. The next day.
Ms. Marvel! This is Commander Timothy Aloysius Cadwallader Dugan of C.R.A.D.L.E.! Cease and desist--you're under arrest!
Really? Things are this bad and you're wasting taxes arresting people who *help* keep everything together?
New Jersey MIN-JKI
I told you before, kid, I don't make those calls. I just do the job that needs doin'.
"Only following orders" is never an excuse.

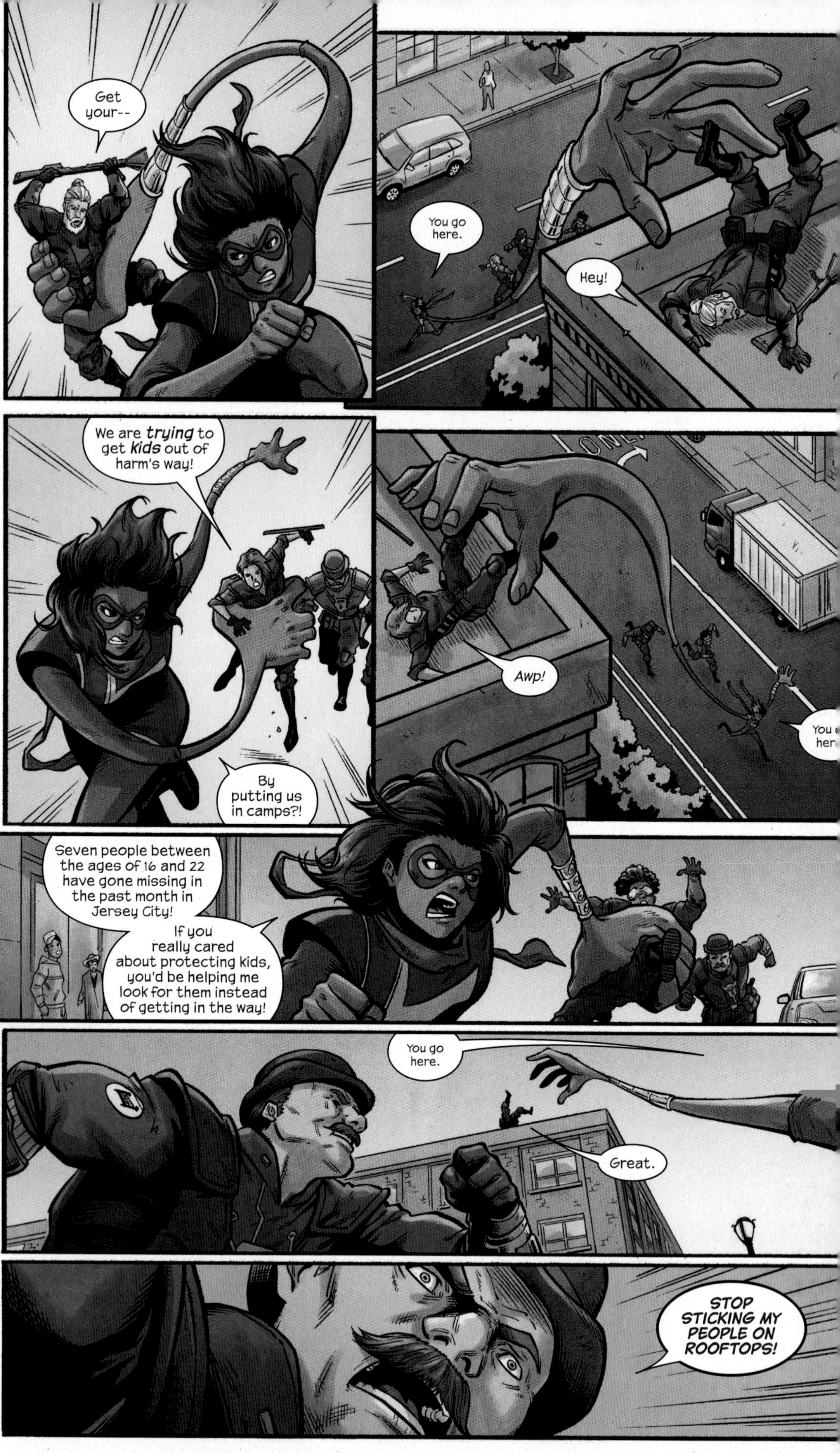
Get your--
You go here.
Hey!
We are *trying* to get *kids* out of harm's way!
By putting us in camps?!
Awp!
Seven people between the ages of 16 and 22 have gone missing in the past month in Jersey City!
If you really cared about protecting kids, you'd be helping me look for them instead of getting in the way!
You go here.
Great.
STOP STICKING MY PEOPLE ON ROOFTOPS!

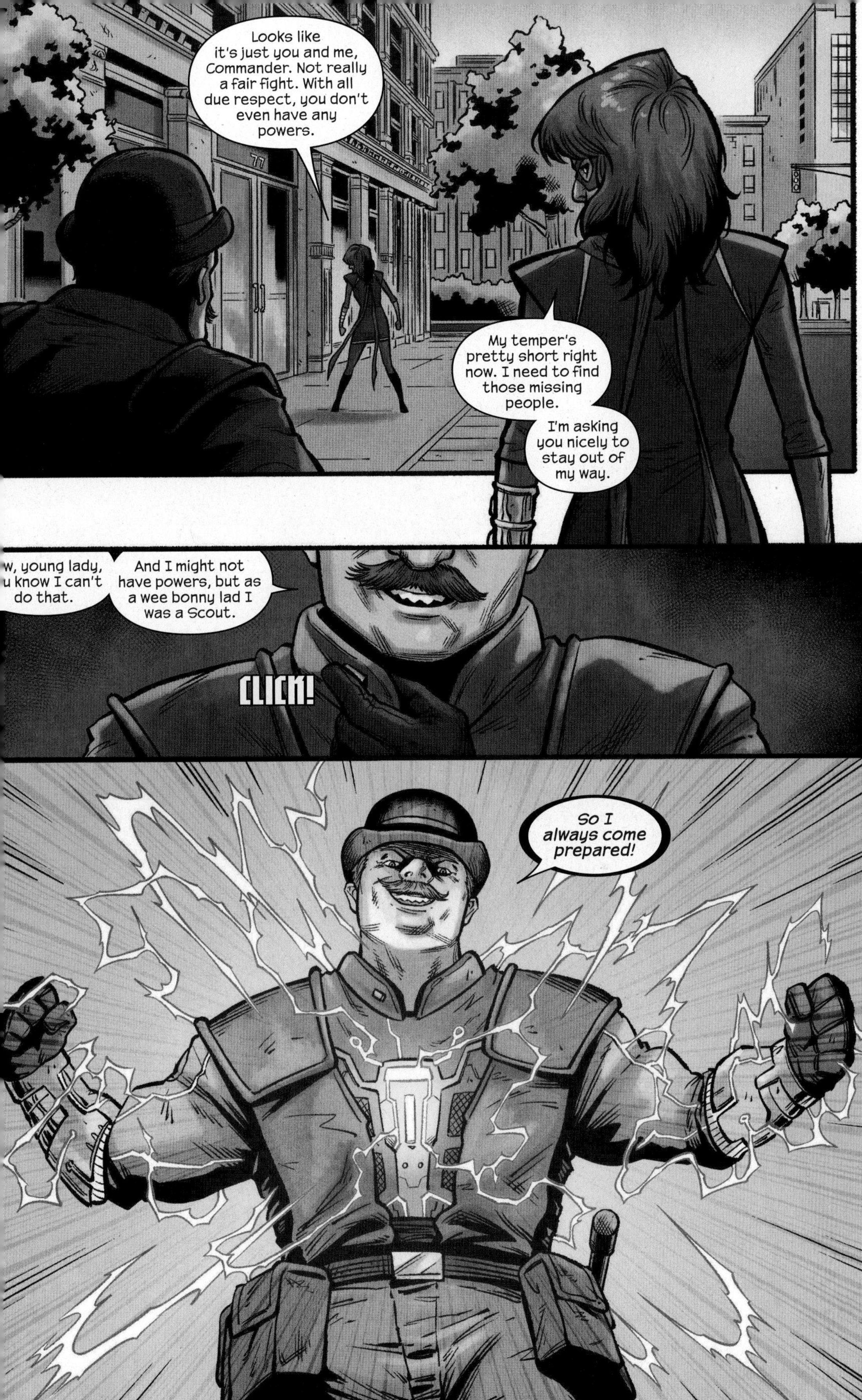
Looks like it's just you and me, Commander. Not really a fair fight. With all due respect, you don't even have any powers.
My temper's pretty short right now. I need to find those missing people.
I'm asking you nicely to stay out of my way.
w, young lady, u know I can't do that.
And I might not have powers, but as a wee bonny lad I was a Scout.
CLICK!
So I always come prepared!

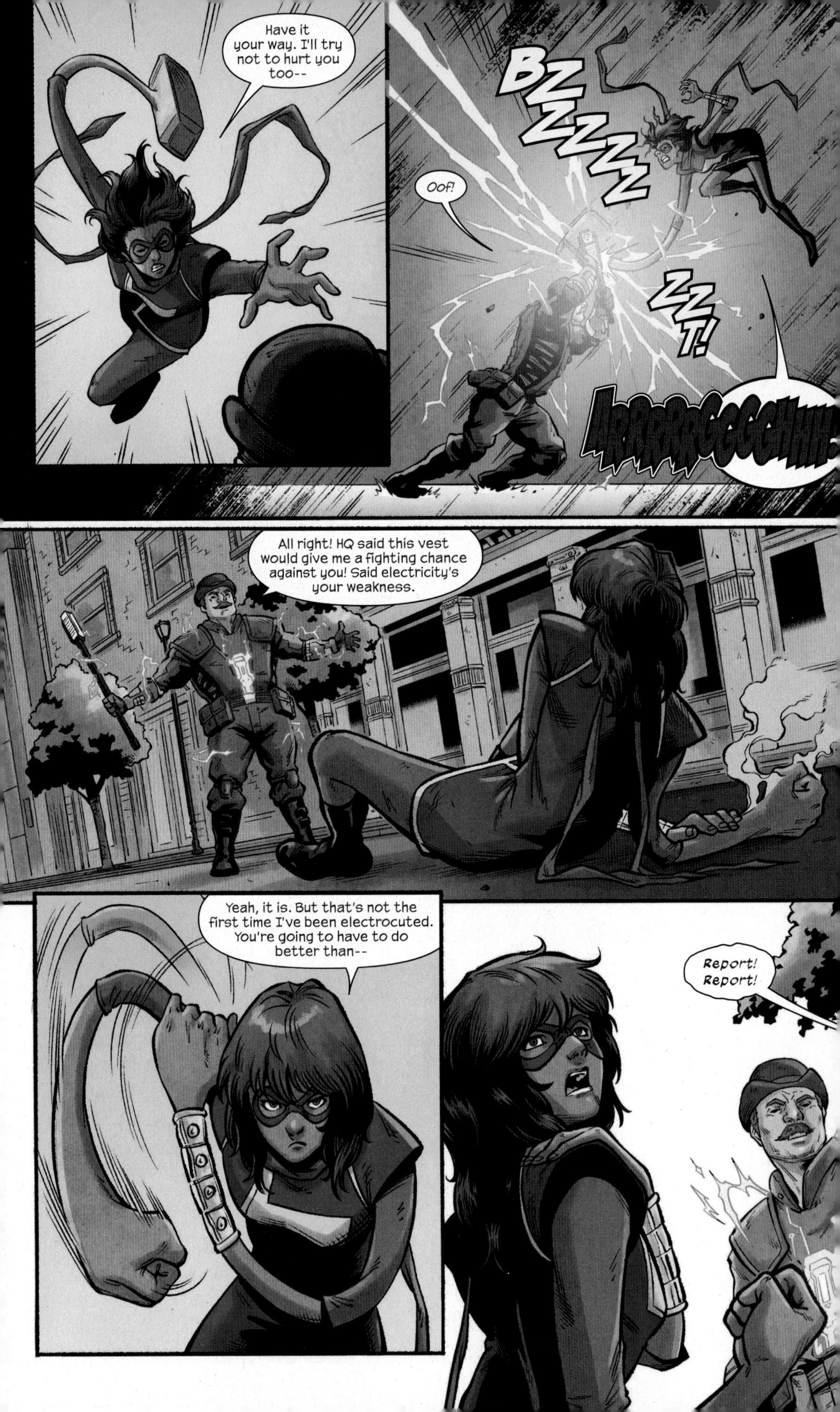
Have it your way. I'll try not to hurt you too--
BZZZZZZ
Oof!
ZZT!
ARRRRRGGGCHHH!
All right! HQ said this vest would give me a fighting chance against you! Said electricity's your weakness.
Yeah, it is. But that's not the first time I've been electrocuted. You're going to have to do better than--
Report! Report!

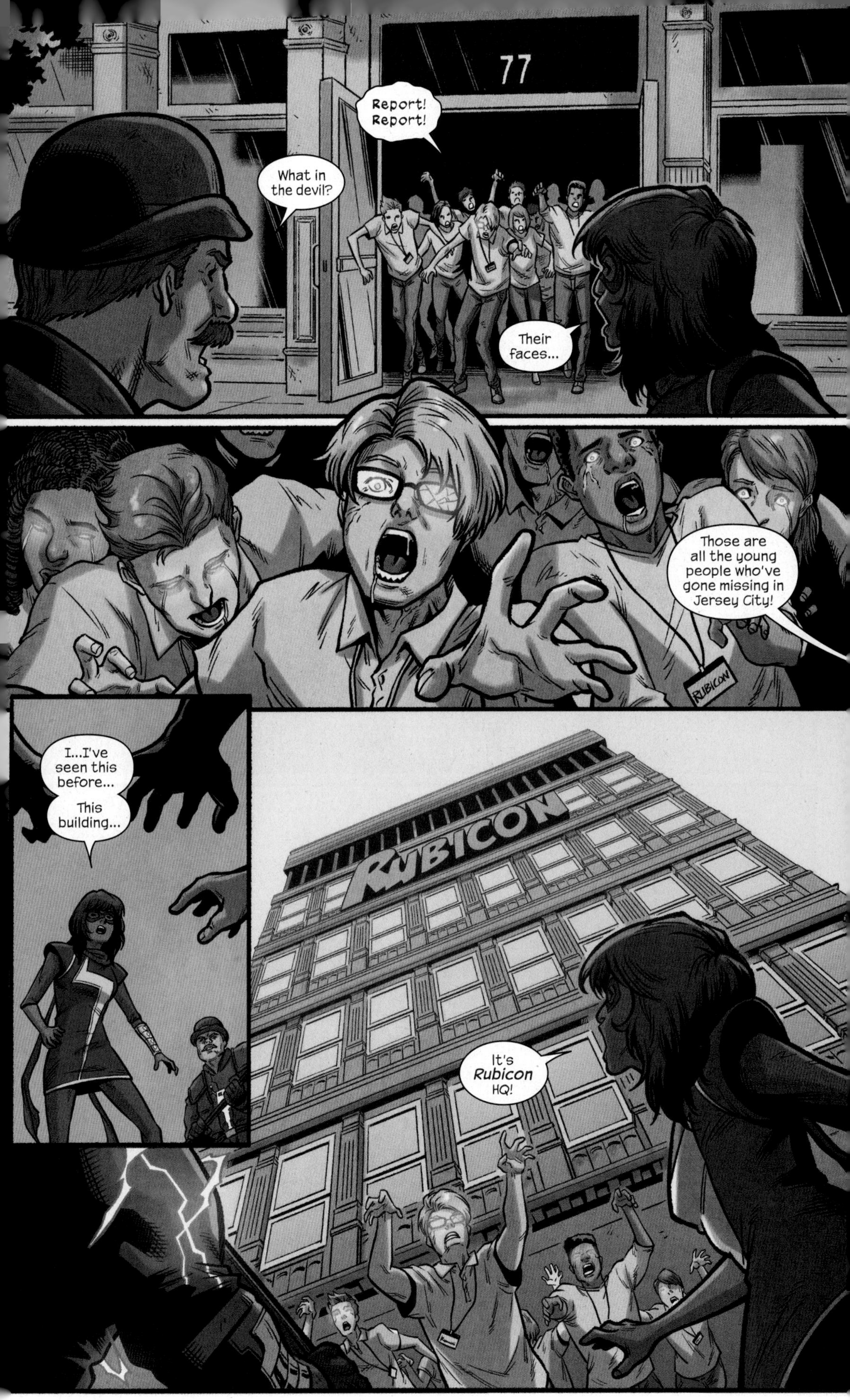

77
Report! Report!
What in the devil?
Their faces...
Those are all the young people who've gone missing in Jersey City!
RUBICON
I...I've seen this before...
This building...
RUBICON
It's *Rubicon* HQ!

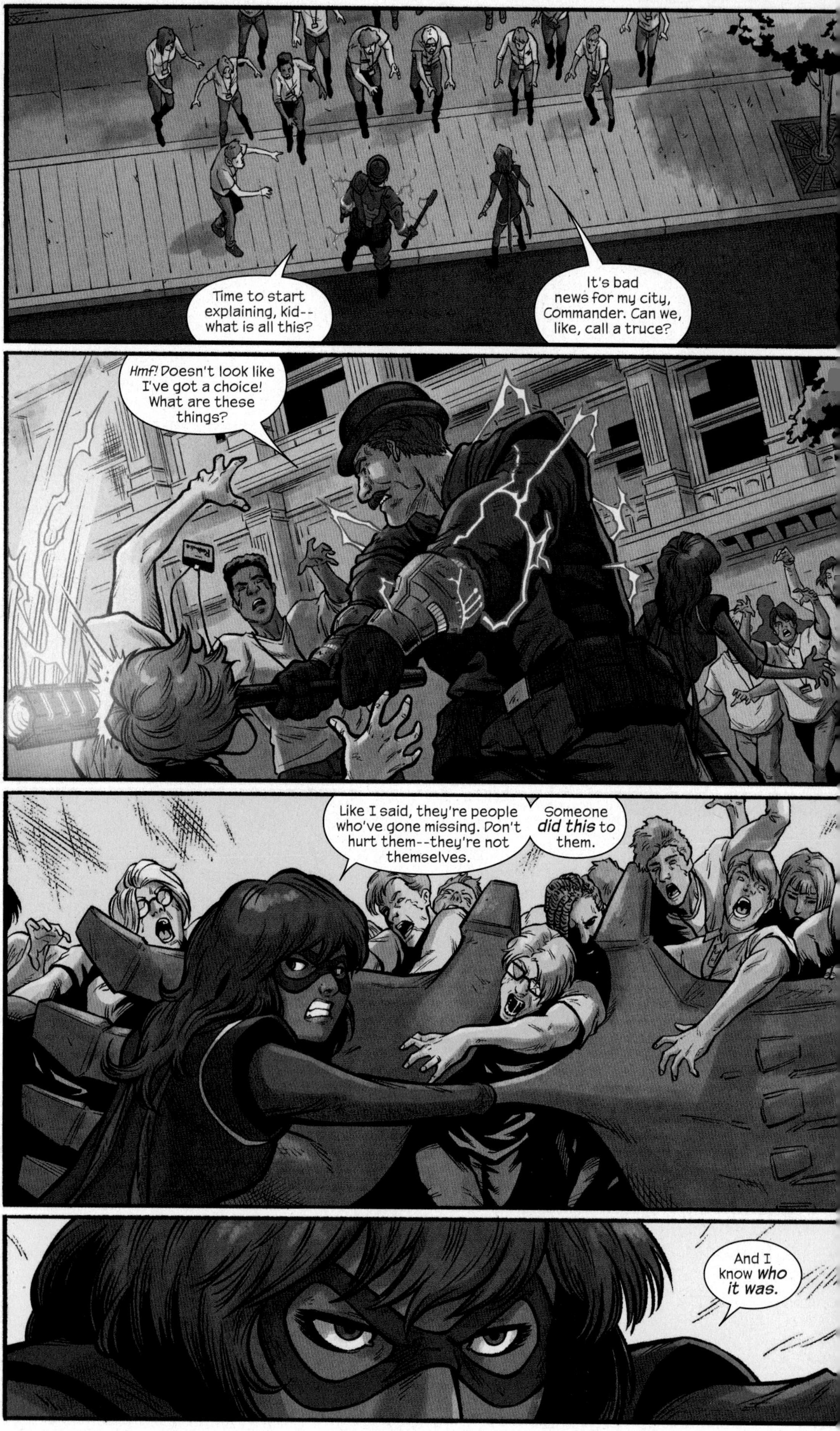
Time to start explaining, kid-- what is all this?
It's bad news for my city, Commander. Can we, like, call a truce?
Hmf! Doesn't look like I've got a choice! What are these things?
Like I said, they're people who've gone missing. Don't hurt them--they're not themselves.
Someone did this to them.
And I know who it was.

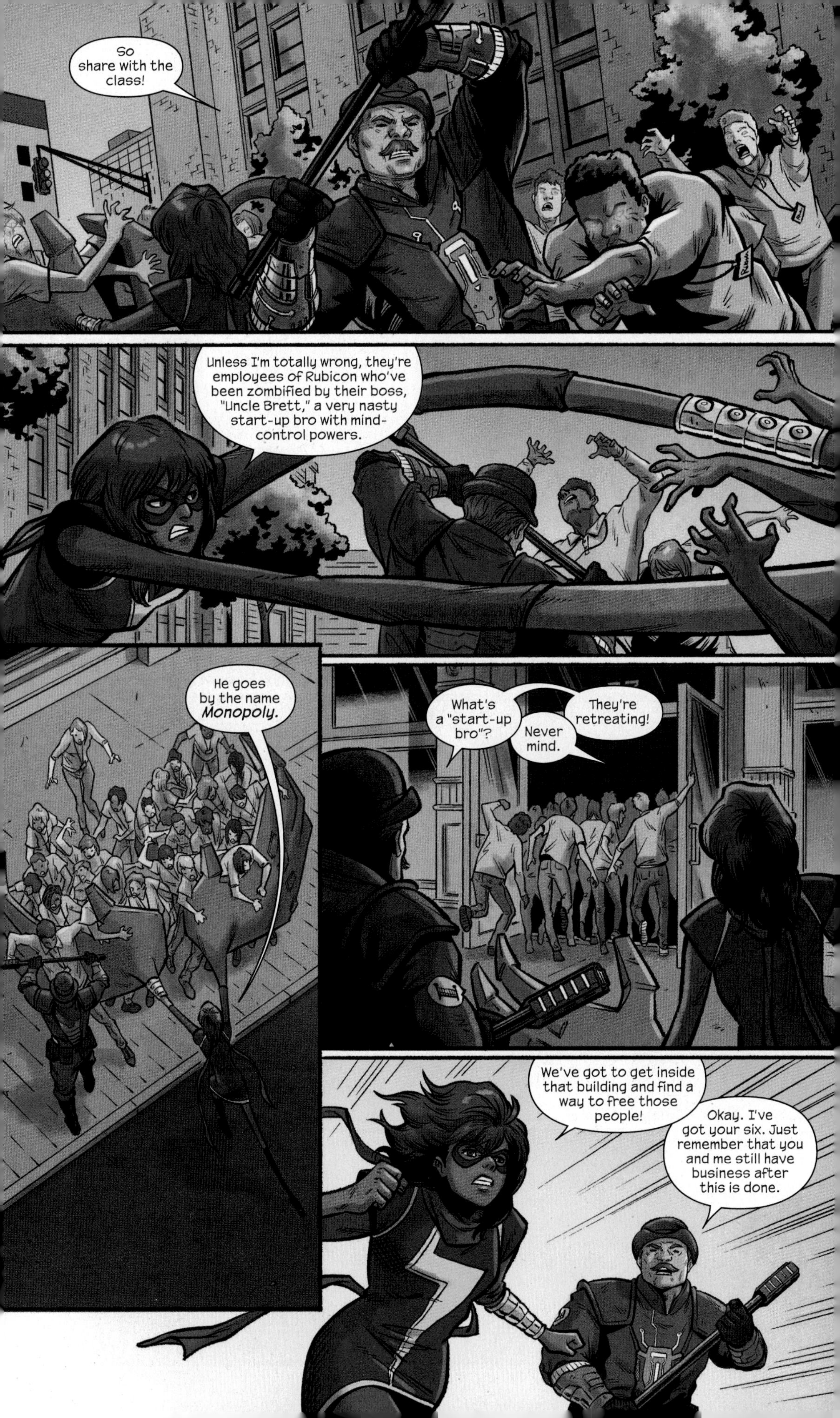
So share with the class!
Unless I'm totally wrong, they're employees of Rubicon who've been zombified by their boss, "Uncle Brett," a very nasty start-up bro with mind-control powers.
He goes by the name *Monopoly*.
What's a "start-up bro"?
They're retreating!
Never mind.
We've got to get inside that building and find a way to free those people!
Okay. I've got your six. Just remember that you and me still have business after this is done.

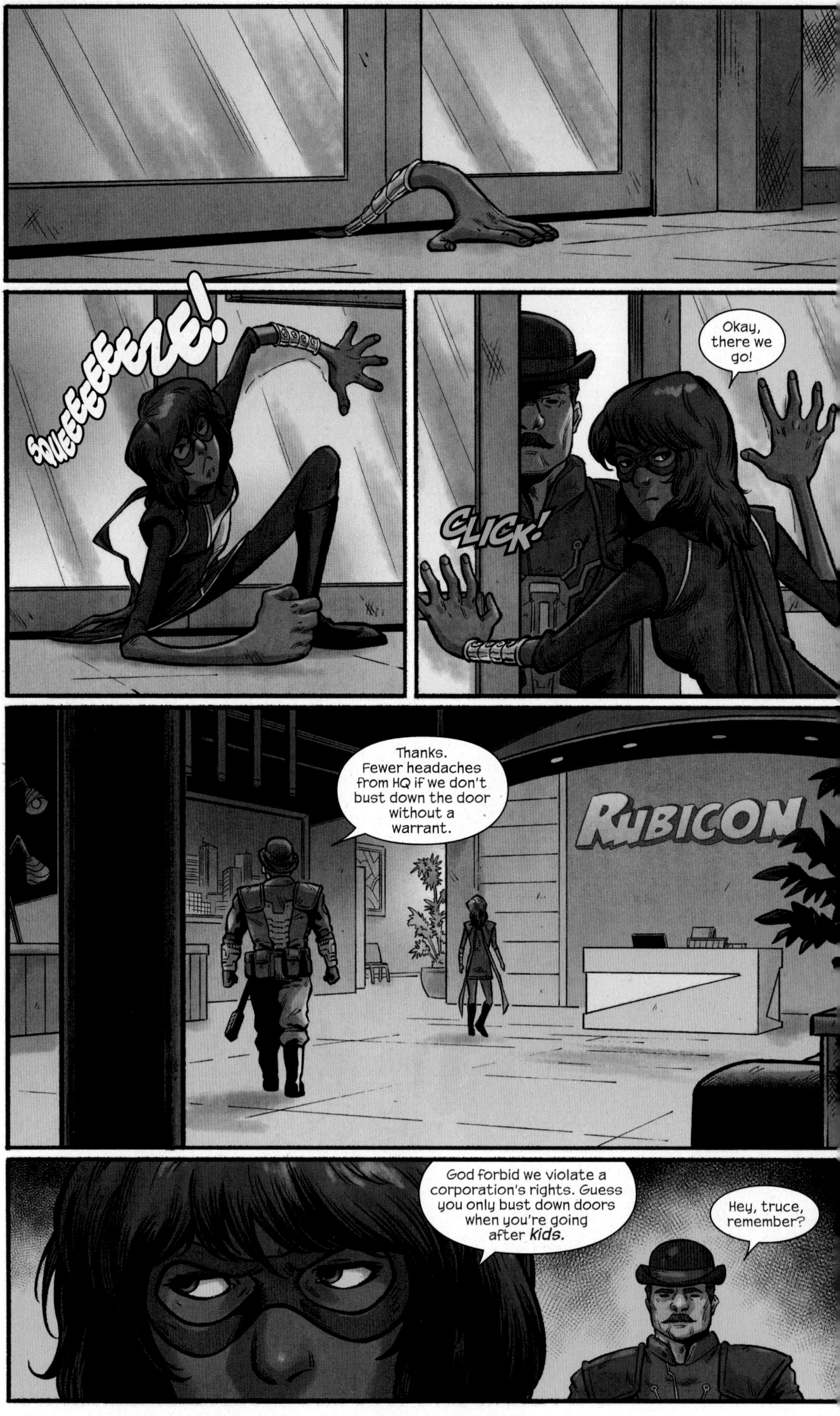
SQUEEEEEEEZE!
Okay, there we go!
CLICK!
Thanks. Fewer headaches from HQ if we don't bust down the door without a warrant.
RUBICON
God forbid we violate a corporation's rights. Guess you only bust down doors when you're going after kids.
Hey, truce, remember?

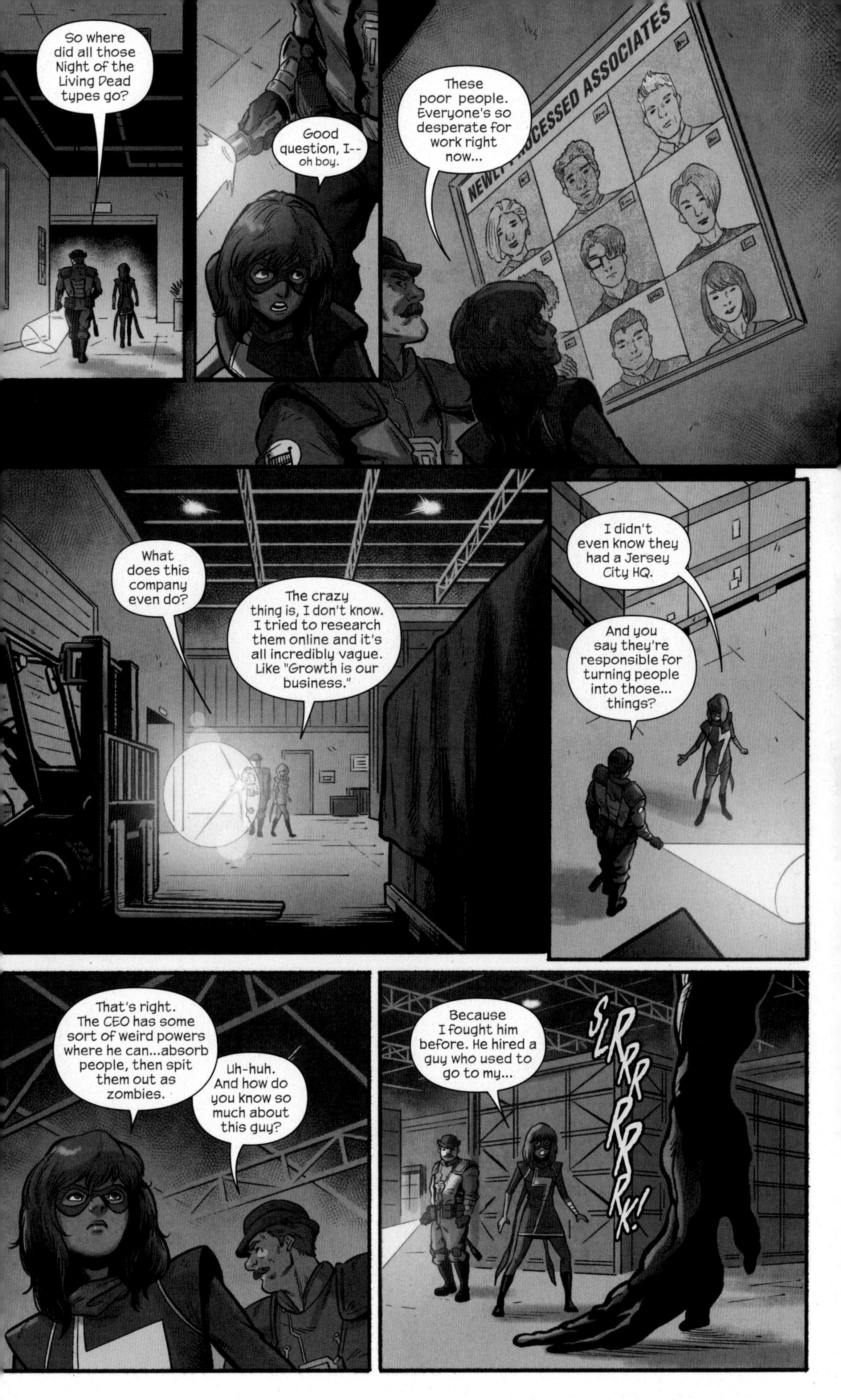
So where did all those Night of the Living Dead types go?
Good question, I-- oh boy.
These poor people. Everyone's so desperate for work right now...
NEWLY PROCESSED ASSOCIATES
What does this company even do?
The crazy thing is, I don't know. I tried to research them online and it's all incredibly vague. Like "Growth is our business."
I didn't even know they had a Jersey City HQ.
And you say they're responsible for turning people into those... things?
That's right. The CEO has some sort of weird powers where he can...absorb people, then spit them out as zombies.
Uh-huh. And how do you know so much about this guy?
Because I fought him before. He hired a guy who used to go to my...
SLRRRRRK!

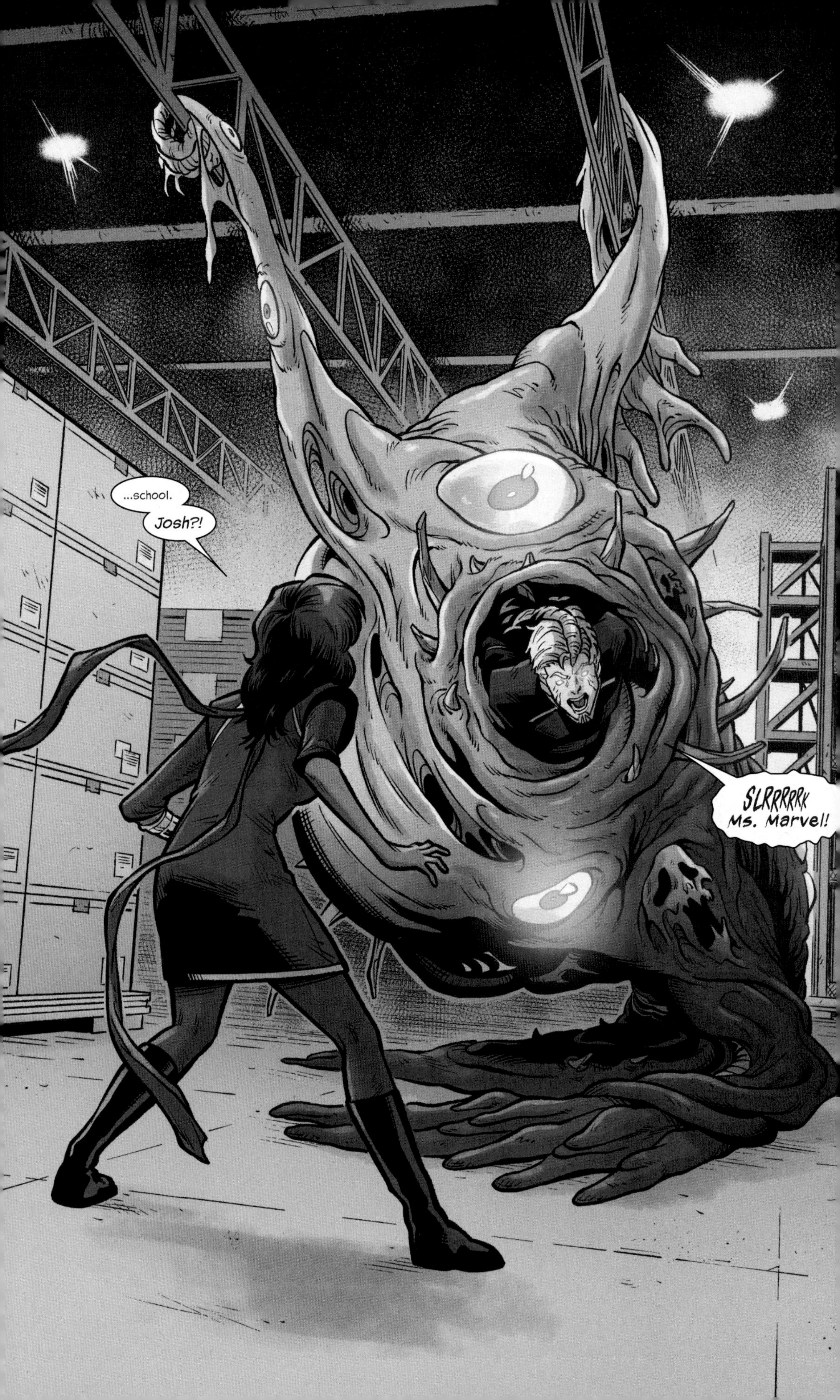
...school.
Josh?!
SLRRRRRK
Ms. Marvel!

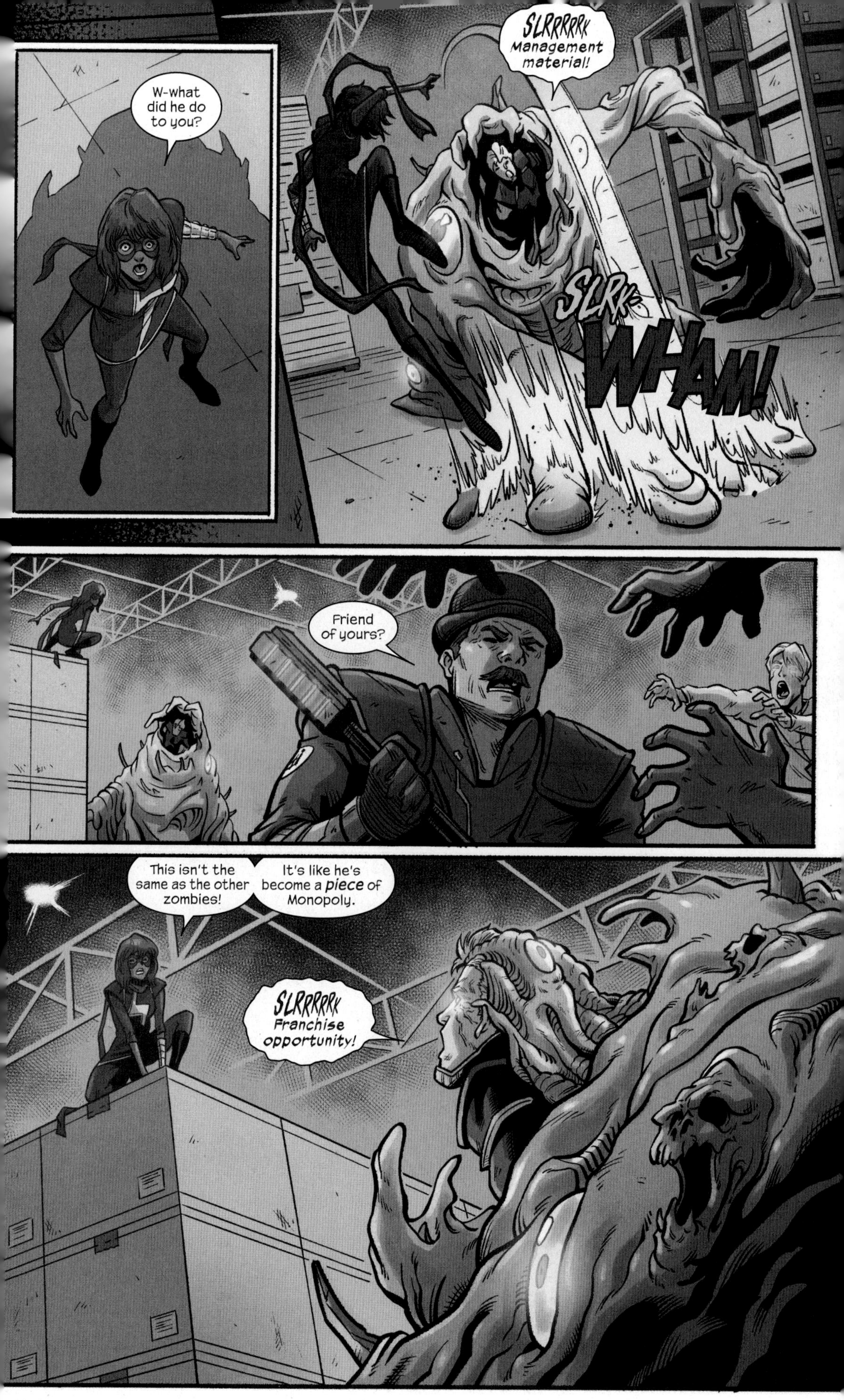
W-what did he do to you?
SLRRRRRK Management material!
SLRK
WHAM!
Friend of yours?
This isn't the same as the other zombies!
It's like he's become a *piece* of Monopoly.
SLRRRRRK Franchise opportunity!

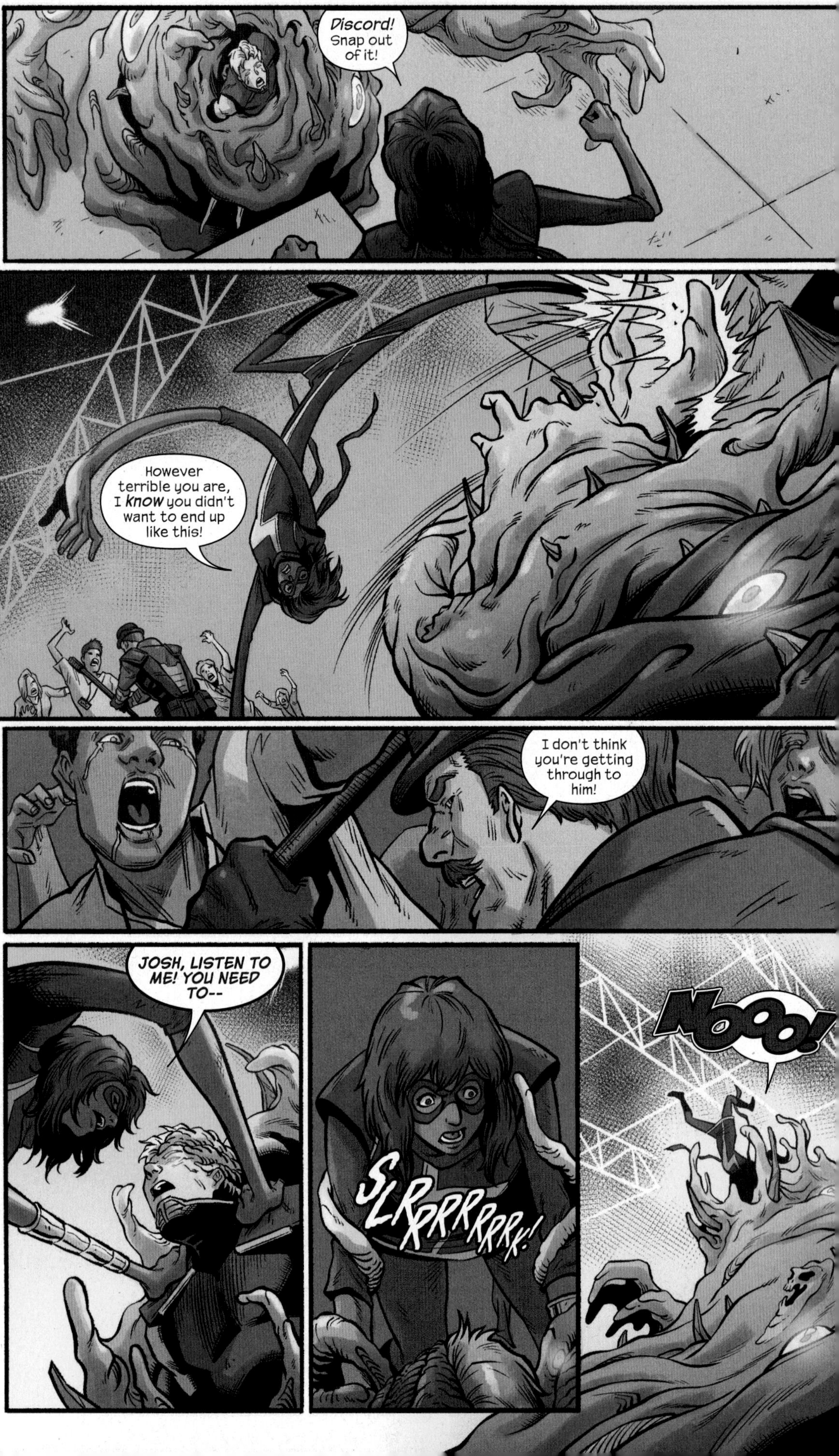
Discord! Snap out of it!
However terrible you are, I KNOW you didn't want to end up like this!
I don't think you're getting through to him!
JOSH, LISTEN TO ME! YOU NEED TO--
SLRRRRRRRK!
NOOO!

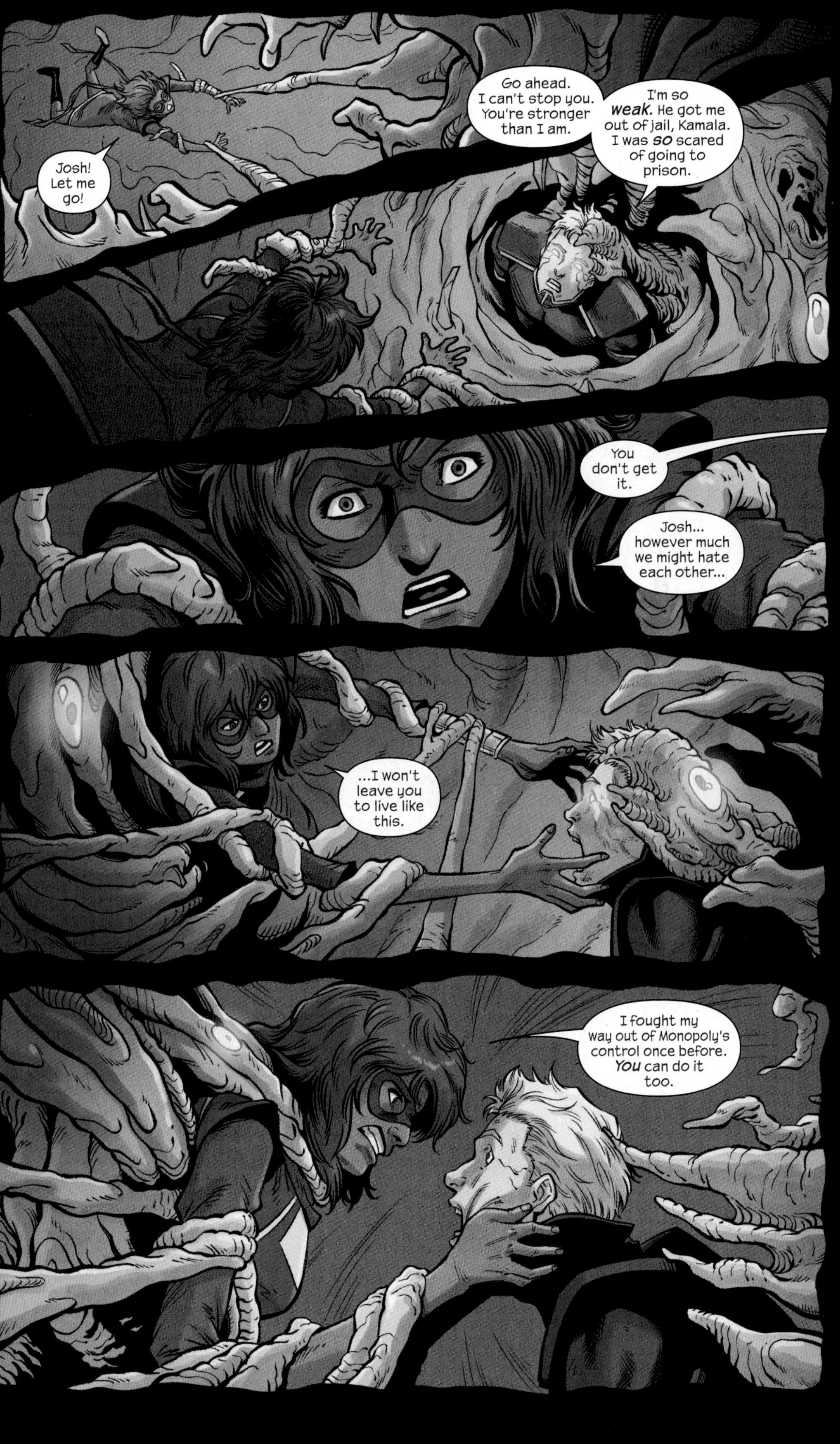
Josh! Let me go!
Go ahead. I can't stop you. You're stronger than I am.
I'm so **weak.** He got me out of jail, Kamala. I was ***SO*** scared of going to prison.
You don't get it.
Josh... however much we might hate each other...
...I won't leave you to live like this.
I fought my way out of Monopoly's control once before. ***YOU*** can do it too.

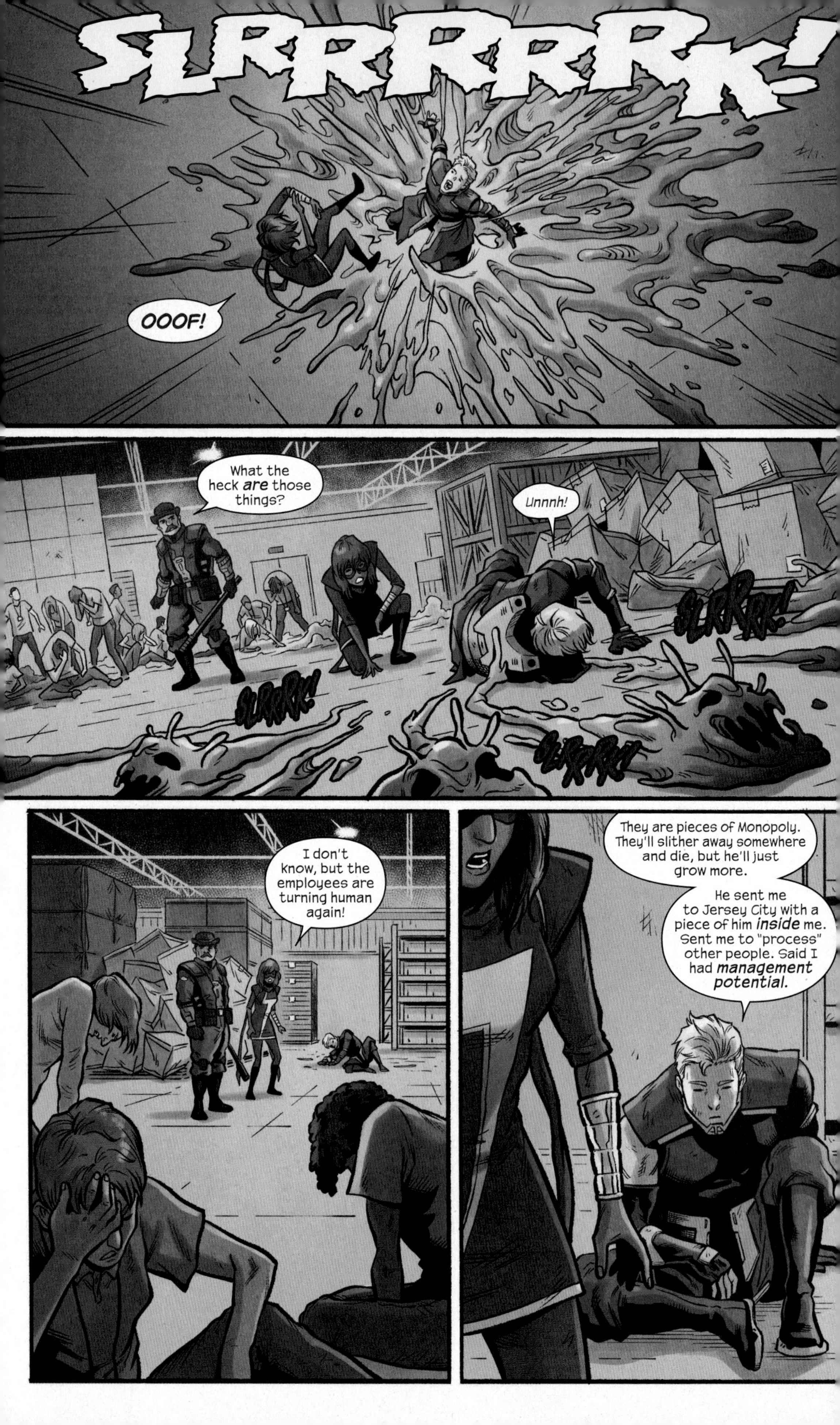
SLRRRRRRK!
OOOF!
What the heck are those things?
Unnnh!
SLRRRK!
SLRRRK!
SLRRRK!
I don't know, but the employees are turning human again!
They are pieces of Monopoly. They'll slither away somewhere and die, but he'll just grow more.
He sent me to Jersey City with a piece of him inside me. Sent me to "process" other people. Said I had management potential.

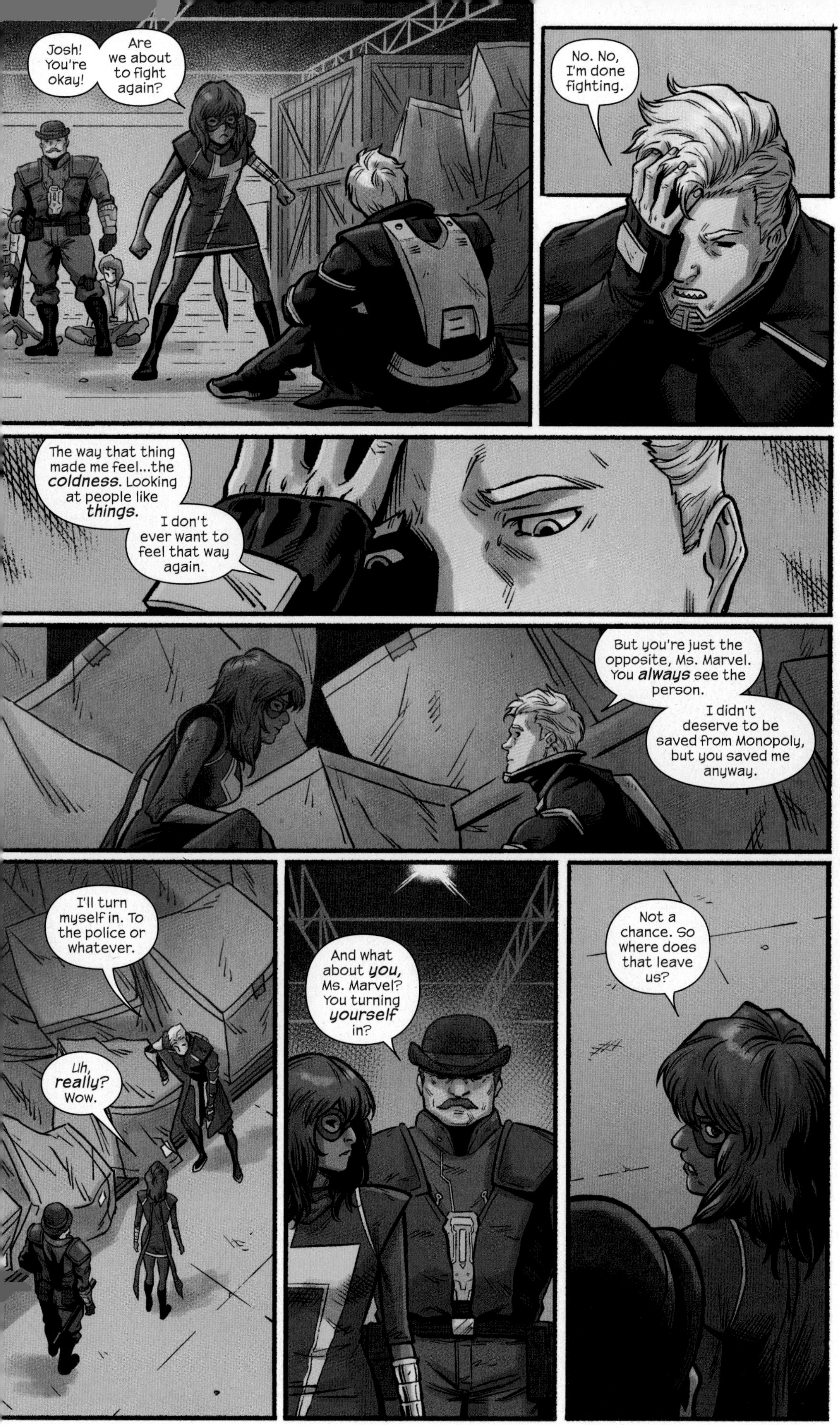
Josh! You're okay!
Are we about to fight again?
No. No, I'm done fighting.
The way that thing made me feel...the *coldness*. Looking at people like *things*.
I don't ever want to feel that way again.
But you're just the opposite, Ms. Marvel. You *always* see the person.
I didn't deserve to be saved from Monopoly, but you saved me anyway.
I'll turn myself in. To the police or whatever.
Uh, *really?* Wow.
And what about *you,* Ms. Marvel? You turning *yourself* in?
Not a chance. So where does that leave us?

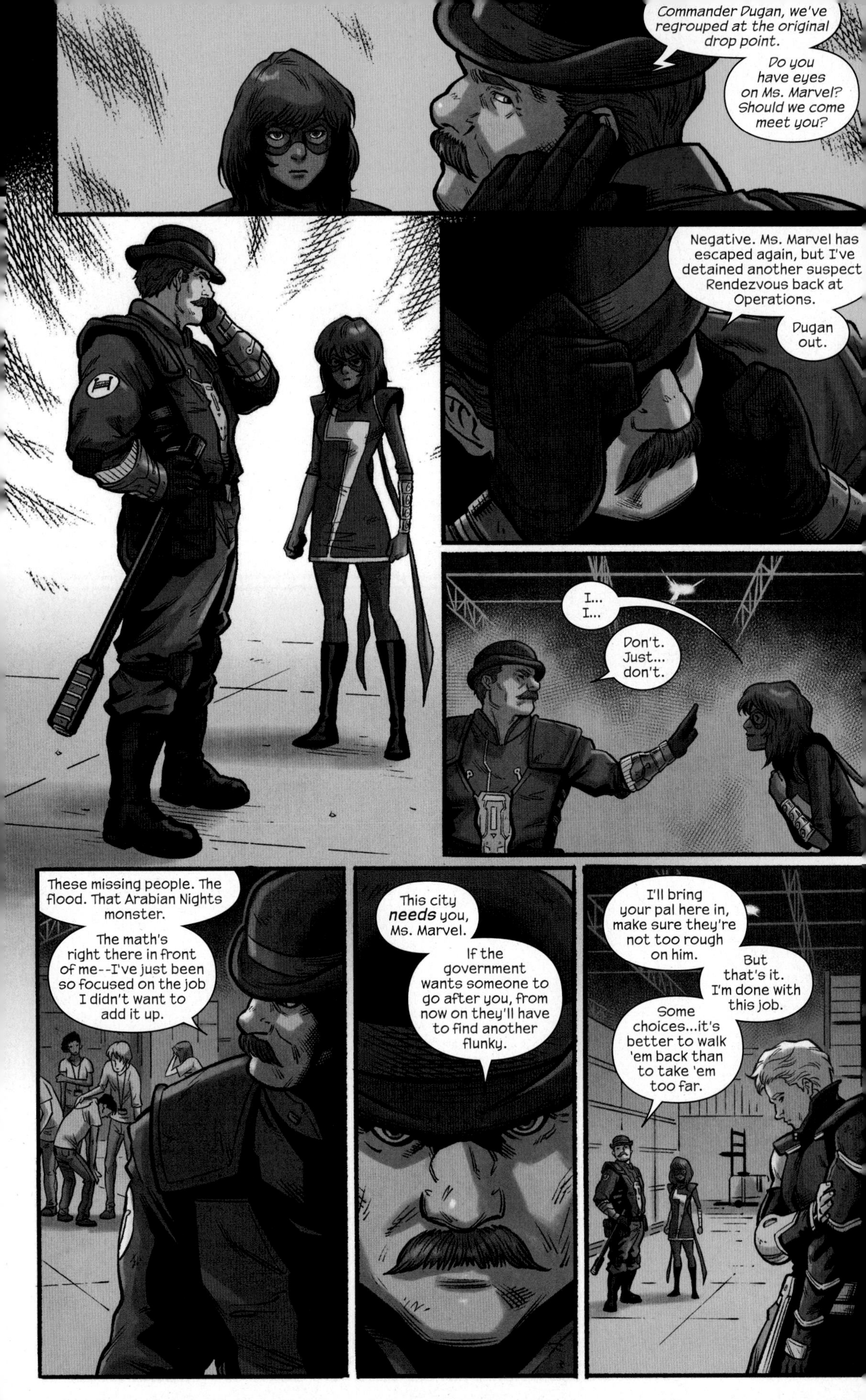

Commander Dugan, we've regrouped at the original drop point.
Do you have eyes on Ms. Marvel? Should we come meet you?
Negative. Ms. Marvel has escaped again, but I've detained another suspect Rendezvous back at Operations.
Dugan out.
I... I...
Don't. Just... don't.
These missing people. The flood. That Arabian Nights monster.
The math's right there in front of me--I've just been so focused on the job I didn't want to add it up.
This city **needs** you, Ms. Marvel.
If the government wants someone to go after you, from now on they'll have to find another flunky.
I'll bring your pal here in, make sure they're not too rough on him.
But that's it. I'm done with this job.
Some choices...it's better to walk 'em back than to take 'em too far.

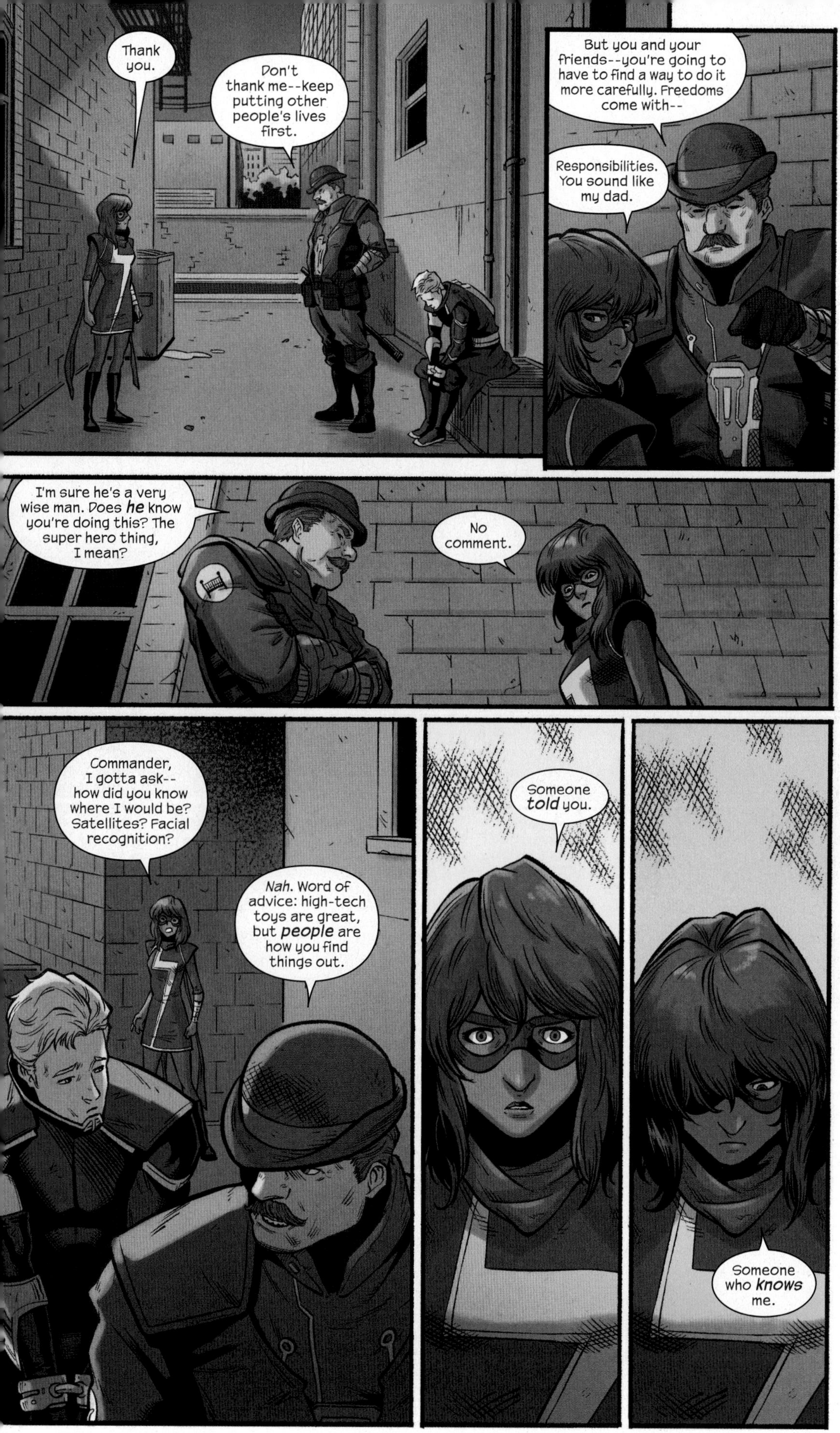
Thank you.
Don't thank me--keep putting other people's lives first.
But you and your friends--you're going to have to find a way to do it more carefully. Freedoms come with--
Responsibilities. You sound like my dad.
I'm sure he's a very wise man. Does *he* know you're doing this? The super hero thing, I mean?
No comment.
Commander, I gotta ask--how did you know where I would be? Satellites? Facial recognition?
Nah. Word of advice: high-tech toys are great, but *people* are how you find things out.
Someone *told* you.
Someone who *knows* me.

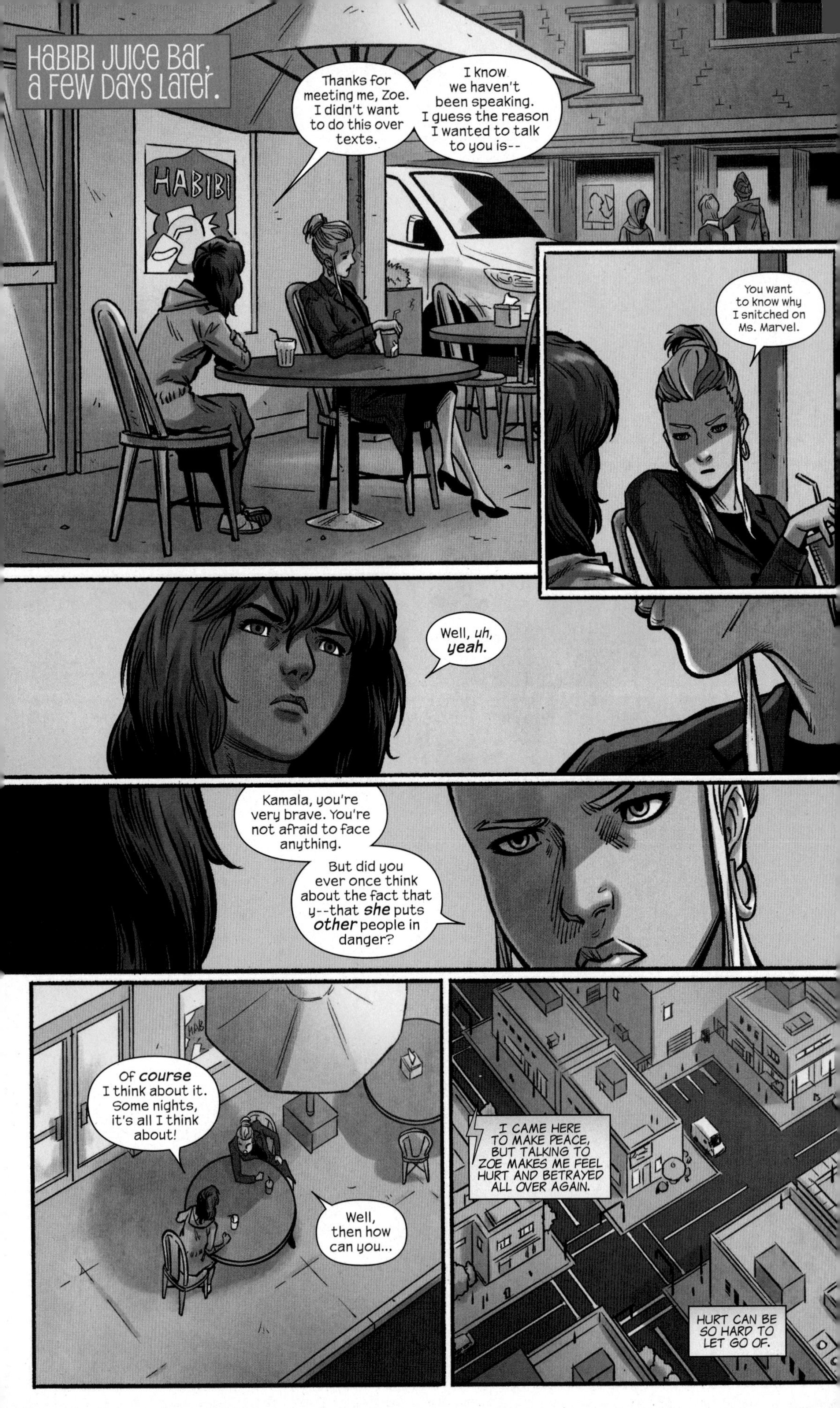
HABIBI JUICE BAR, A FEW DAYS LATER.
Thanks for meeting me, Zoe. I didn't want to do this over texts.
I know we haven't been speaking. I guess the reason I wanted to talk to you is--
HABIBI
You want to know why I snitched on Ms. Marvel.
Well, uh, *yeah.*
Kamala, you're very brave. You're not afraid to face anything.
But did you ever once think about the fact that y--that *she* puts *other* people in danger?
Of *course* I think about it. Some nights, it's all I think about!
Well, then how can you...
I CAME HERE TO MAKE PEACE, BUT TALKING TO ZOE MAKES ME FEEL HURT AND BETRAYED ALL OVER AGAIN.
HURT CAN BE SO HARD TO LET GO OF.

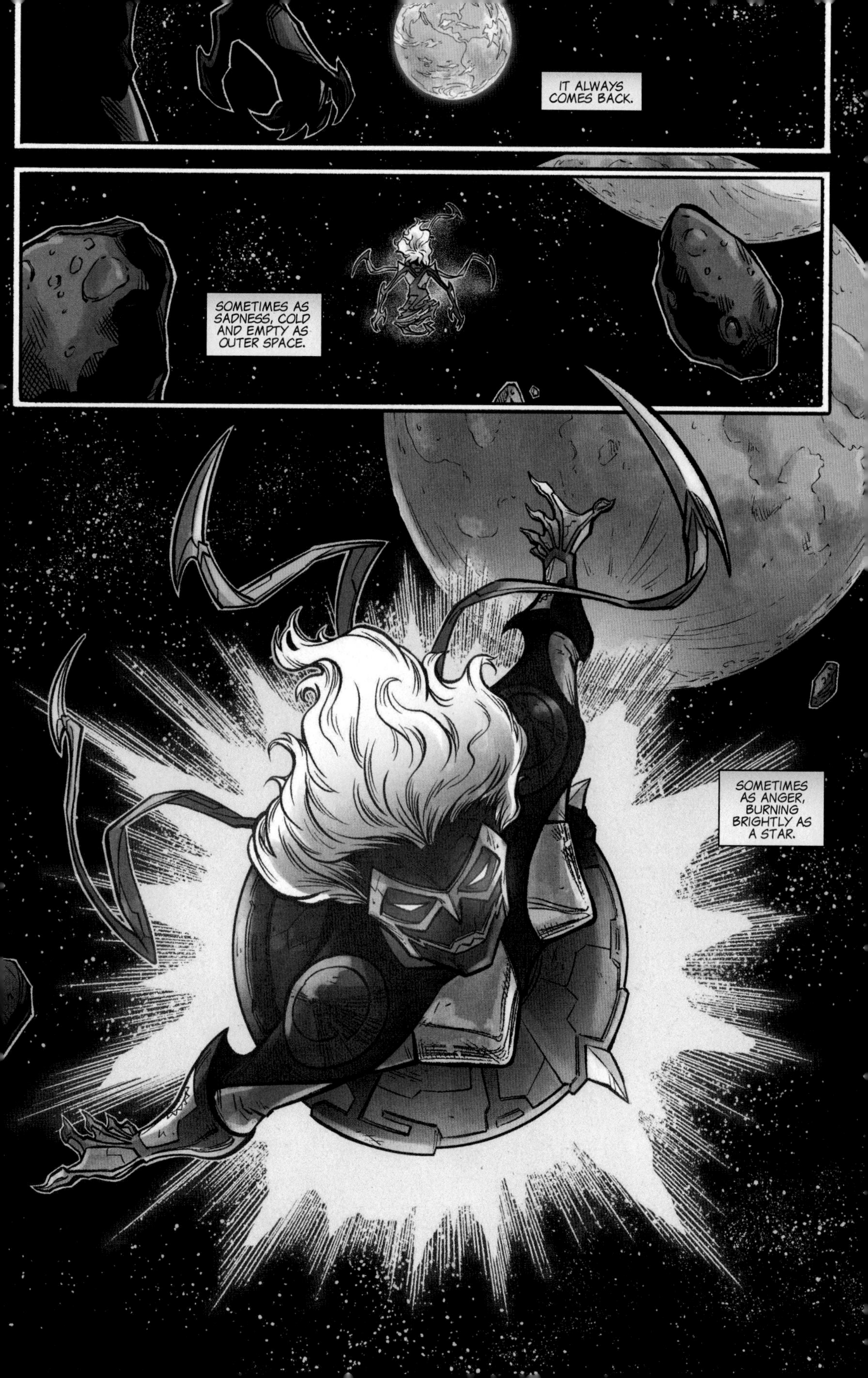
IT ALWAYS COMES BACK.
SOMETIMES AS SADNESS, COLD AND EMPTY AS OUTER SPACE.
SOMETIMES AS ANGER, BURNING BRIGHTLY AS A STAR.

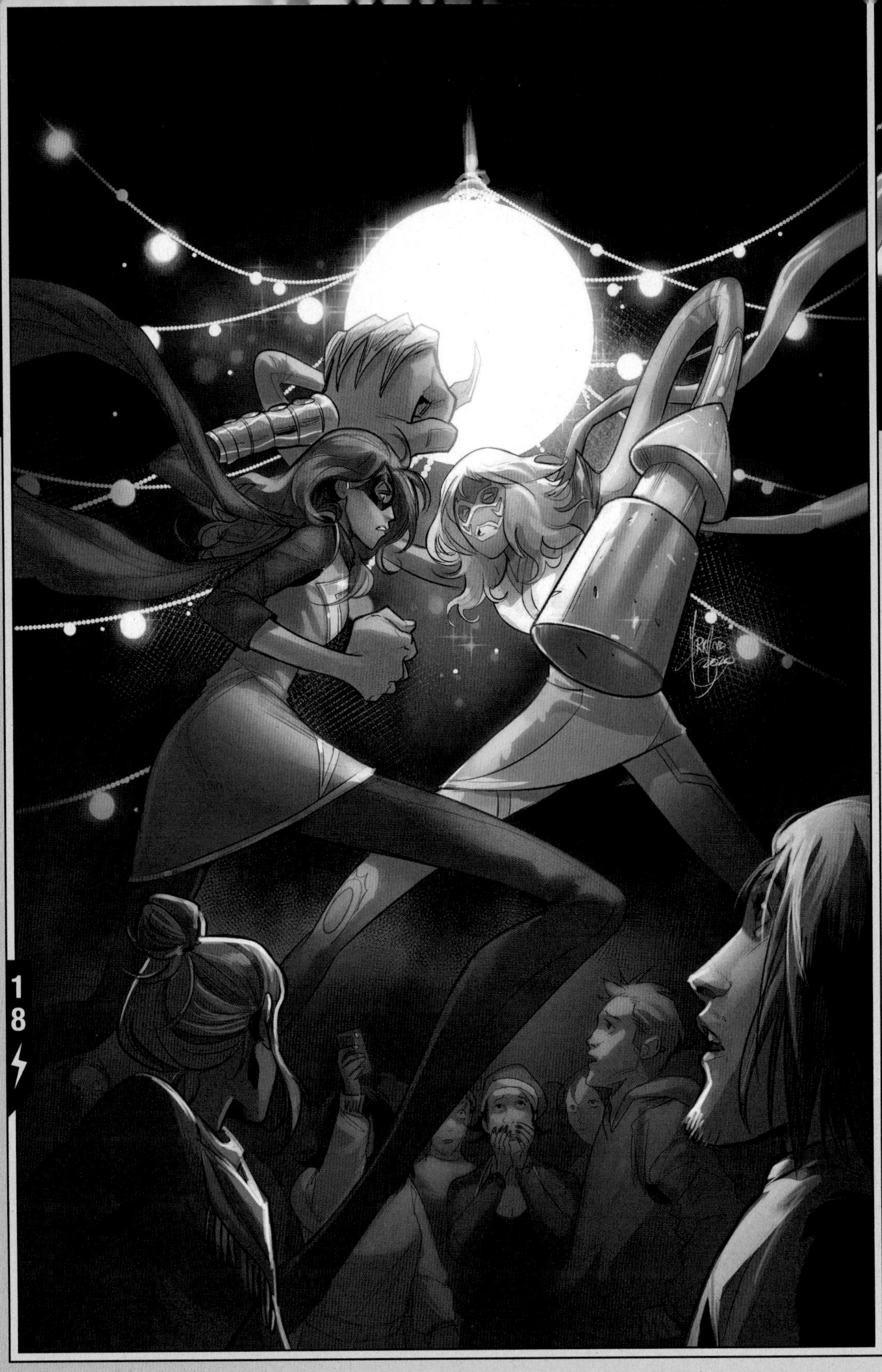18

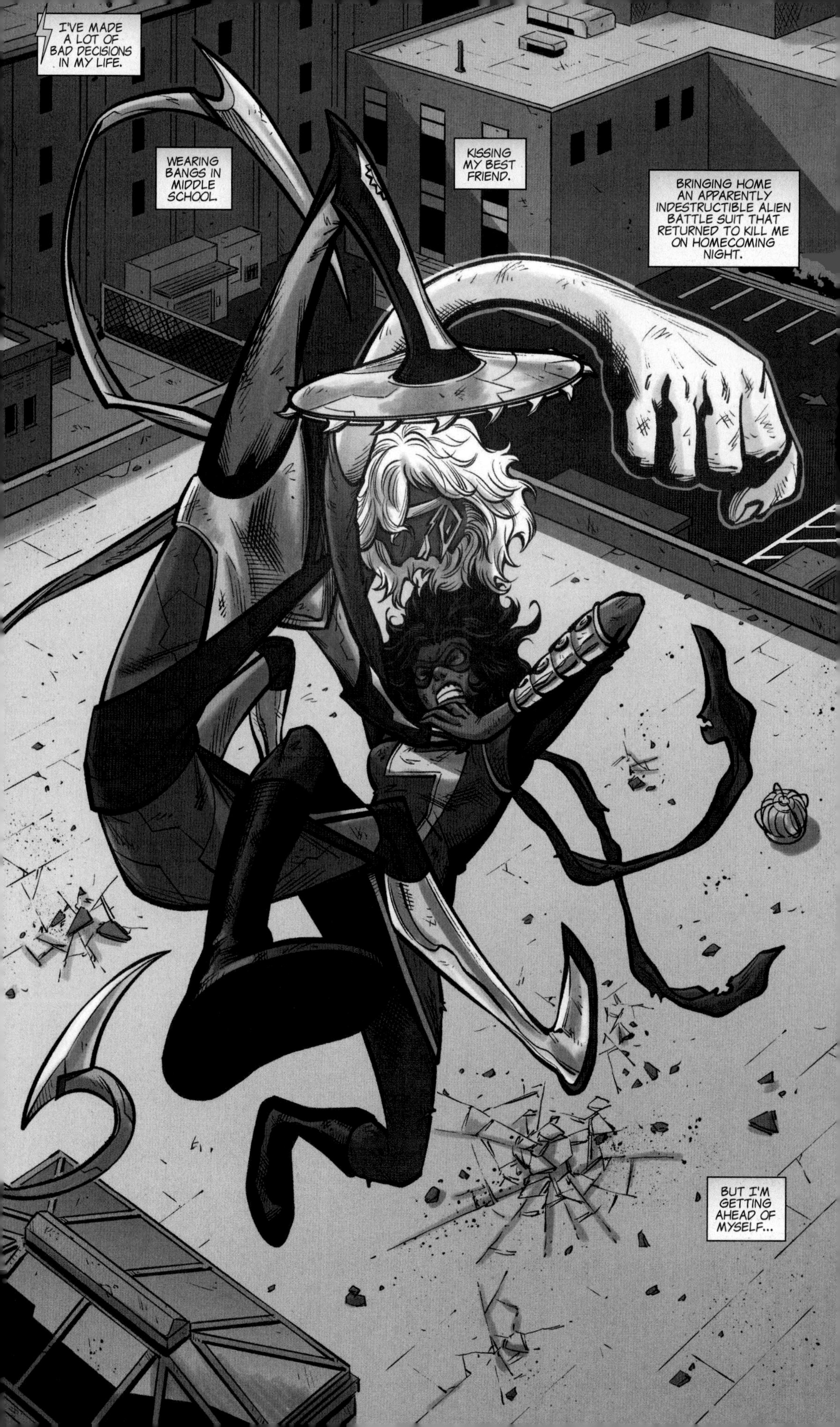
I'VE MADE A LOT OF BAD DECISIONS IN MY LIFE.
WEARING BANGS IN MIDDLE SCHOOL.
KISSING MY BEST FRIEND.
BRINGING HOME AN APPARENTLY INDESTRUCTIBLE ALIEN BATTLE SUIT THAT RETURNED TO KILL ME ON HOMECOMING NIGHT.
BUT I'M GETTING AHEAD OF MYSELF...

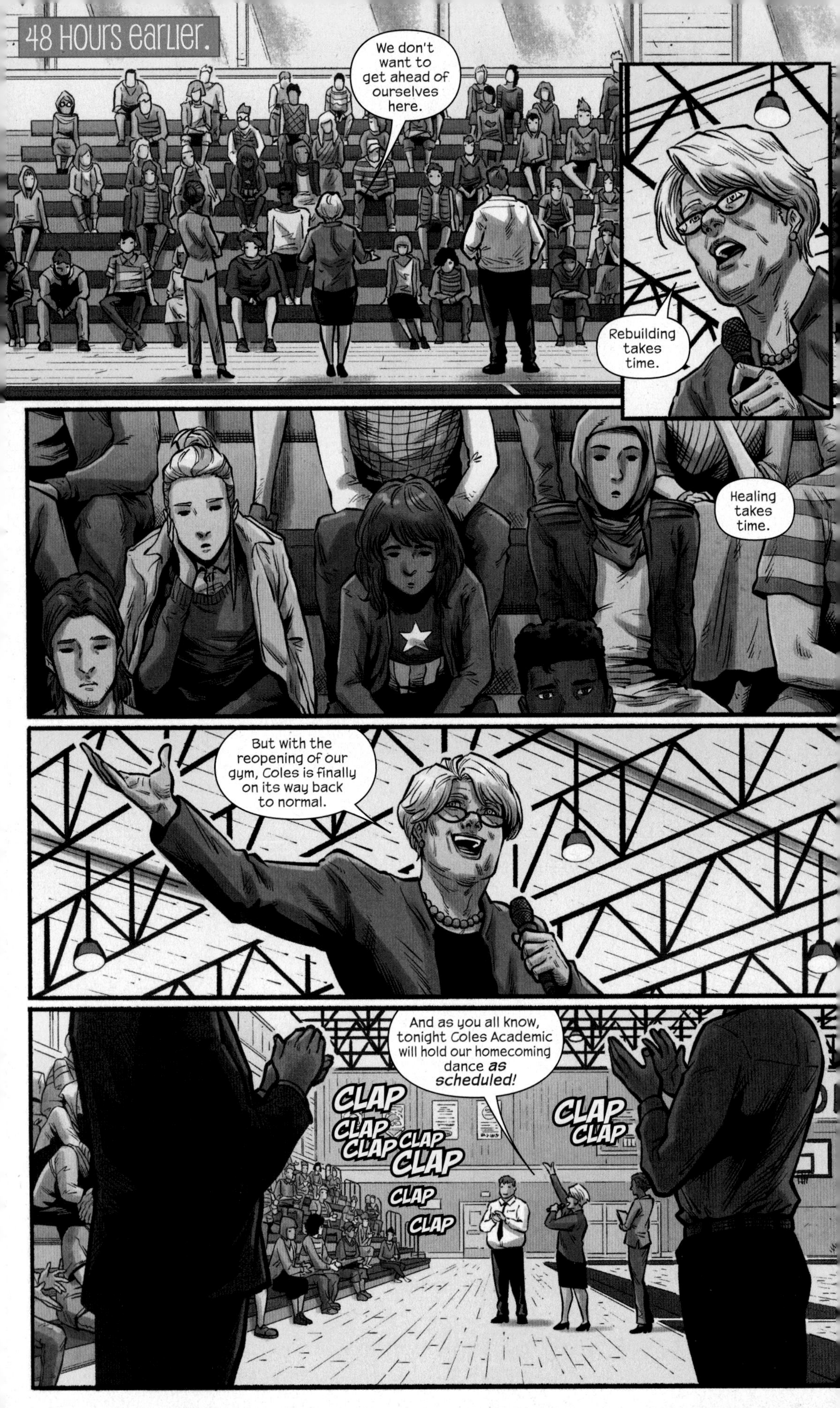
48 Hours earlier.
We don't want to get ahead of ourselves here.
Rebuilding takes time.
Healing takes time.
But with the reopening of our gym, Coles is finally on its way back to normal.
And as you all know, tonight Coles Academic will hold our homecoming dance *as scheduled!*
CLAP CLAP CLAP CLAP CLAP CLAP CLAP
CLAP CLAP

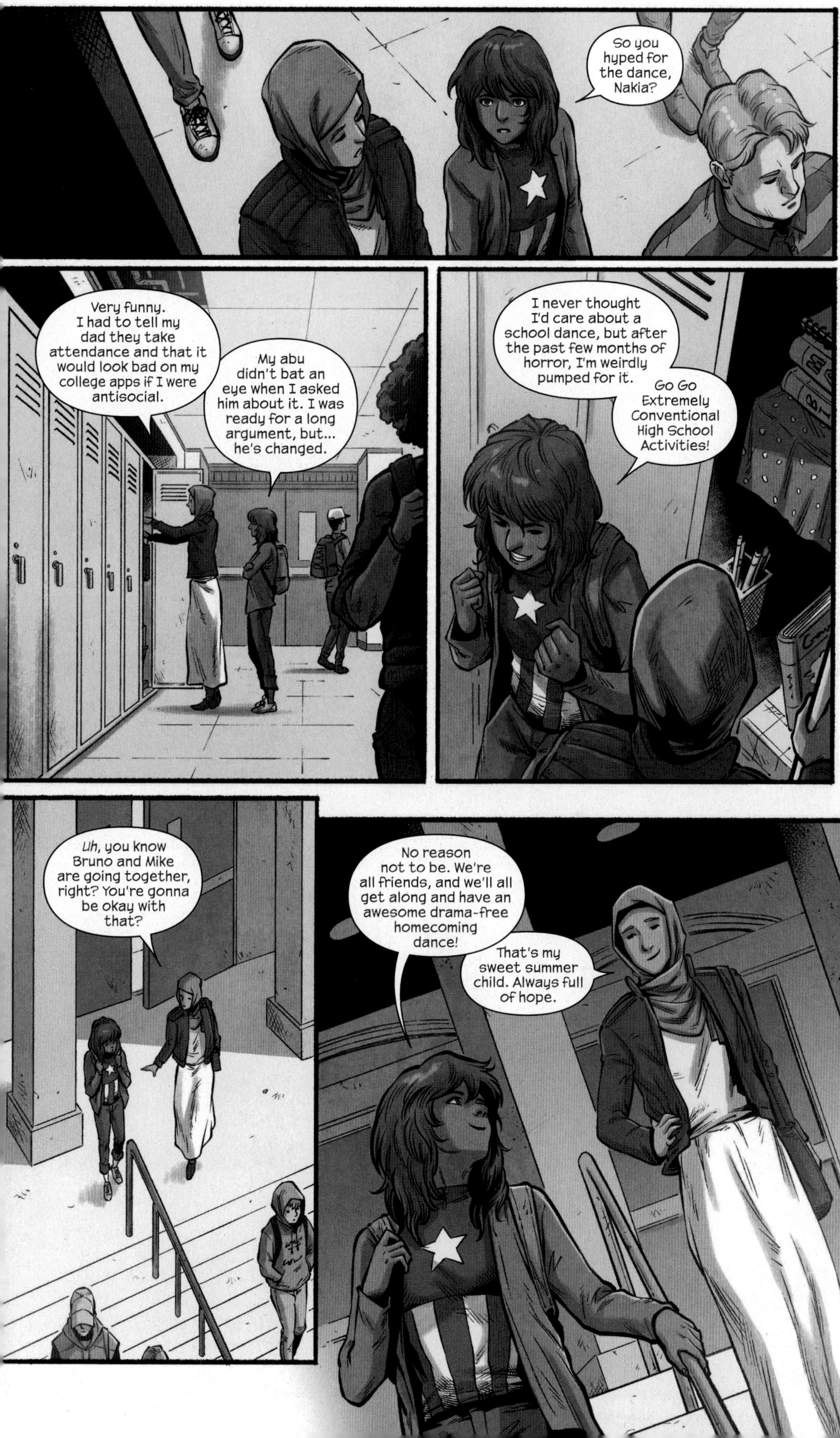
So you hyped for the dance, Nakia?
Very funny. I had to tell my dad they take attendance and that it would look bad on my college apps if I were antisocial.
My abu didn't bat an eye when I asked him about it. I was ready for a long argument, but... he's changed.
I never thought I'd care about a school dance, but after the past few months of horror, I'm weirdly pumped for it.
Go Go Extremely Conventional High School Activities!
Uh, you know Bruno and Mike are going together, right? You're gonna be okay with that?
No reason not to be. We're all friends, and we'll all get along and have an awesome drama-free homecoming dance!
That's my sweet summer child. Always full of hope.

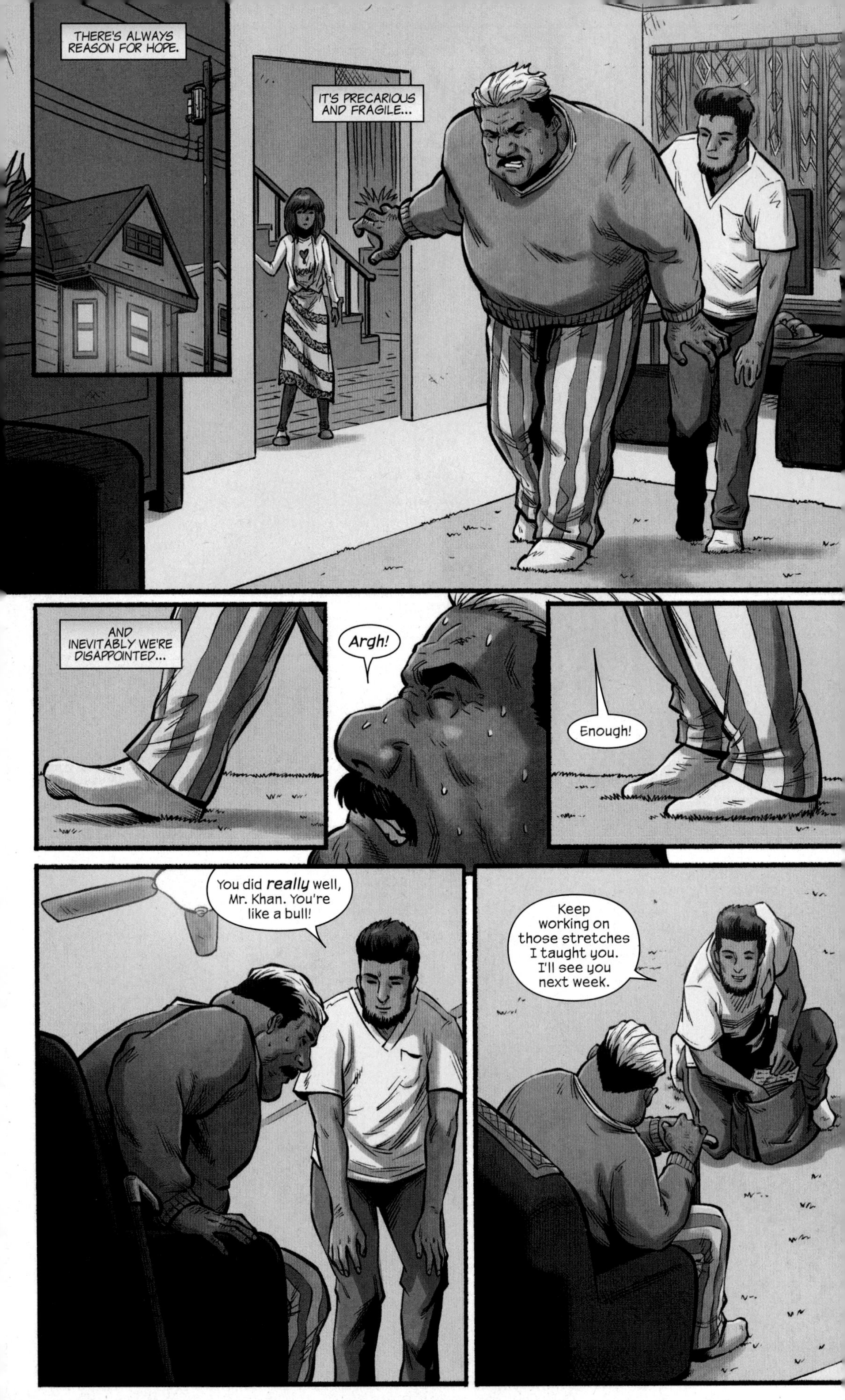
THERE'S ALWAYS REASON FOR HOPE.
IT'S PRECARIOUS AND FRAGILE...
AND INEVITABLY WE'RE DISAPPOINTED...
Argh!
Enough!
You did *really* well, Mr. Khan. You're like a bull!
Keep working on those stretches I taught you. I'll see you next week.

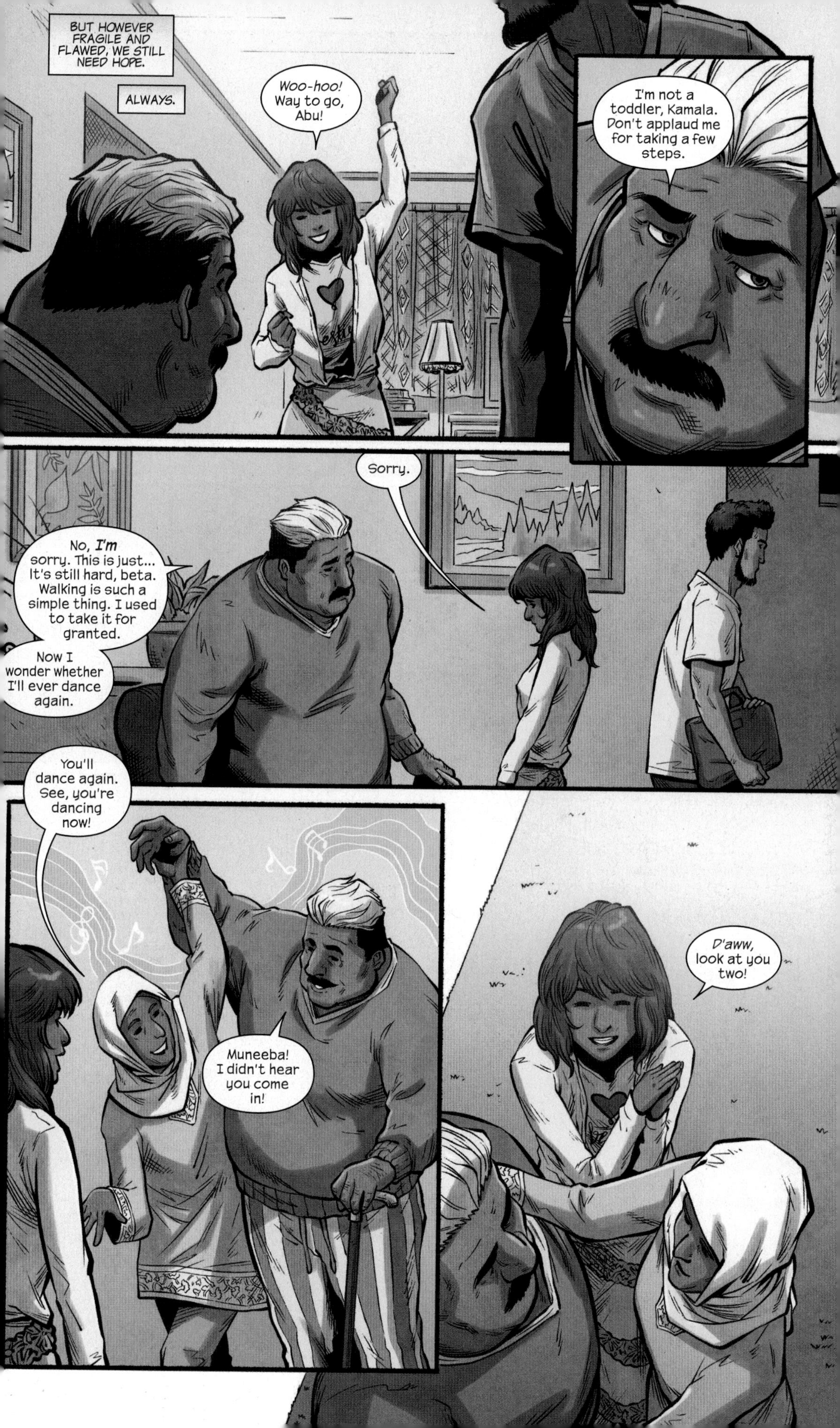
BUT HOWEVER FRAGILE AND FLAWED, WE STILL NEED HOPE.
ALWAYS.
Woo-hoo! Way to go, Abu!
I'm not a toddler, Kamala. Don't applaud me for taking a few steps.
Sorry.
No, ***I'm*** sorry. This is just... It's still hard, beta. Walking is such a simple thing. I used to take it for granted.
Now I wonder whether I'll ever dance again.
You'll dance again. See, you're dancing now!
Muneeba! I didn't hear you come in!
D'aww, look at you two!

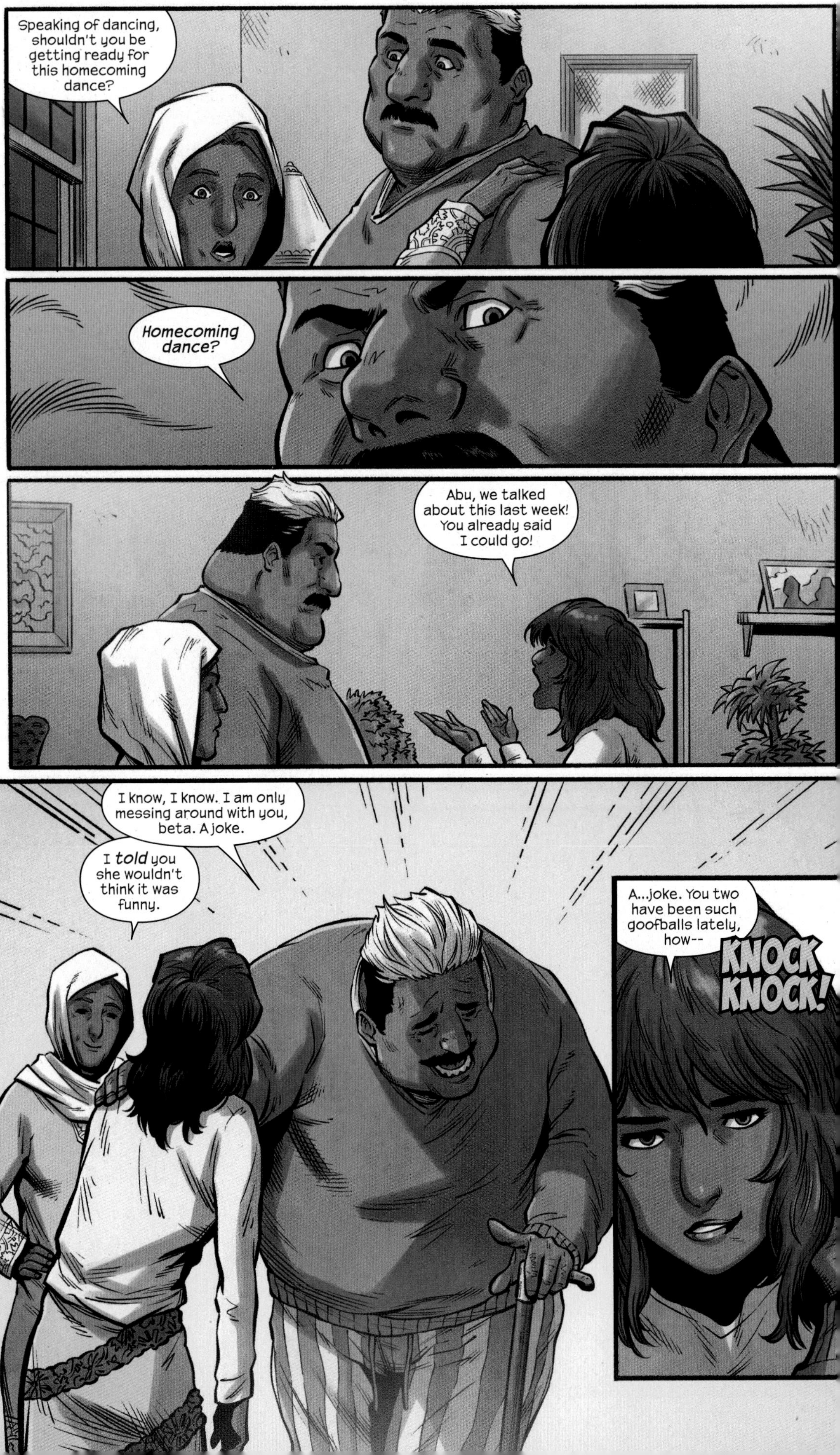
Speaking of dancing, shouldn't you be getting ready for this homecoming dance?
Homecoming dance?
Abu, we talked about this last week! You already said I could go!
I know, I know. I am only messing around with you, beta. A joke.
I told you she wouldn't think it was funny.
A...joke. You two have been such goofballs lately, how--
KNOCK KNOCK!

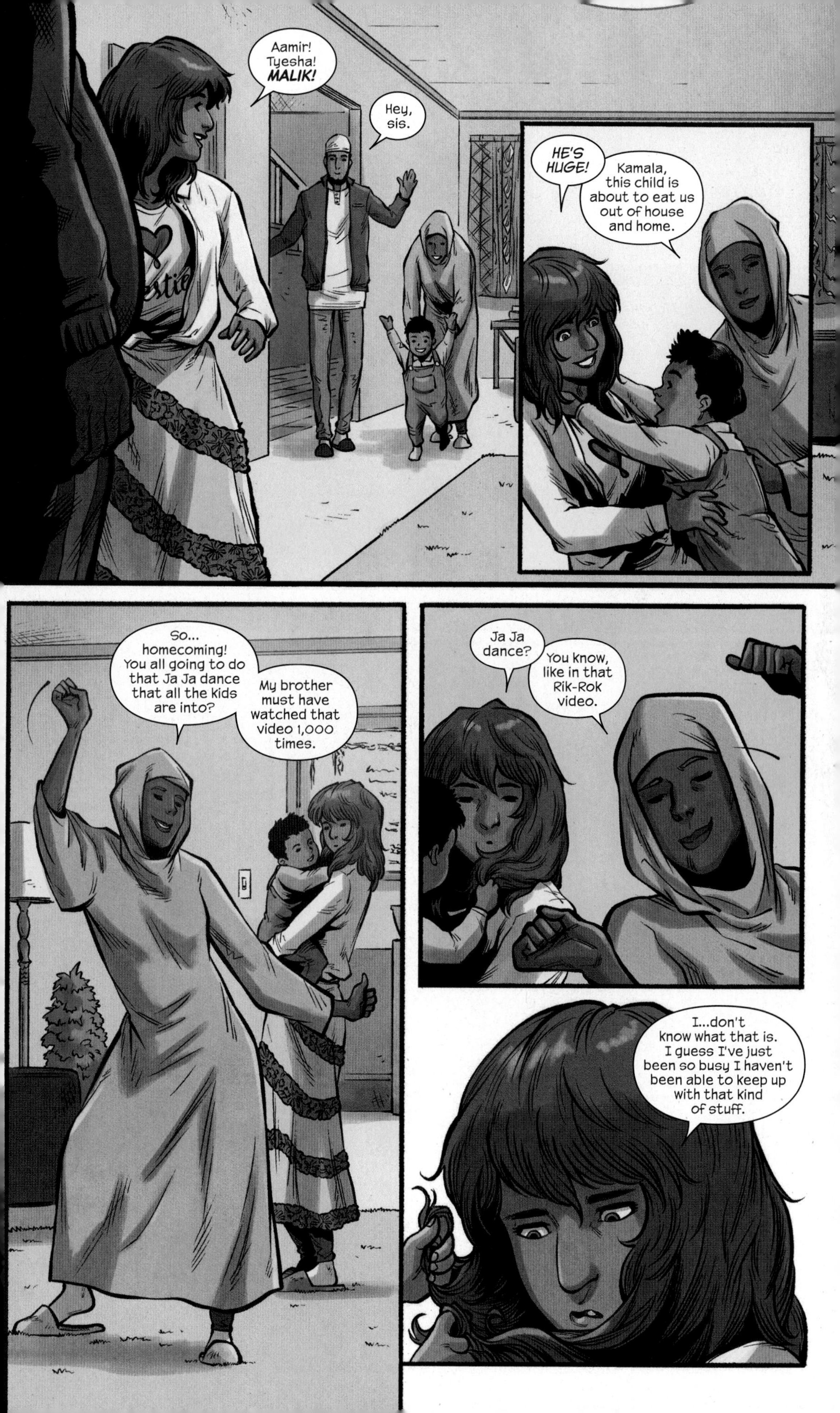
Aamir! Tyesha! MALIK!
Hey, sis.
HE'S HUGE!
Kamala, this child is about to eat us out of house and home.
So... homecoming! You all going to do that Ja Ja dance that all the kids are into?
My brother must have watched that video 1,000 times.
Ja Ja dance?
You know, like in that Rik-Rok video.
I...don't know what that is. I guess I've just been so busy I haven't been able to keep up with that kind of stuff.

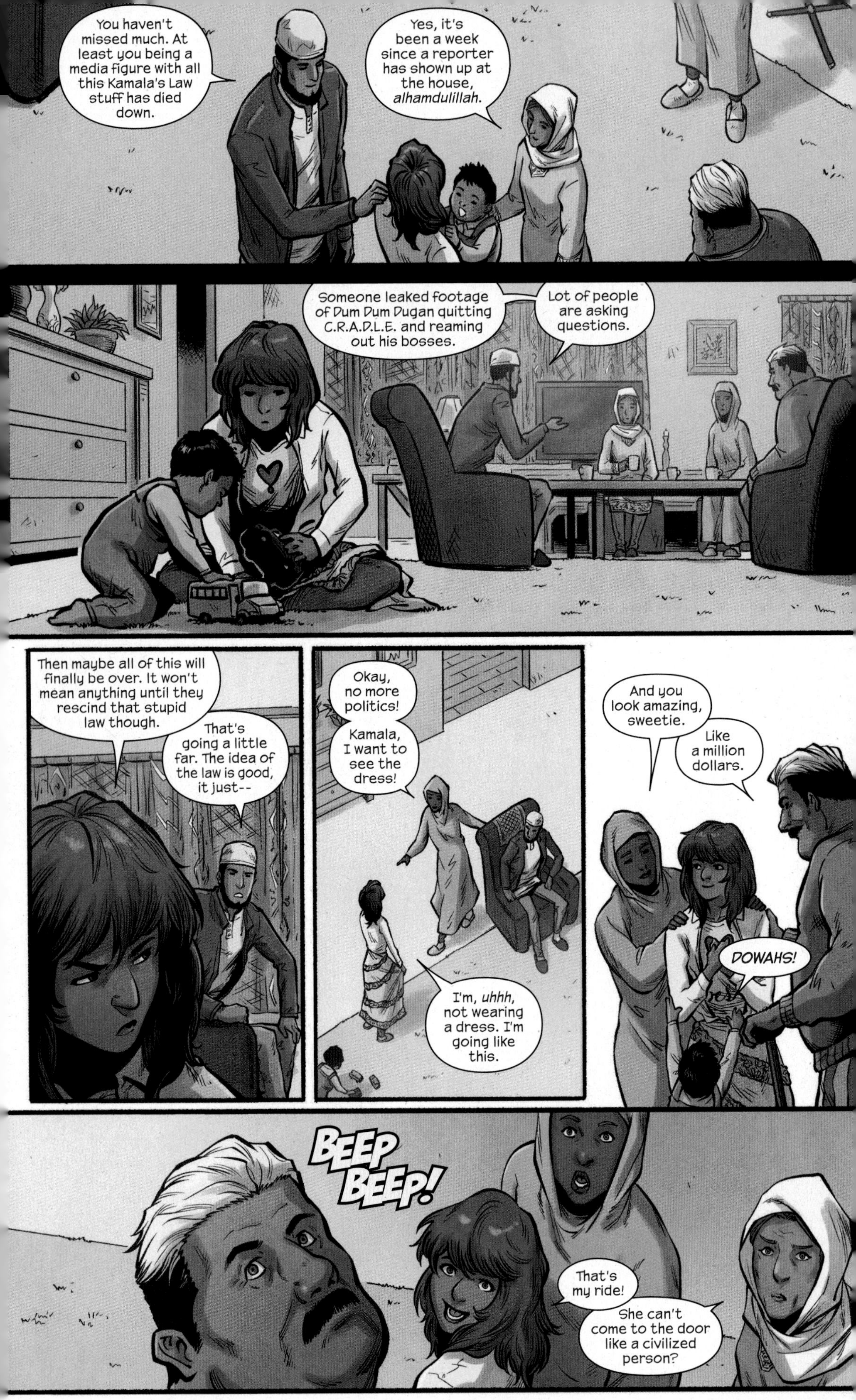

You haven't missed much. At least you being a media figure with all this Kamala's Law stuff has died down.
Yes, it's been a week since a reporter has shown up at the house, *alhamdulillah*.
Someone leaked footage of Dum Dum Dugan quitting C.R.A.D.L.E. and reaming out his bosses.
Lot of people are asking questions.
Then maybe all of this will finally be over. It won't mean anything until they rescind that stupid law though.
That's going a little far. The idea of the law is good, it just--
Okay, no more politics!
Kamala, I want to see the dress!
I'm, *uhhh*, not wearing a dress. I'm going like this.
And you look amazing, sweetie.
Like a million dollars.
DOWAHS!
BEEP BEEP!
That's my ride!
She can't come to the door like a civilized person?

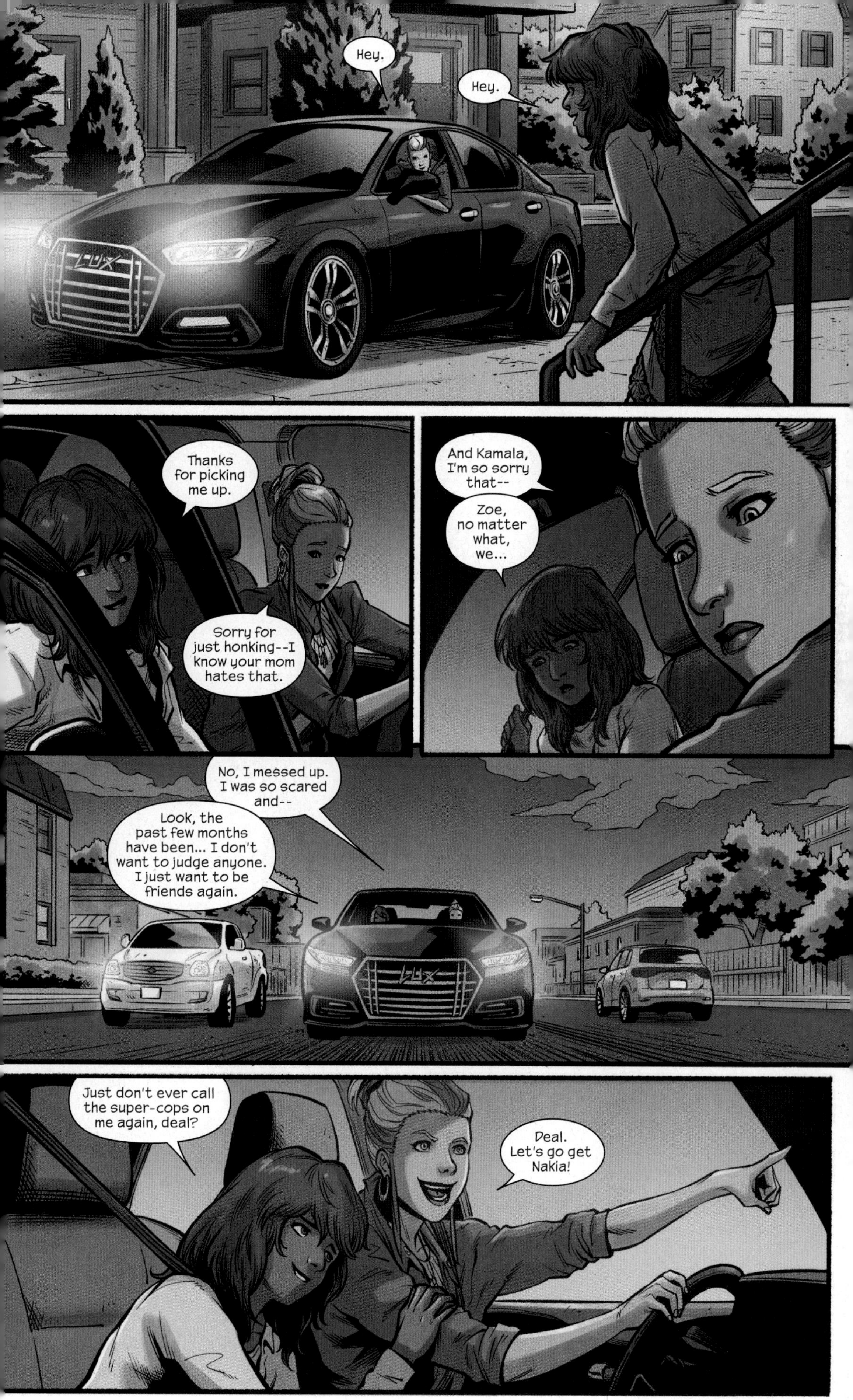
Hey.
Hey.
Thanks for picking me up.
Sorry for just honking--I know your mom hates that.
And Kamala, I'm so sorry that--
Zoe, no matter what, we...
No, I messed up. I was so scared and--
Look, the past few months have been... I don't want to judge anyone. I just want to be friends again.
Just don't ever call the super-cops on me again, deal?
Deal. Let's go get Nakia!

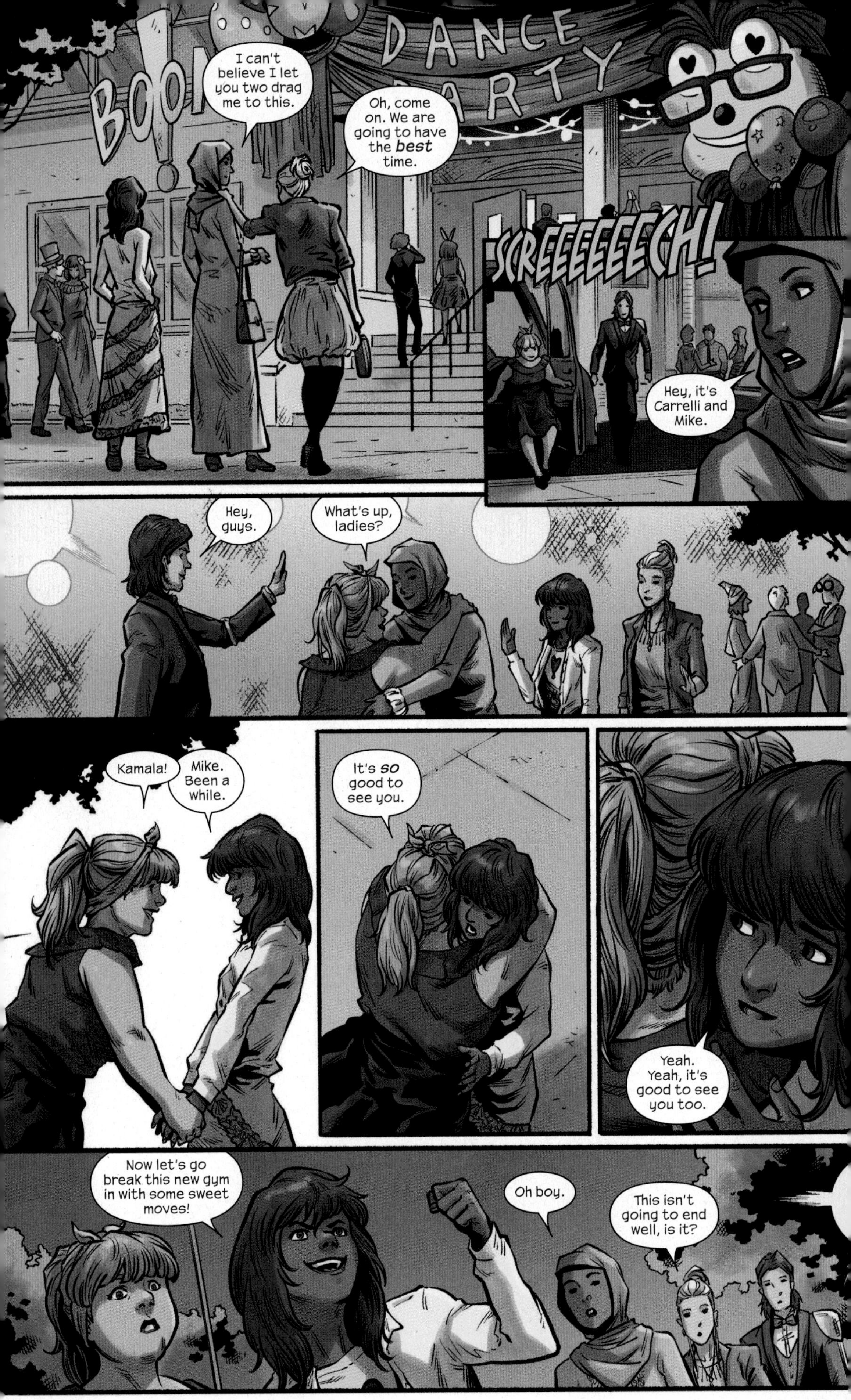
DANCE PARTY
BOO
I can't believe I let you two drag me to this.
Oh, come on. We are going to have the **best** time.
SCREEEEEEECH!
Hey, it's Carrelli and Mike.
Hey, guys.
What's up, ladies?
Kamala!
Mike. Been a while.
It's *so* good to see you.
Yeah. Yeah, it's good to see you too.
Now let's go break this new gym in with some sweet moves!
Oh boy.
This isn't going to end well, is it?

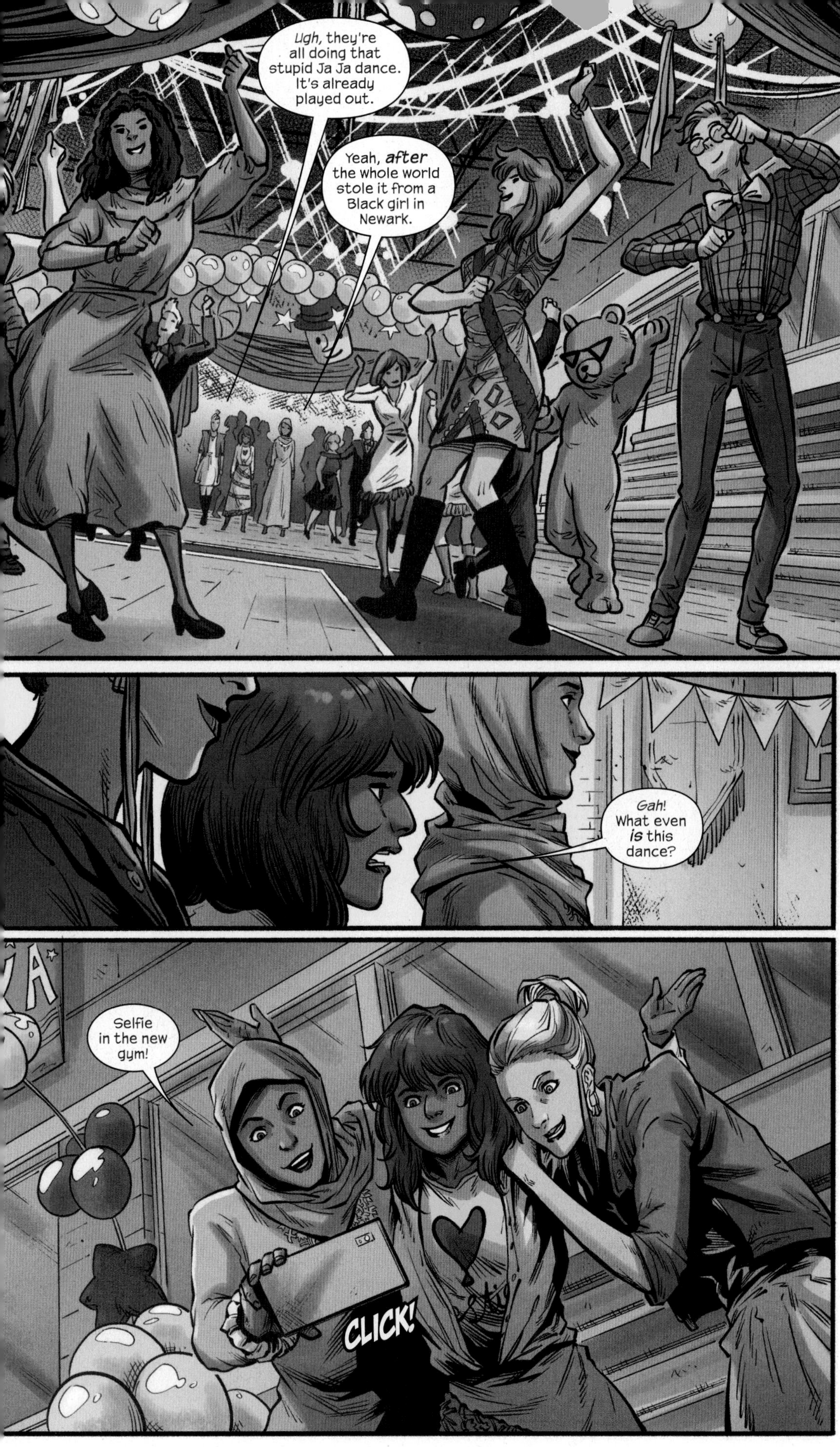
Ugh, they're all doing that stupid Ja Ja dance. It's already played out.
Yeah, after the whole world stole it from a Black girl in Newark.
Gah! What even is this dance?
Selfie in the new gym!
CLICK!

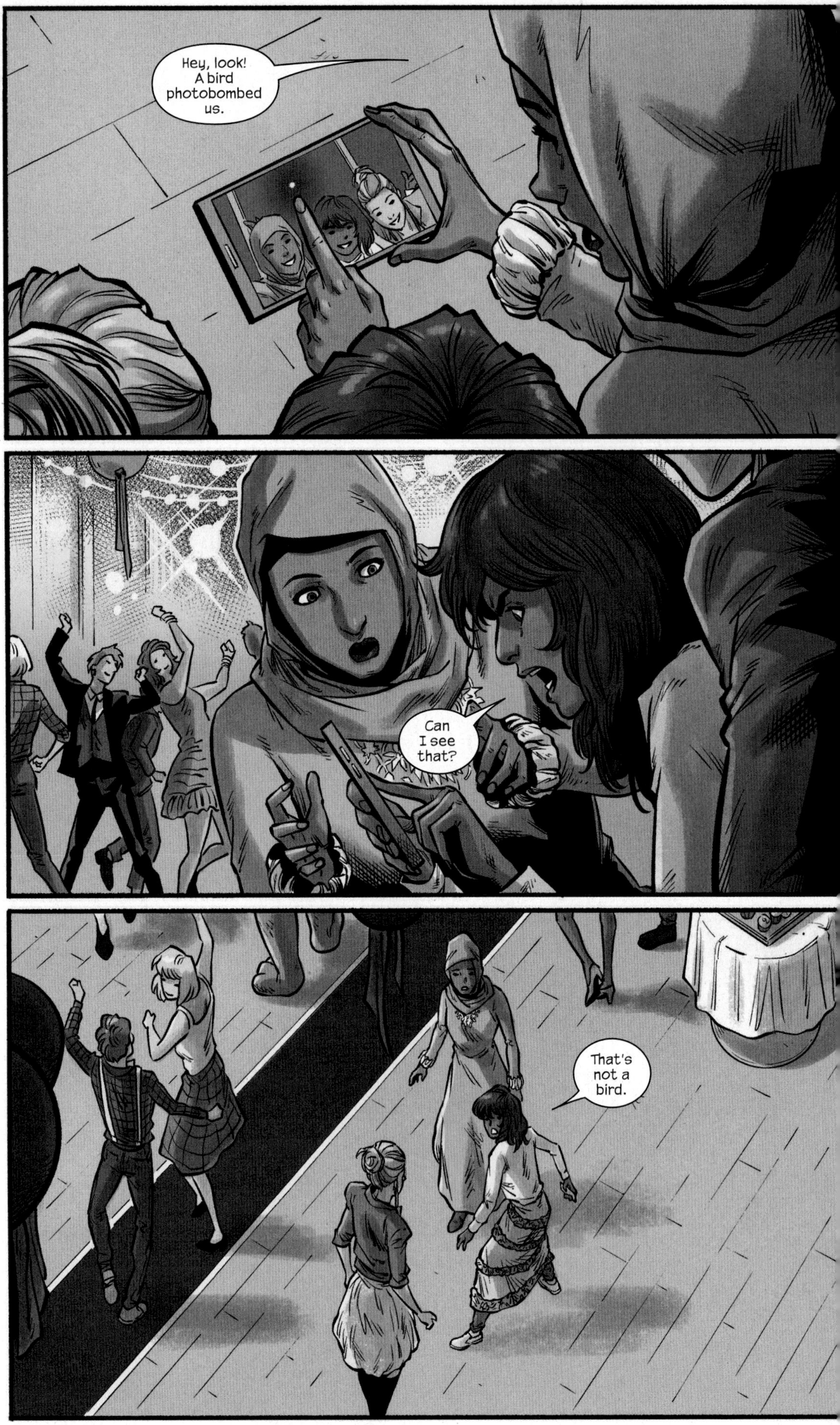
Hey, look! A bird photobombed us.
Can I see that?
That's not a bird.

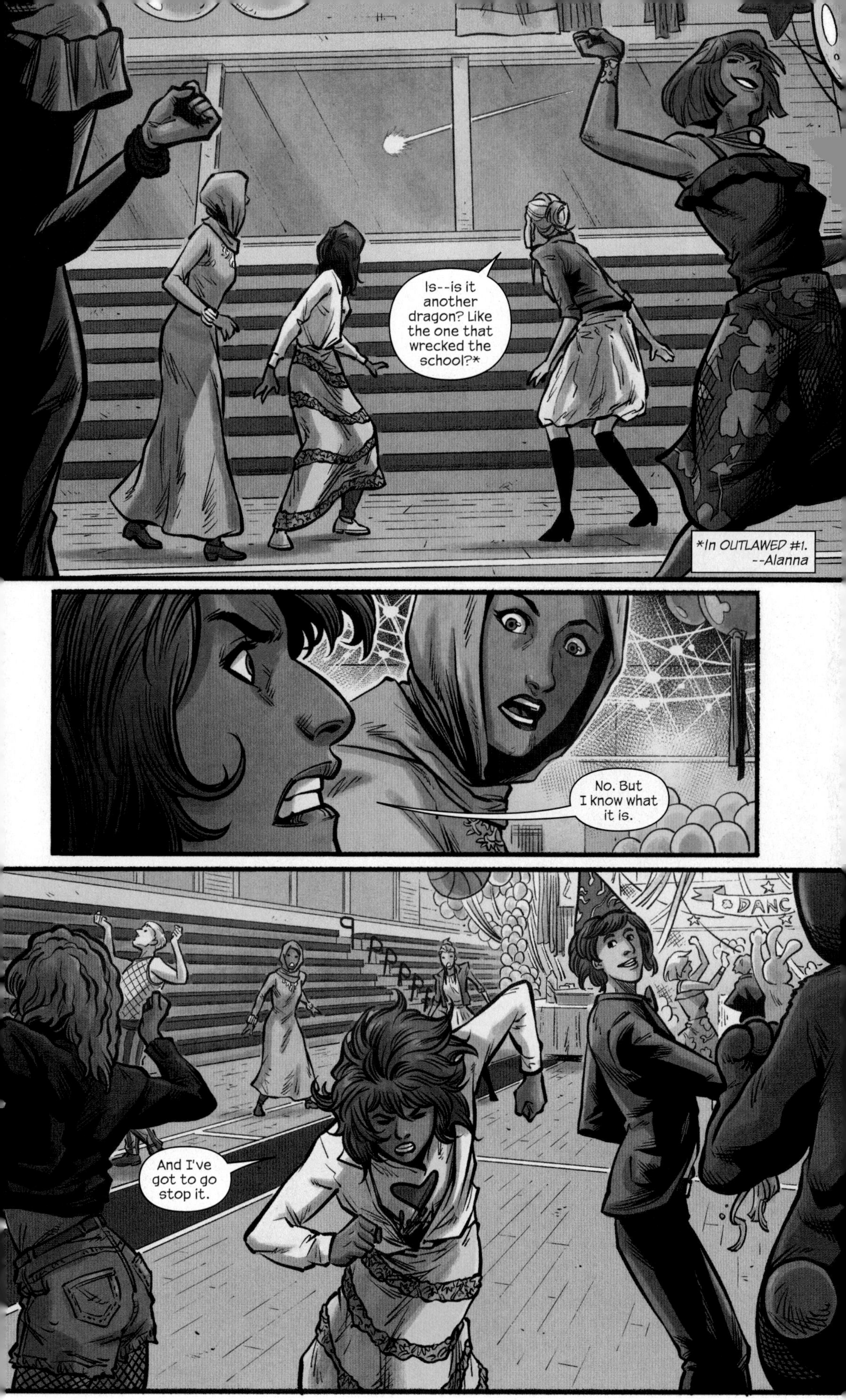
Is--is it another dragon? Like the one that wrecked the school?*
*In OUTLAWED #1. --Alanna
No. But I know what it is.
And I've got to go stop it.

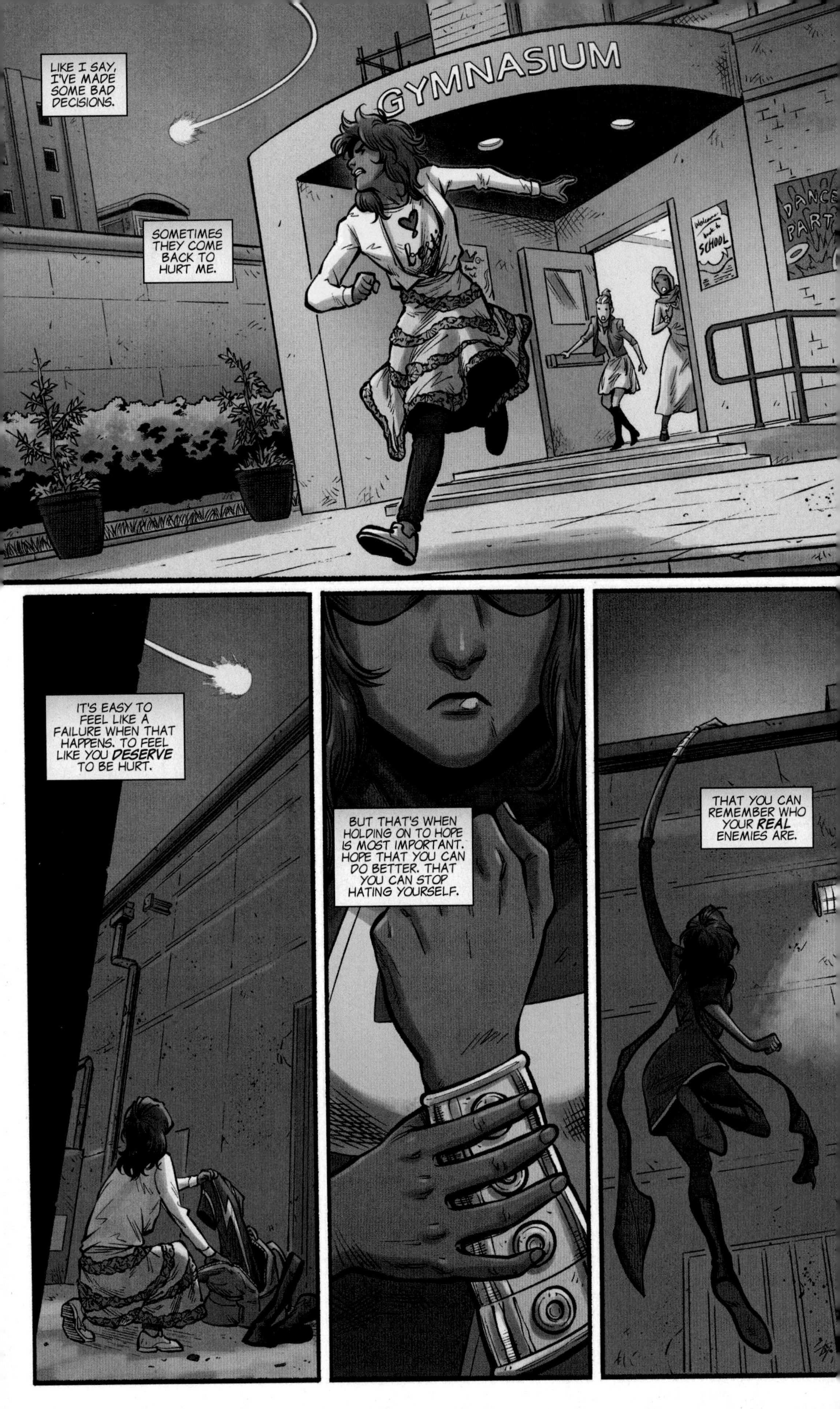

LIKE I SAY, I'VE MADE SOME BAD DECISIONS.
GYMNASIUM
SOMETIMES THEY COME BACK TO HURT ME.
DANCE PARTY
SCHOOL
IT'S EASY TO FEEL LIKE A FAILURE WHEN THAT HAPPENS. TO FEEL LIKE YOU DESERVE TO BE HURT.
BUT THAT'S WHEN HOLDING ON TO HOPE IS MOST IMPORTANT. HOPE THAT YOU CAN DO BETTER. THAT YOU CAN STOP HATING YOURSELF.
THAT YOU CAN REMEMBER WHO YOUR REAL ENEMIES ARE.

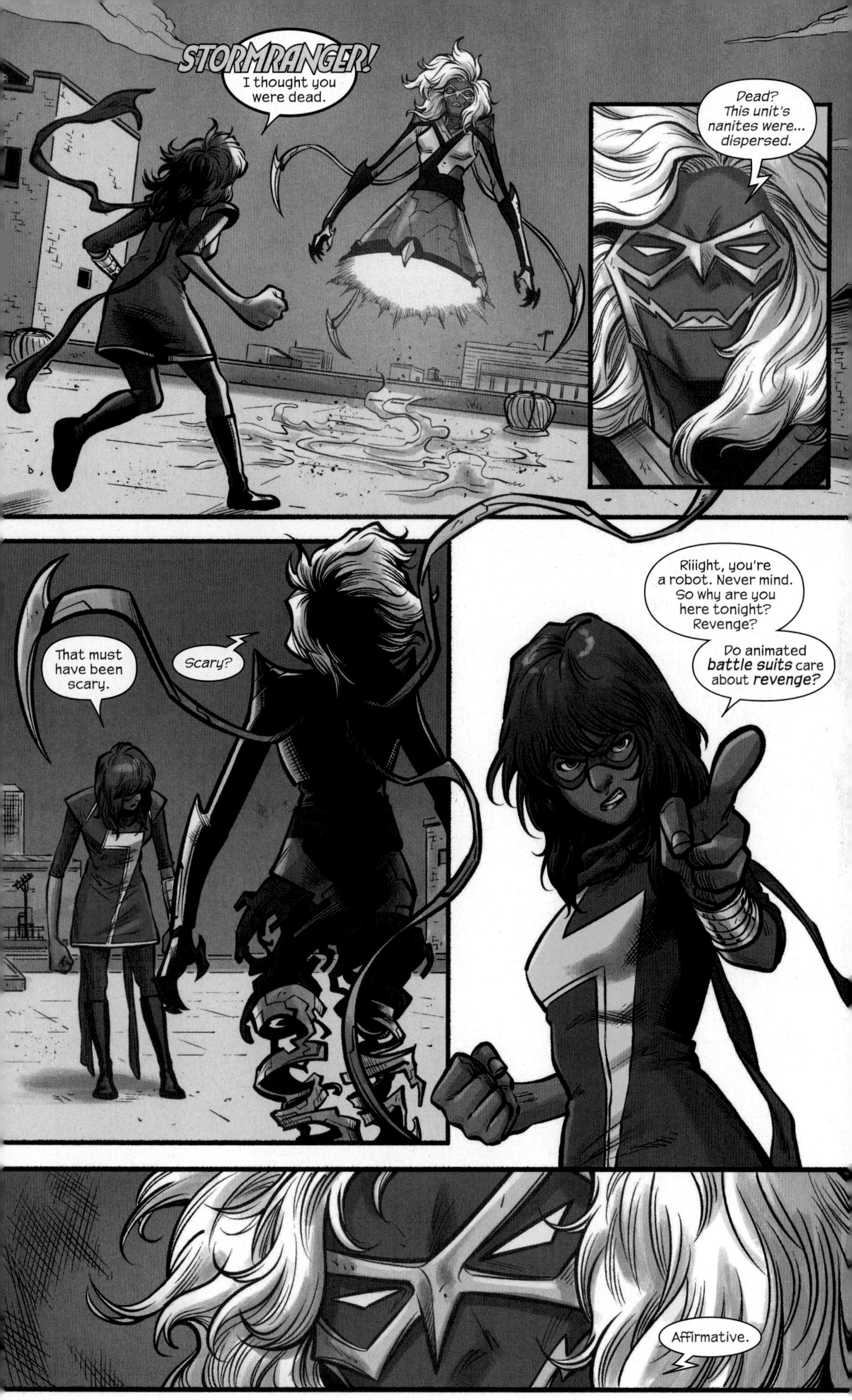
STORMRANGER!
I thought you were dead.
Dead? This unit's nanites were... dispersed.
That must have been scary.
Scary?
Riiight, you're a robot. Never mind. So why are you here tonight? Revenge?
Do animated **battle suits** care about **revenge?**
Affirmative.

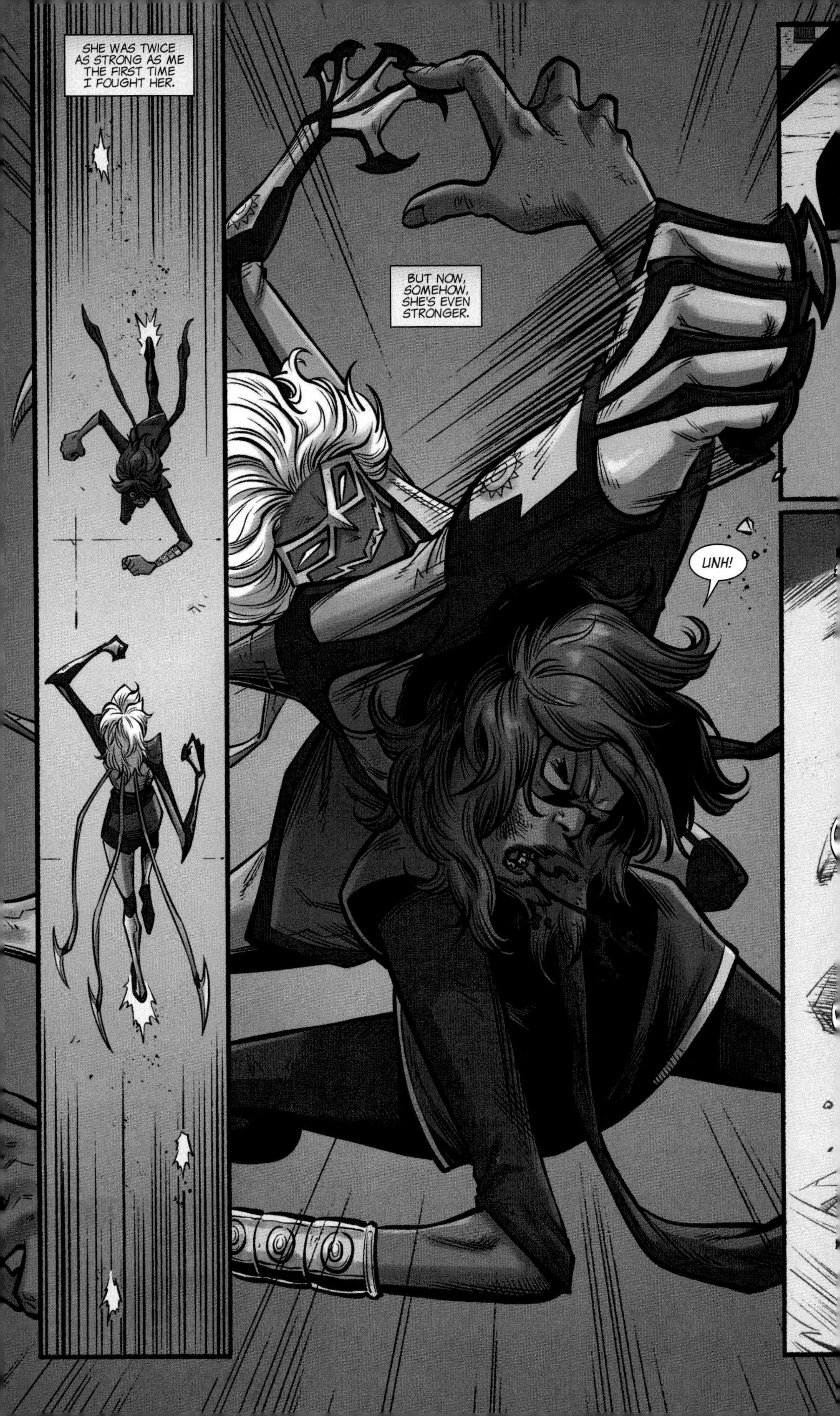

SHE WAS TWICE AS STRONG AS ME THE FIRST TIME I FOUGHT HER.
BUT NOW, SOMEHOW, SHE'S EVEN STRONGER.
UNH!

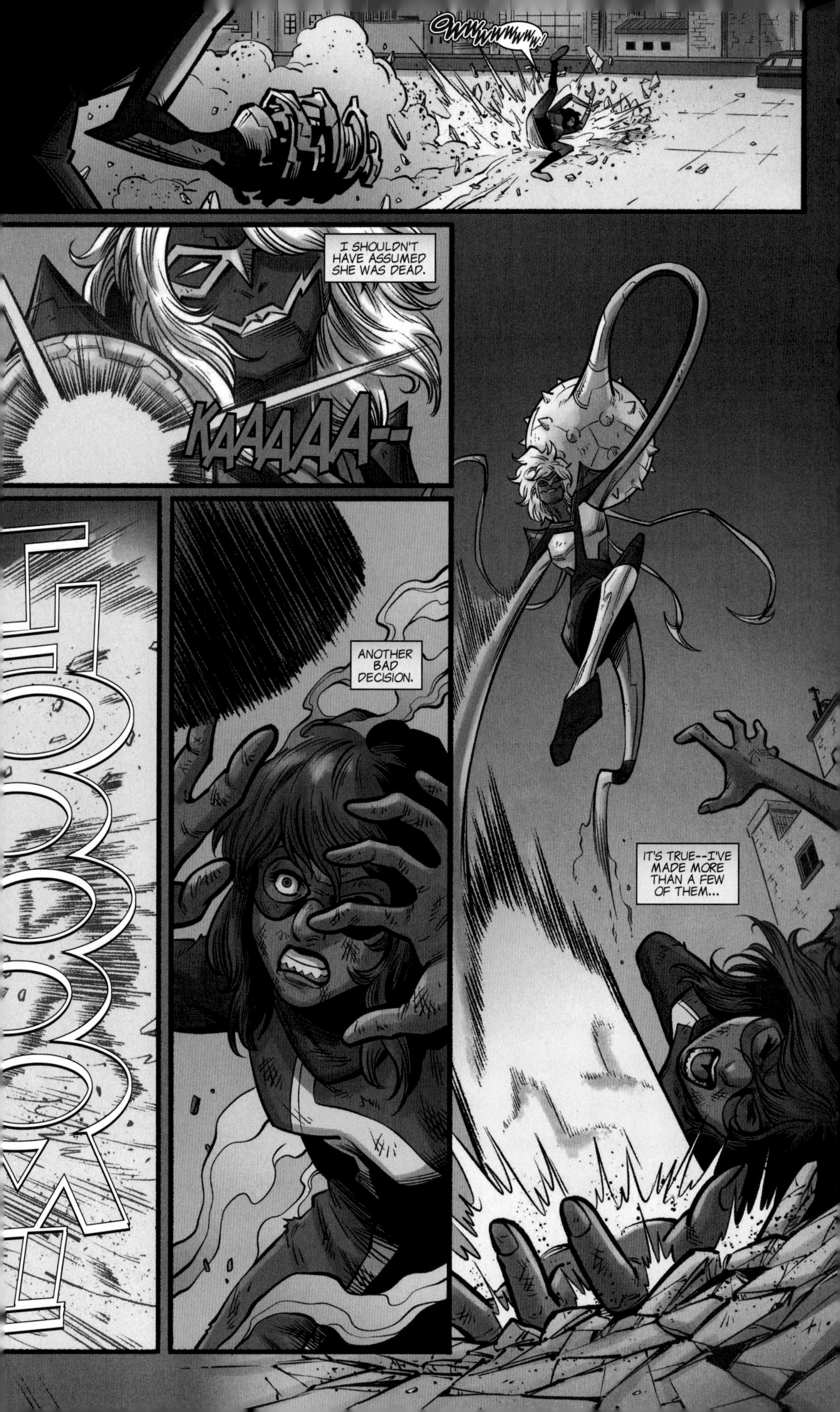
I SHOULDN'T HAVE ASSUMED SHE WAS DEAD.
KAAAAAA--
ANOTHER BAD DECISION.
IT'S TRUE--I'VE MADE MORE THAN A FEW OF THEM...

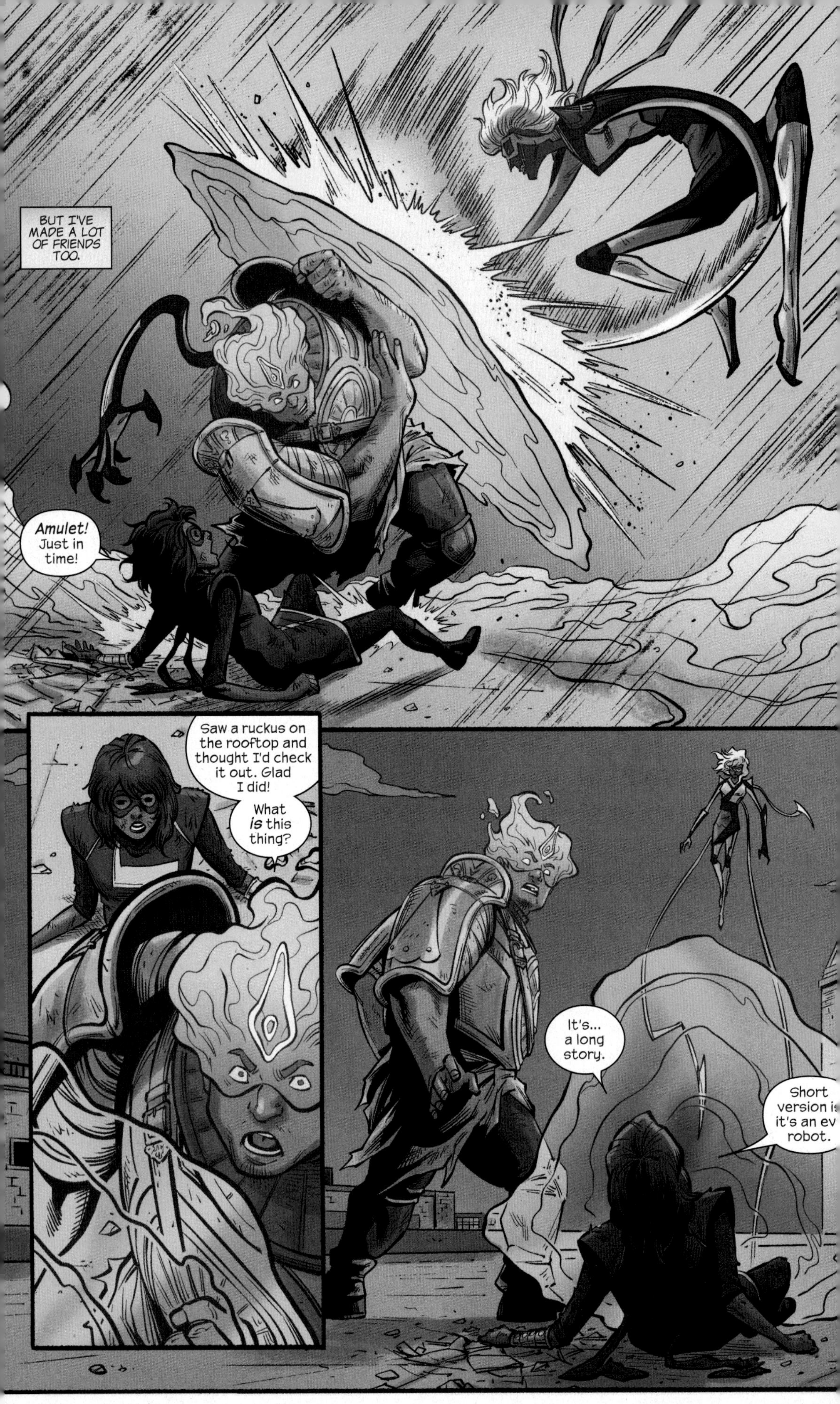

BUT I'VE MADE A LOT OF FRIENDS TOO.
Amulet! Just in time!
Saw a ruckus on the rooftop and thought I'd check it out. Glad I did!
What *is* this thing?
It's... a long story.
Short version is it's an ev robot.

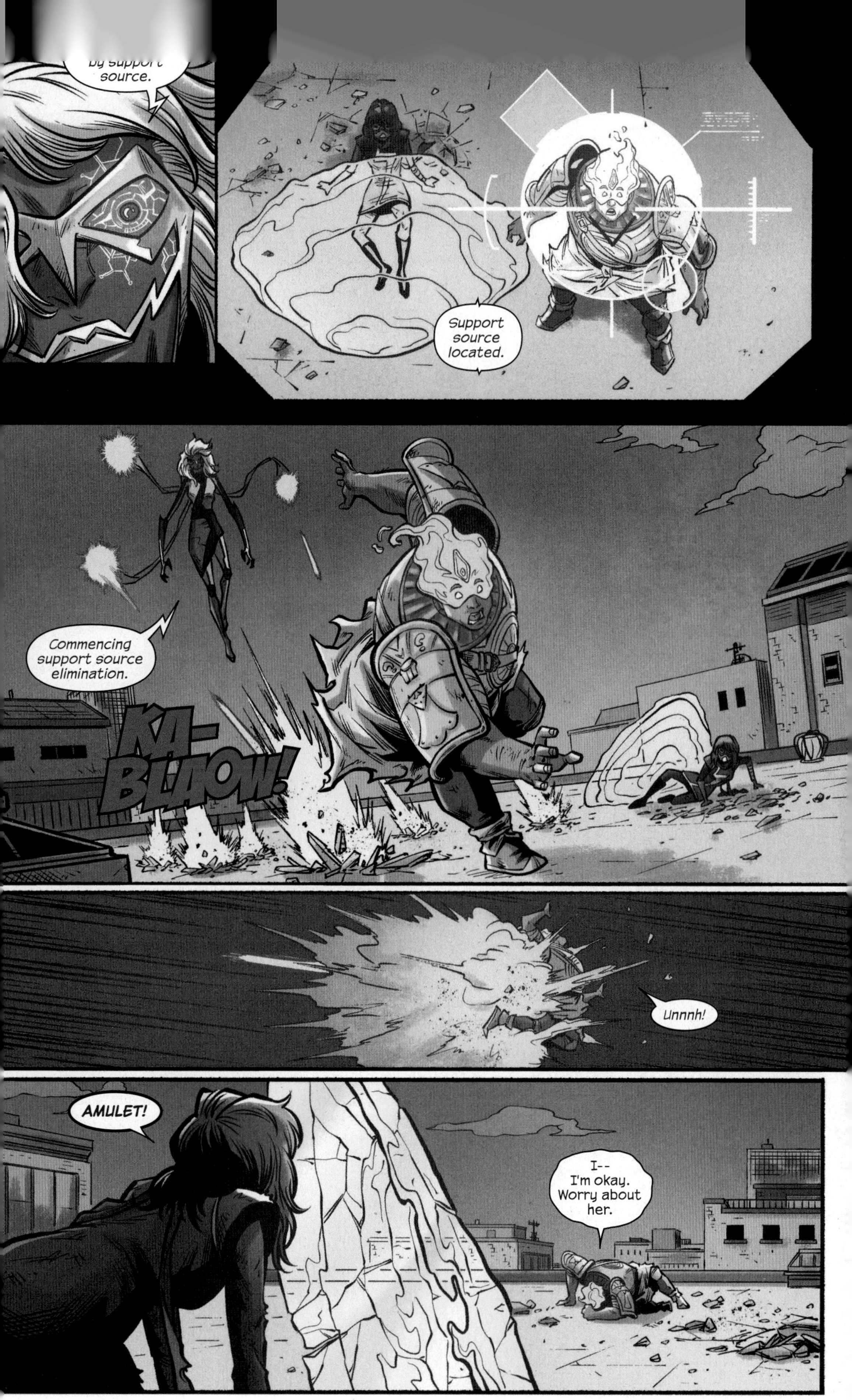

source.
Support source located.
Commencing support source elimination.
KA-BLAOW!
Unnnh!
AMULET!
I-- I'm okay. Worry about her.

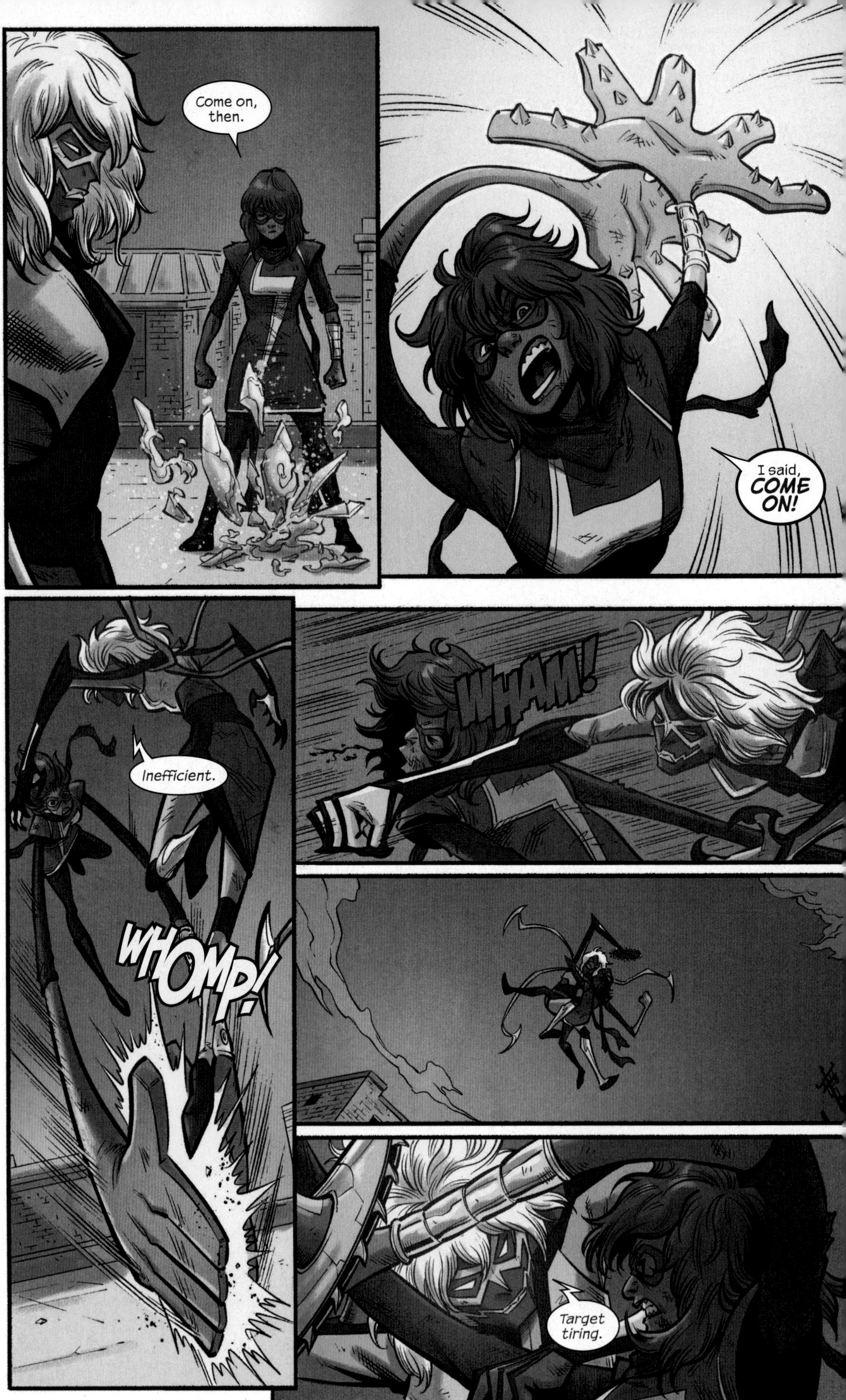

Come on, then.
I said, COME ON!
Inefficient.
WHOMP!
WHAM!
Target tiring.

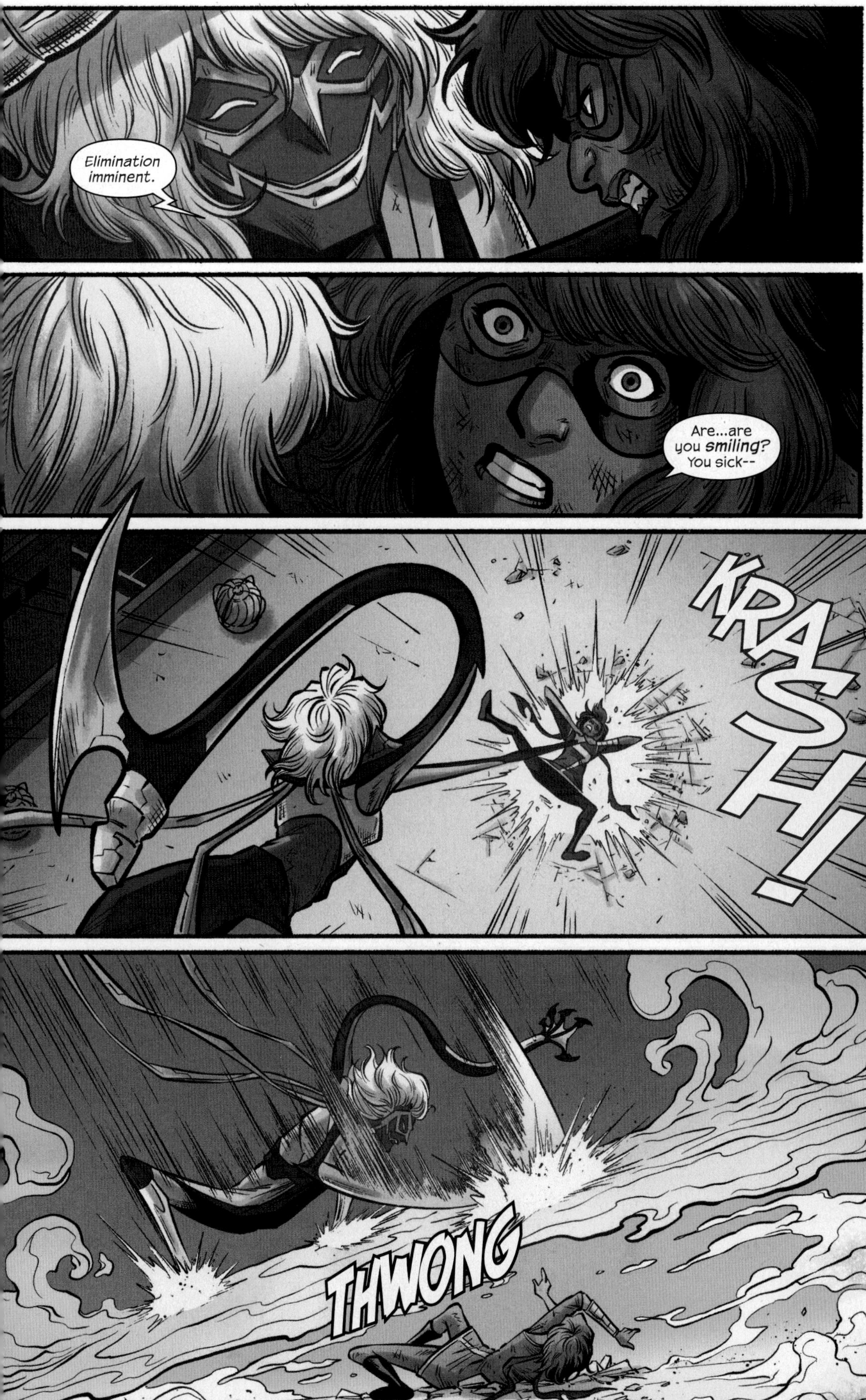
Elimination imminent.
Are...are you *smiling*? You sick--
KRASH!
THWONG

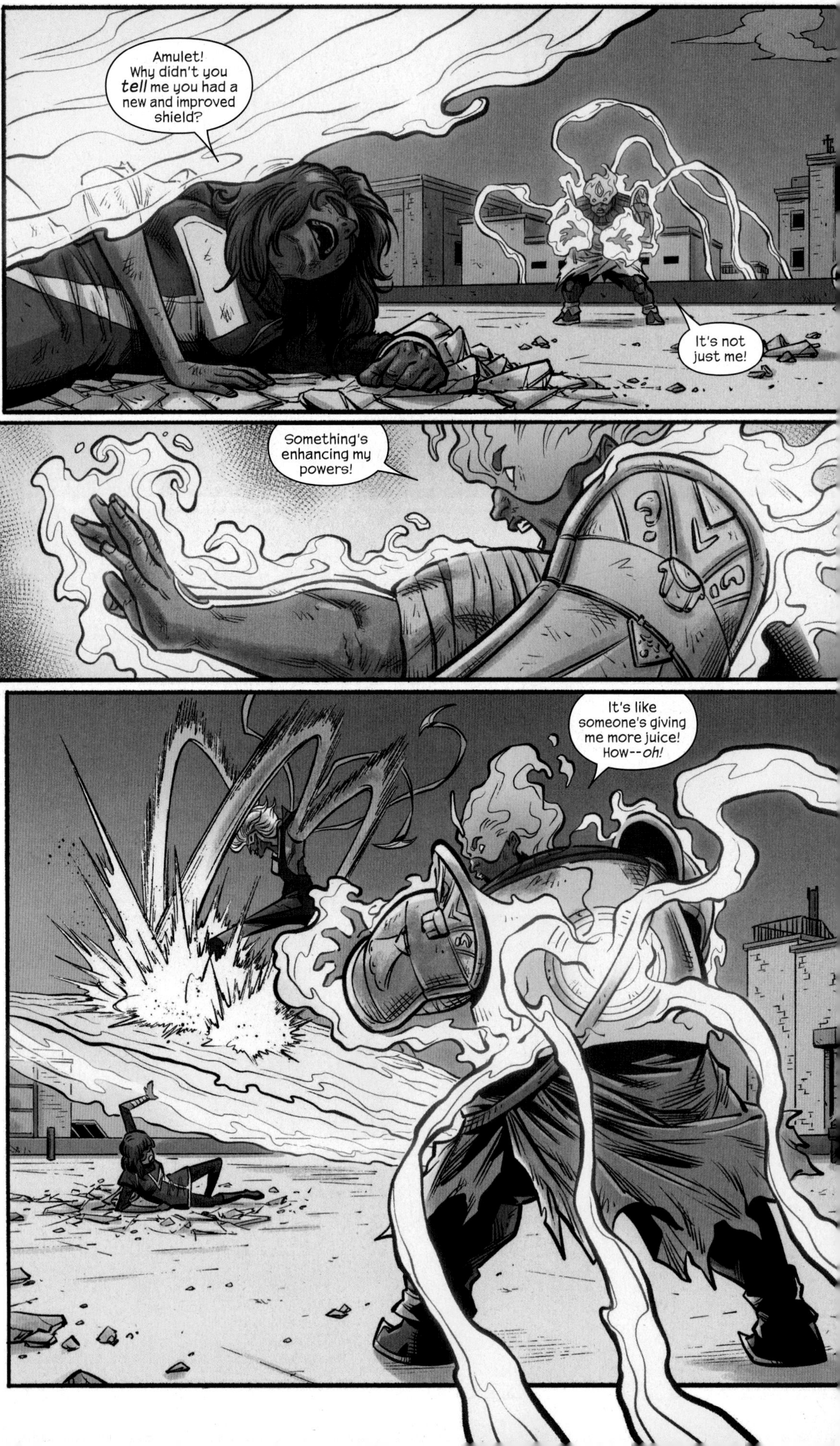

Amulet! Why didn't you *tell* me you had a new and improved shield?
It's not just me!
Something's enhancing my powers!
It's like someone's giving me more juice! How--*oh!*

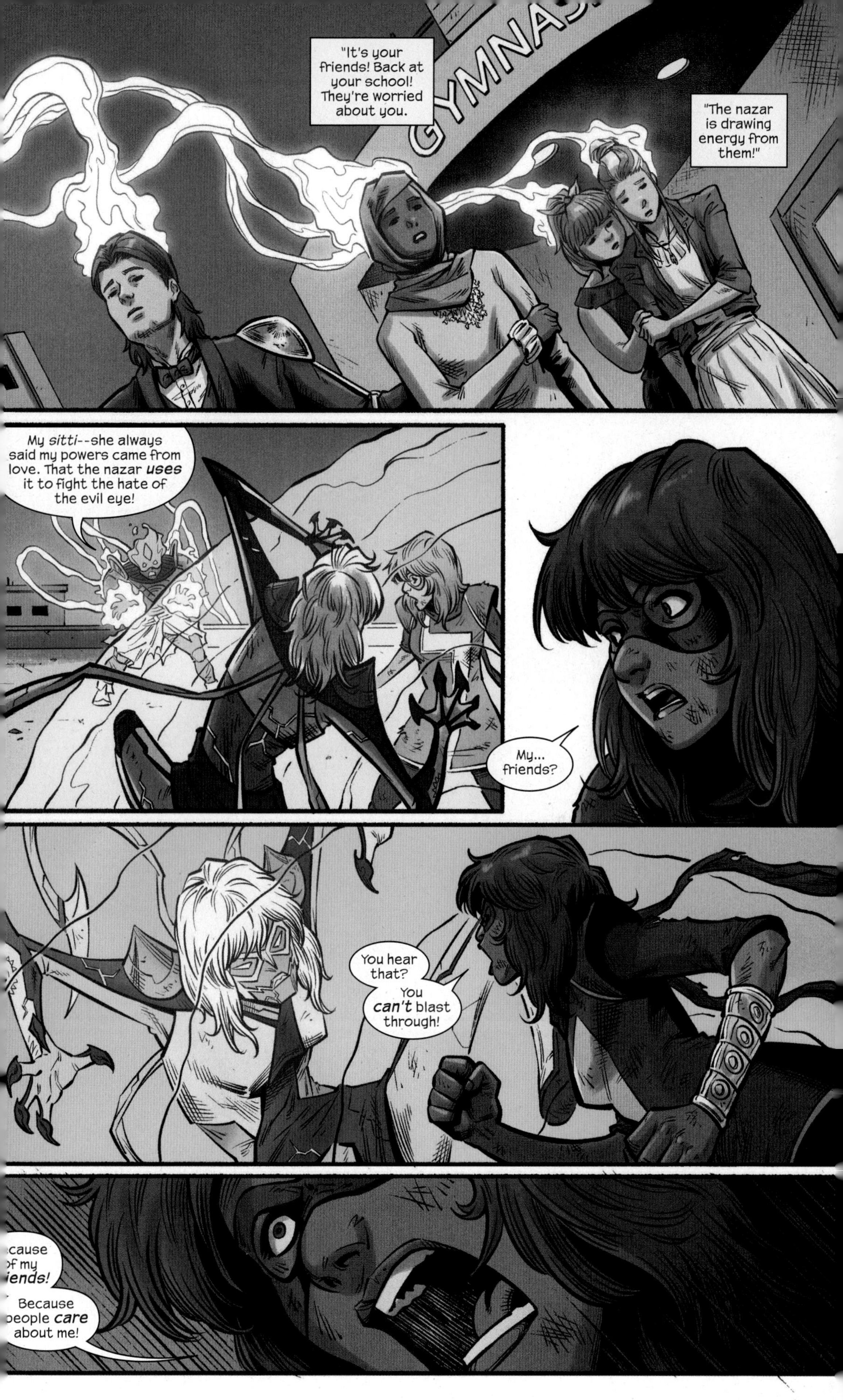
GYMNAS
"It's your friends! Back at your school! They're worried about you.
"The nazar is drawing energy from them!"
My *sitti*--she always said my powers came from love. That the nazar ***uses*** it to fight the hate of the evil eye!
My... friends?
You hear that?
You ***can't*** blast through!
cause of my iends!
Because people ***care*** about me!

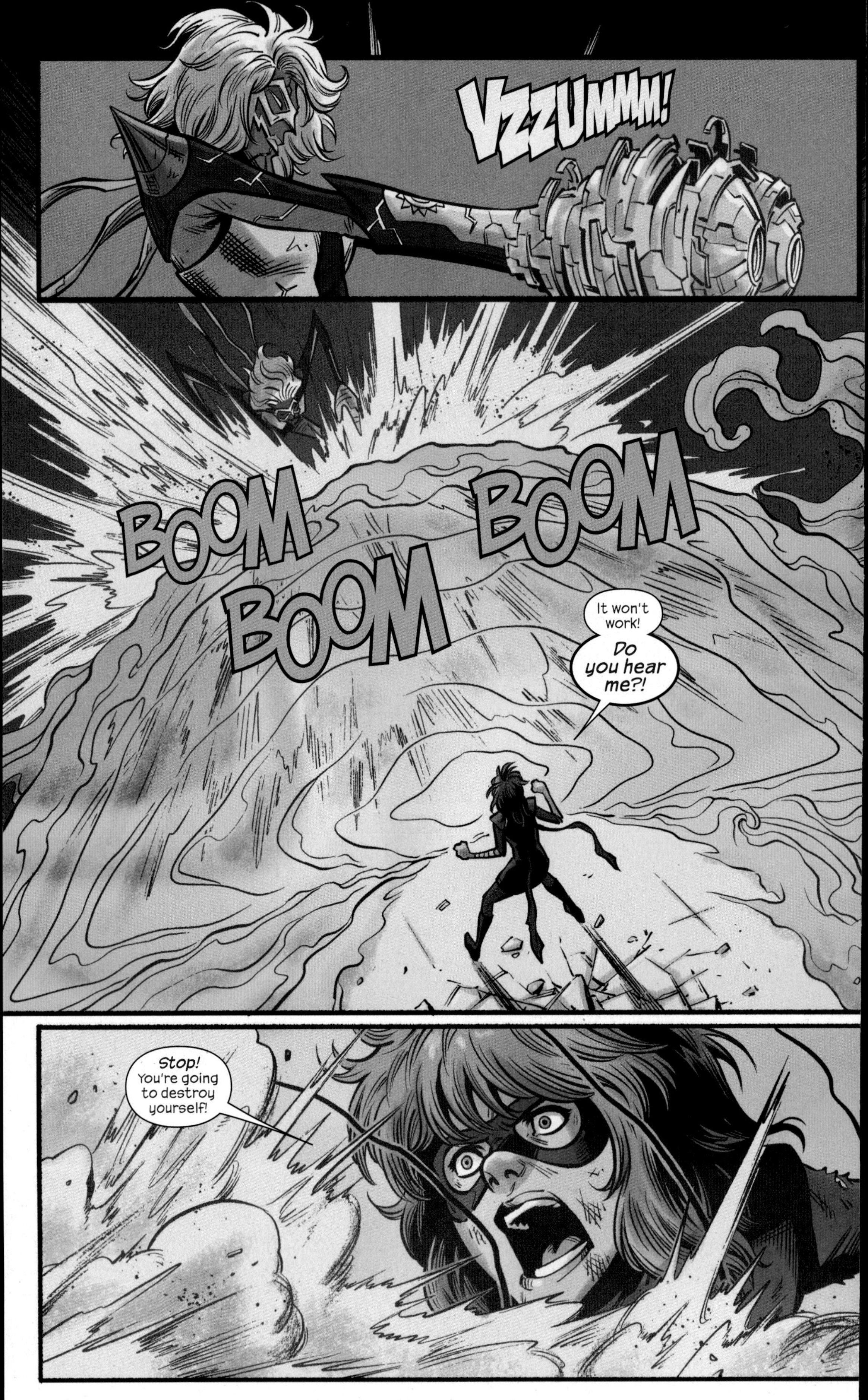
VZZUMMM!
BOOM BOOM BOOM
It won't work!
Do you hear me?!
Stop! You're going to destroy yourself!

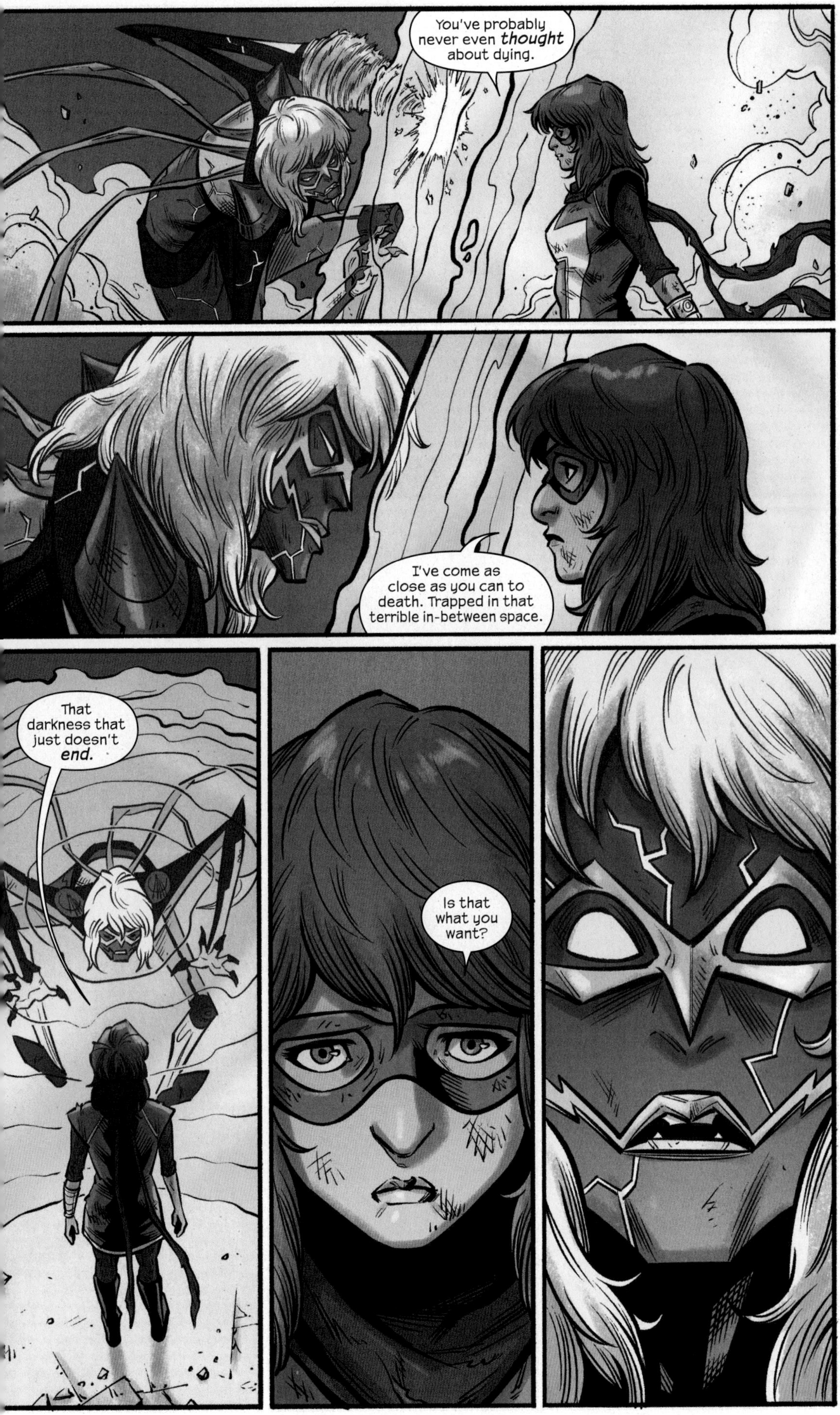
You've probably never even *thought* about dying.
I've come as close as you can to death. Trapped in that terrible in-between space.
That darkness that just doesn't *end.*
Is that what you want?

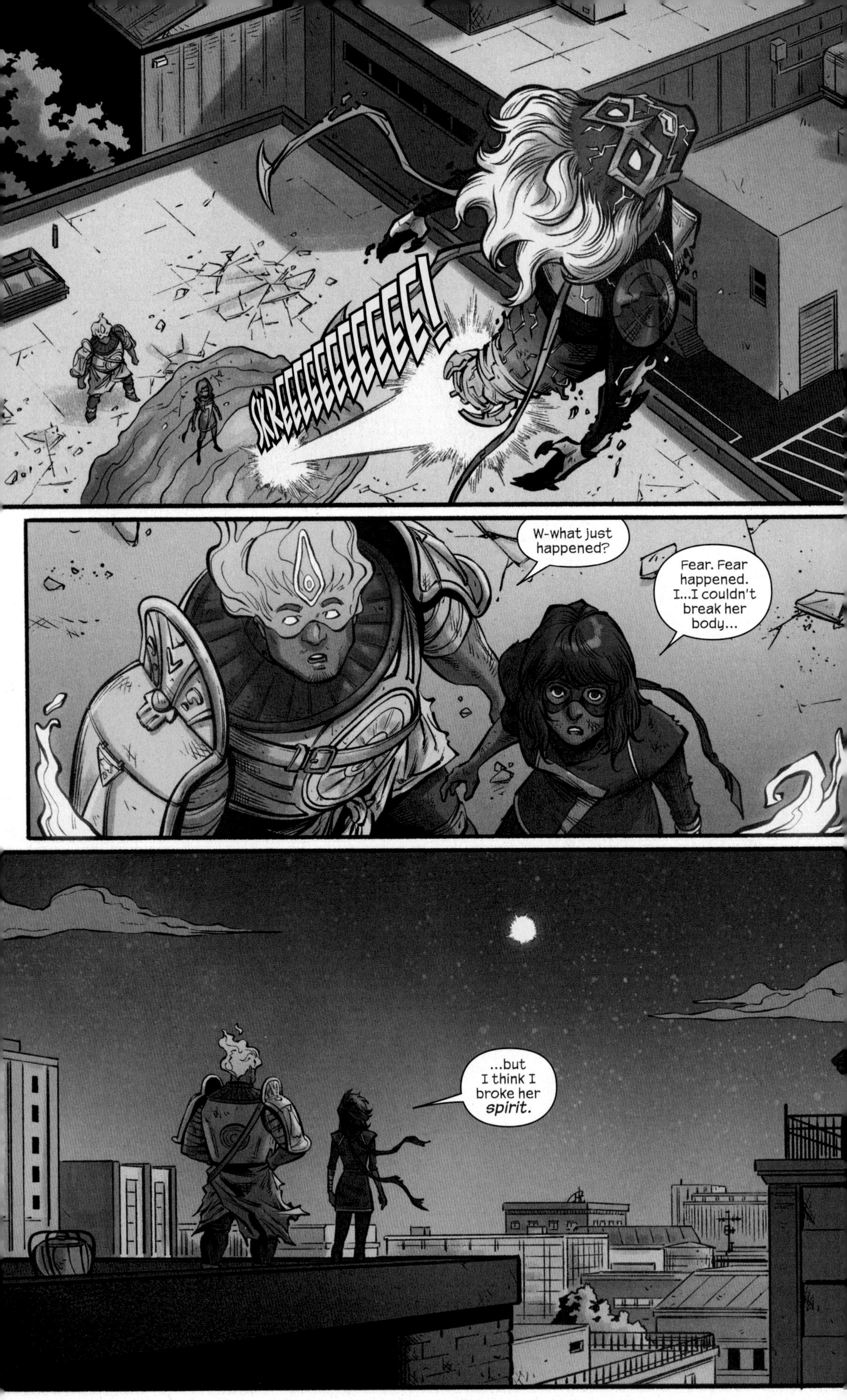
SKREEEEEEEEEEEE!
W-what just happened?
Fear. Fear happened. I...I couldn't break her body...
...but I think I broke her *spirit*.

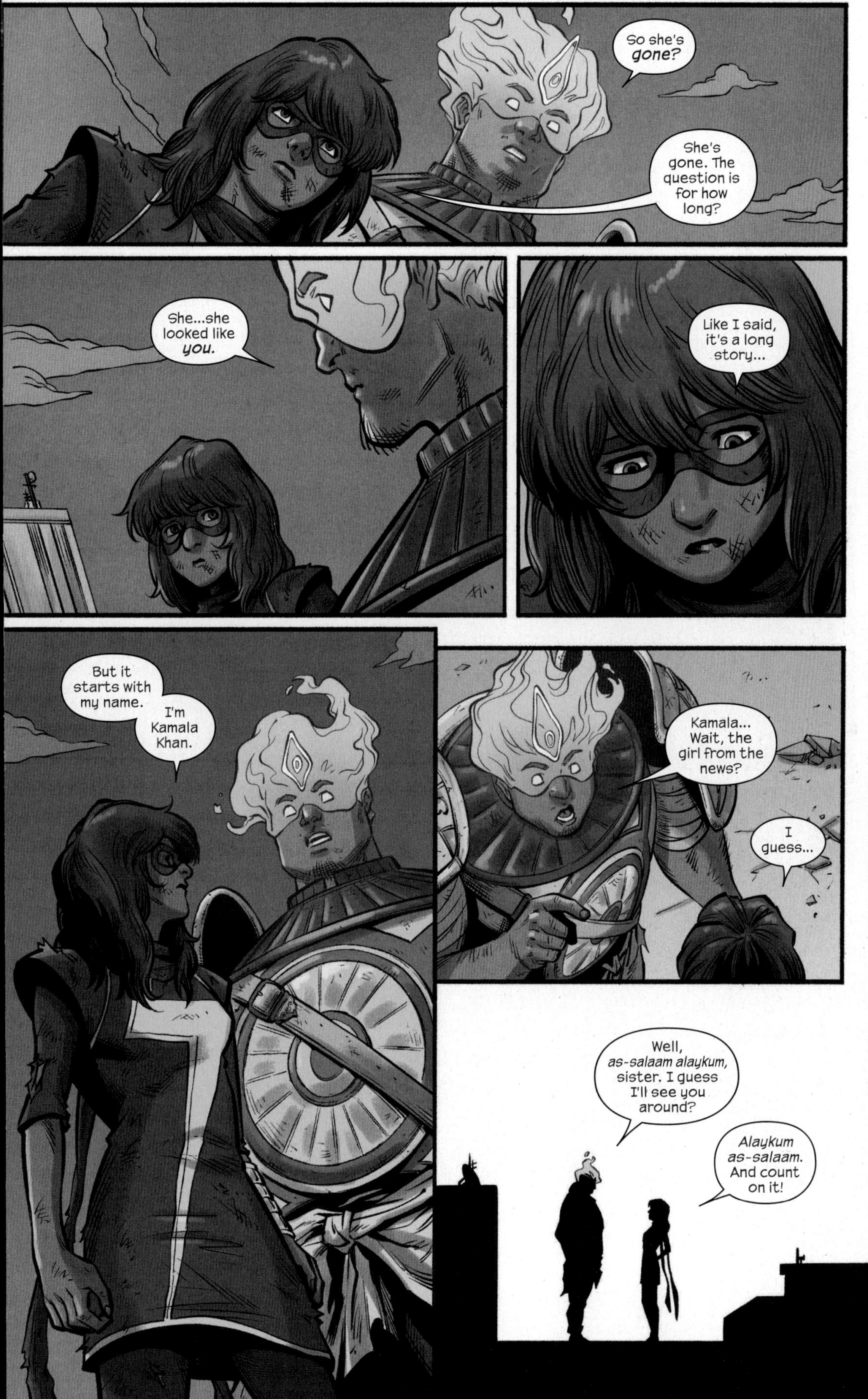

So she's *gone?*
She's gone. The question is for how long?
She...she looked like *you.*
Like I said, it's a long story...
But it starts with my name.
I'm Kamala Khan.
Kamala... Wait, the girl from the news?
I guess...
Well, *as-salaam alaykum,* sister. I guess I'll see you around?
Alaykum as-salaam. And count on it!

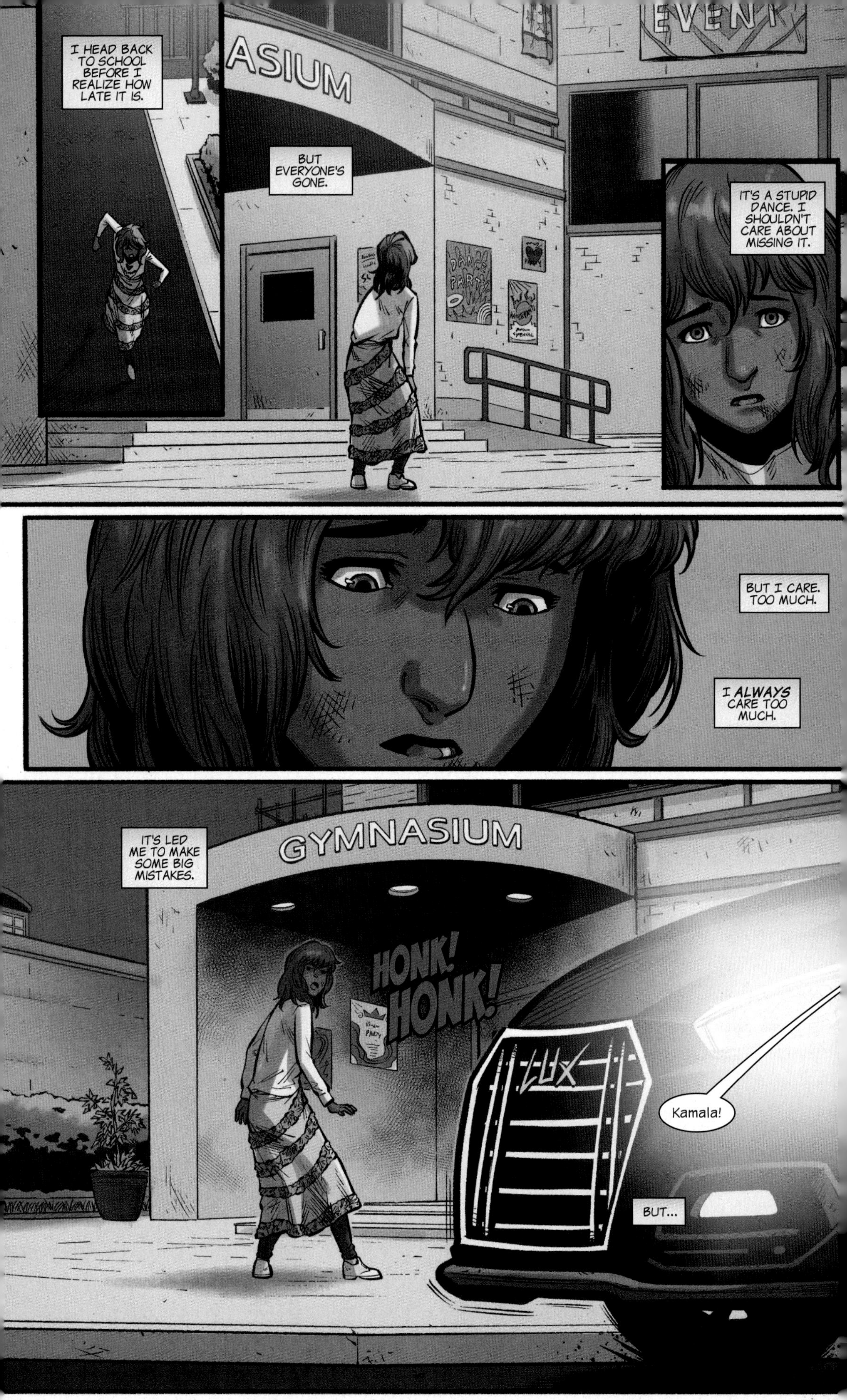

I HEAD BACK TO SCHOOL BEFORE I REALIZE HOW LATE IT IS.
ASIUM
BUT EVERYONE'S GONE.
EVENT
DANCE PARTY
IT'S A STUPID DANCE. I SHOULDN'T CARE ABOUT MISSING IT.
BUT I CARE. TOO MUCH.
I *ALWAYS* CARE TOO MUCH.
GYMNASIUM
IT'S LED ME TO MAKE SOME BIG MISTAKES.
HONK! HONK!
LUX
Kamala!
BUT...

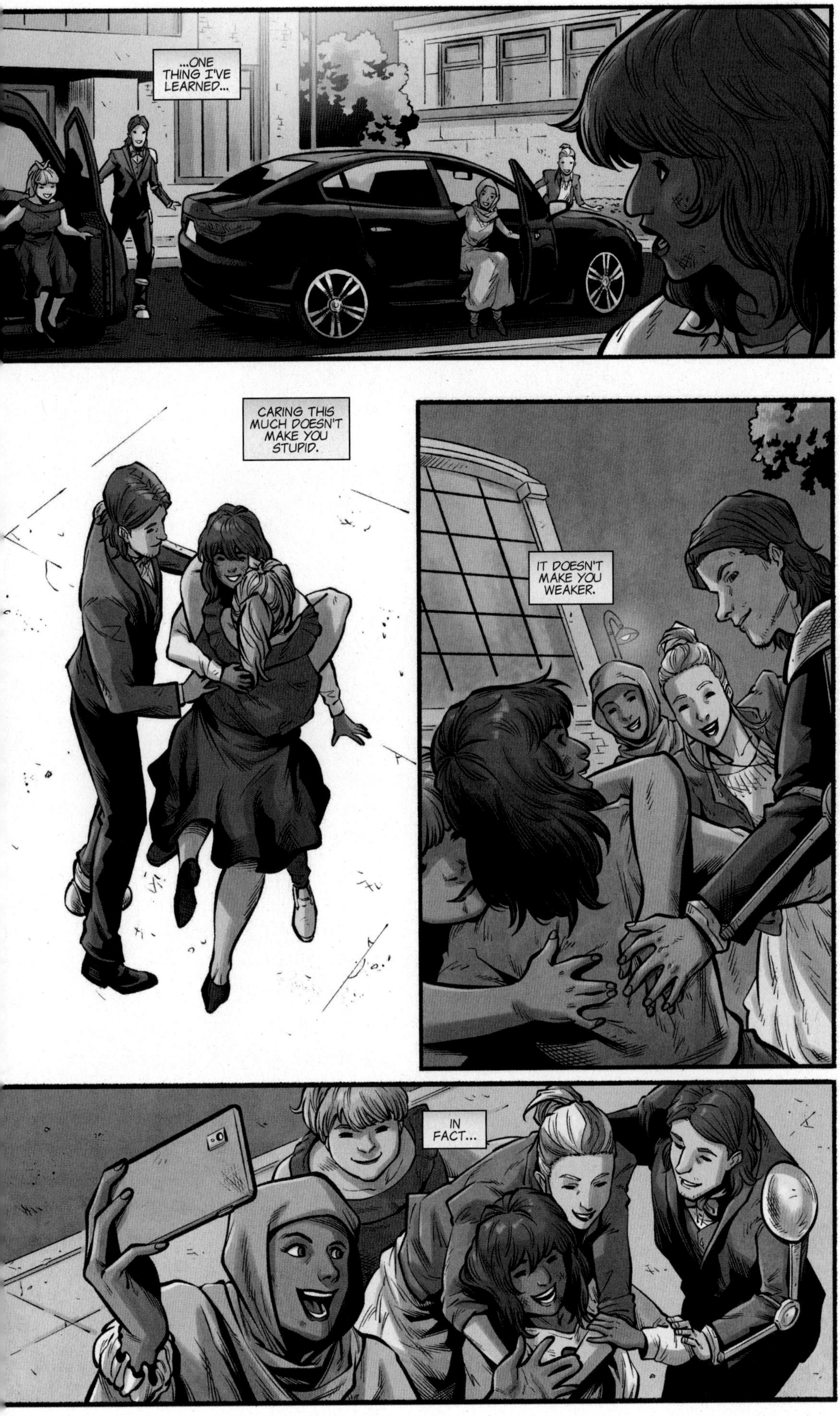
...ONE THING I'VE LEARNED...
CARING THIS MUCH DOESN'T MAKE YOU STUPID.
IT DOESN'T MAKE YOU WEAKER.
IN FACT...

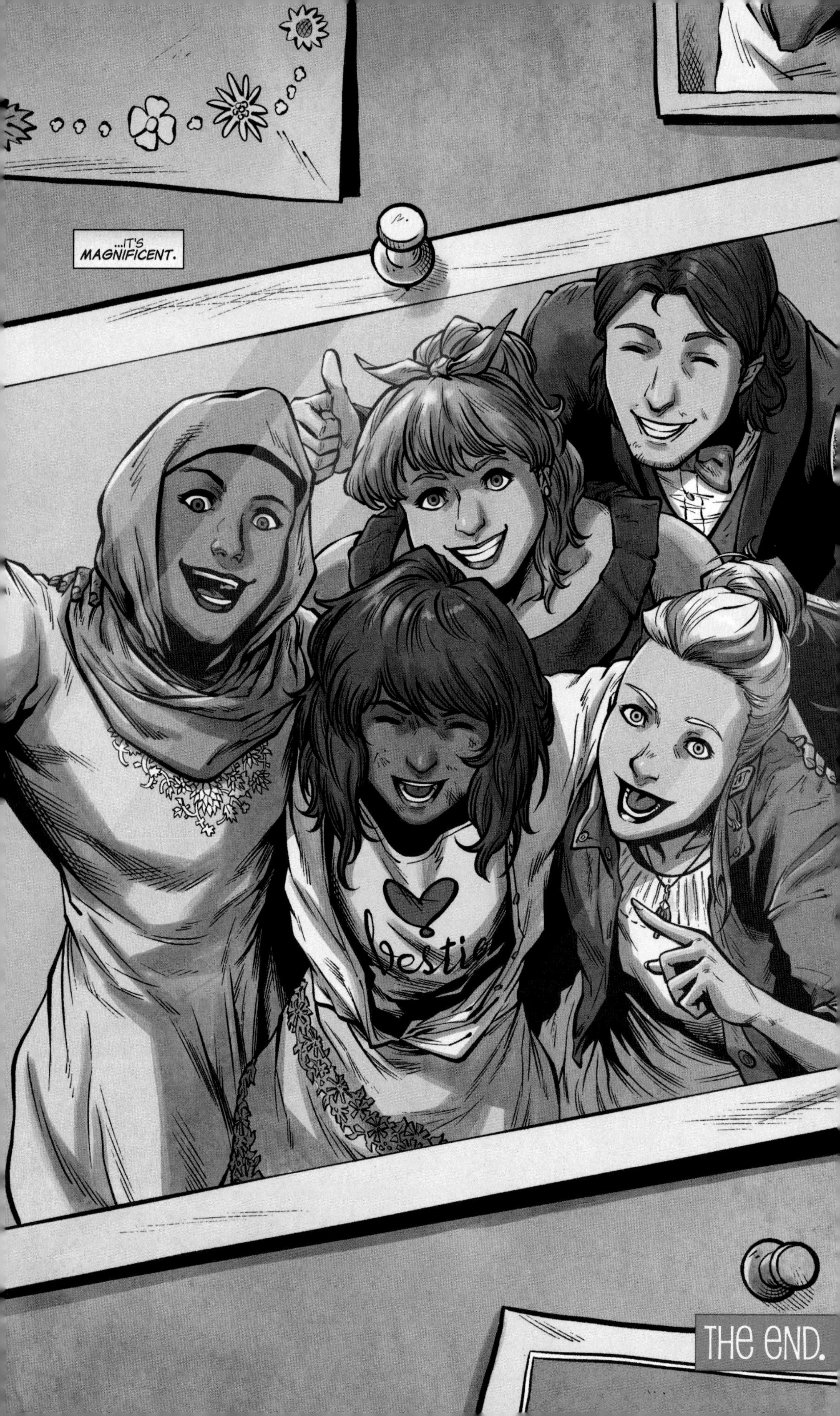
...IT'S MAGNIFICENT.
bestie
THE END.

HOLLA @ KAMALA

Send letters to MHEROES@MARVEL.COM
marked "okay to print"!

Oh my goodness, has it really been eighteen issues?!

A little over two years ago, Kamala Khan's co-creators G. Willow Wilson and Sana Amanat approached me about taking over MS. MARVEL when Willow finished her legendary run. It seems appropriate to Kamala's story that I immediately felt like a video game adventurer who'd been given a rewarding but daunting quest.

I was thrilled and honored, and my mind immediately began planting story seeds. But I was also profoundly intimidated. For personal, cultural, even religious reasons, I knew this would be the hardest project I've ever worked on.

But the quest has been wonderfully worth it, and the treasures discovered along the way have been rich indeed!

Forget super heroes, Kamala Khan is just plain one of the most important fictional characters of her generation. I knew that was true even before I came to write comics. But meeting and hearing from fans since launching THE MAGNIFICENT MS. MARVEL has made it clearer and clearer. Kamala means so much to so many! Muslim readers. South Asian readers. But also people of all ages and cultures from all over

the world who want to root for a selfless, kindhearted (possibly slightly dorky) hero in this grim, stingy era.

Of course, a hero's myth becomes most fully realized when it is passed between storytellers, changing with each telling. We've brought Kamala face-to-face with new enemies and to new places in her personal life, sent her to space and to the edge of the law. Now others will tell her story their way. I can't wait to see what that looks like.

THE MAGNIFICENT MS. MARVEL literally wouldn't exist without a dedicated team of brilliant creators:

Minkyu Jung's pencils and designs went effortlessly from the streets of Jersey City to the alien plains of Saffa to night-sky battles, always maintaining the human emotion that drives this book. From homicidal battle suits to awkward conversations, he constantly pushed our story in new visual directions. I can't imagine a more perfect artist for this run, and I'm so happy we got to work together.

Ian Herring's colors have been a dazzling compass for the book, connecting it back to Willow's run while charting out new territory. From the comforting tones of the Khans' living room to the eerie shades of Ms. Marvel's

enemies, Ian's work has been flawless throughout.

Joe Caramagna's letters have given voice to Kamala's friends and family as well as set the tone for her allies and enemies. Joe's been a pitch-perfect constant on this book, conveying robotic cruelty and super villainous speechifying then bringing us back home with the coziest of fonts.

A special shout-out to our editor Alanna Smith, who understood why this book is important in a way many editors might not. Alanna's eye for balancing timely storytelling with traditional comic book action has been essential to MMM, and I couldn't be happier with the way she both productively challenged me and helped me build every step of the way.

Finally, I'd like to hold in light the late Juan Vlasco, who inked most issues of MMM. As we worked on the book, Juan was always a wonderful balance of buoyant enthusiasm and veteran professionalism. His inks were by turns muscular and fluid, enriching the art of this book immeasurably. The world of comics is poorer for Juan's passing, but I'm thankful we got to make something magnificent with him.

Saladin Ahmed

#18 LETTERS PAGE FEATURING
SALADIN AHMED'S FAREWELL

AMULET CHARACTER DESIGNS BY
SARA ALFAGEEH

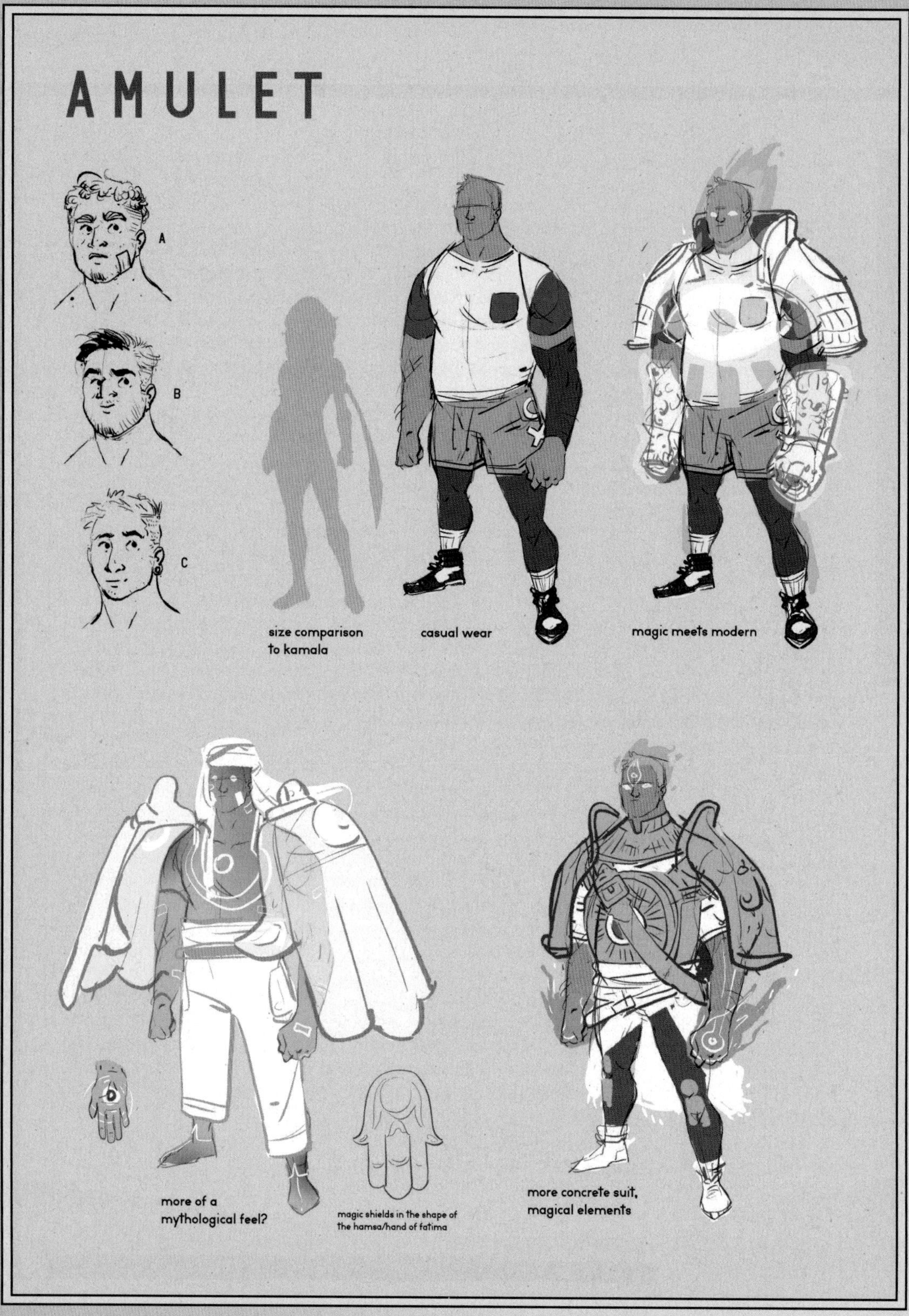
AMULET
A
B
C
size comparison to kamala
casual wear
magic meets modern
more of a mythological feel?
magic shields in the shape of the hamsa/hand of fatima
more concrete suit, magical elements

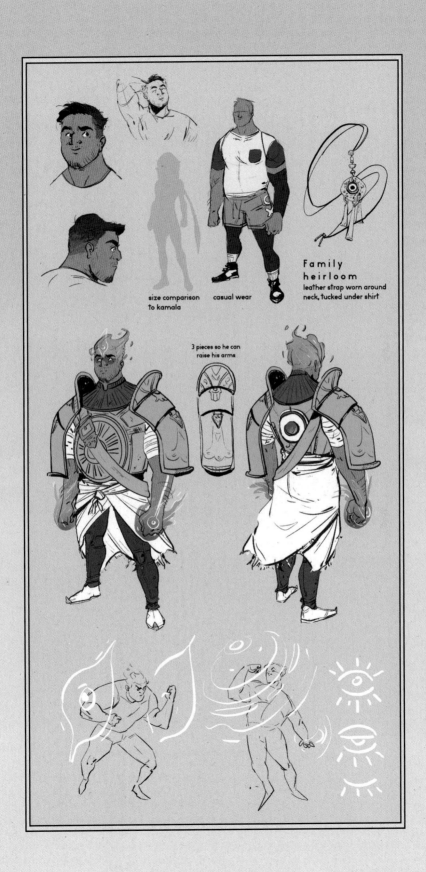

size comparison to kamala

casual wear

Family heirloom
leather strap worn around neck, tucked under shirt

3 pieces so he can raise his arms